Cyber Intelligence: AI and Machine Learning Approaches to Security

Aloïs Lavigne

In an increasingly digital world, where data flows freely across borders and networks, the need for robust cybersecurity has never been more urgent. Cyber threats are evolving at a pace that challenges even the most sophisticated defenses, with attackers leveraging complex tactics, tools, and technologies to breach, disrupt, and manipulate sensitive systems. Traditional cybersecurity measures, while effective to some extent, are often reactive, leaving systems vulnerable to advanced threats that conventional methods struggle to identify and mitigate.

Artificial Intelligence (AI) and Machine Learning (ML) are revolutionizing the field of cybersecurity, bringing unprecedented levels of adaptability, speed, and predictive power to cyber defenses. With AI and ML, we're moving from static defenses to dynamic, intelligence-driven security systems that not only detect threats in real-time but also adapt and evolve as new threats emerge. However, integrating AI into cybersecurity comes with its own set of challenges, from ethical considerations to model robustness and the ongoing arms race with adversaries who exploit vulnerabilities in AI.

This book explores the intersection of cyber intelligence and AI, guiding readers through the foundational concepts, techniques, and future directions in AI-powered security. It provides both a technical understanding and practical insights, making it an essential read for cybersecurity professionals, data scientists, and anyone interested in the future of digital security.

Chapter 1: Introduction to Cyber Intelligence and the Role of AI

This chapter lays the foundation by exploring the concepts of cyber intelligence and the evolving role of AI in enhancing cybersecurity measures. It introduces the reader to the types of threats AI can address and why traditional security approaches are increasingly insufficient.

Chapter 2: Fundamentals of Machine Learning and AI in Cybersecurity

A deep dive into the essential ML and AI concepts necessary for understanding how these technologies work in security contexts. This chapter covers algorithms, data processing, feature engineering, and the various tools and frameworks widely used in cybersecurity.

Chapter 3: Threat Detection Using Machine Learning

Examines the application of machine learning in detecting malware, intrusions, and other cyber threats. This chapter discusses specific ML techniques and how they are tailored for real-time threat detection, backed by practical case studies.

Chapter 4: Anomaly Detection and Behavioral Analysis

Focusing on unsupervised learning and anomaly detection, this chapter explores techniques for identifying irregular patterns in network and user behavior. It provides insights into how behavioral analysis is used to detect potential threats before they escalate.

Chapter 5: Natural Language Processing for Threat Intelligence

Covers the role of Natural Language Processing (NLP) in extracting insights from unstructured data sources like threat reports, news, and social media. Readers will learn how NLP is applied in sentiment analysis, entity recognition, and open-source intelligence (OSINT) for threat identification.

Chapter 6: Predictive Analytics in Cybersecurity

This chapter explains predictive modeling techniques for assessing risk and forecasting potential attacks. Through case studies, it showcases how predictive analytics enable proactive defense by identifying vulnerabilities and trends before they become major issues.

Chapter 7: AI-Driven Security Automation and Incident Response

Explores AI's role in Security Orchestration, Automation, and Response (SOAR) systems, illustrating how automated responses are improving incident response times and accuracy. It discusses where human expertise meets machine efficiency in modern security operations.

Chapter 8: Reinforcement Learning for Adaptive Security

Introduces reinforcement learning and its applications in creating adaptive security policies that respond dynamically to changing threats. This chapter discusses building and training RL agents for cyber defense, emphasizing evolving protection strategies.

Chapter 9: Deep Learning and Advanced Neural Networks in Cyber Defense

Dives into deep learning architectures such as convolutional and recurrent neural networks, explaining their use in detecting phishing, analyzing logs, and enhancing overall defense mechanisms. The chapter also discusses the challenges of deploying deep learning models in real-world security settings.

Chapter 10: Ethical and Legal Implications of AI in Cybersecurity

Addresses the ethical concerns and regulatory compliance issues associated with AI in security, including privacy risks, model bias, and surveillance ethics. This chapter reviews the global legal landscape and provides best practices for ethical AI use.

Chapter 11: Building Robust Cyber Intelligence Systems

Offers guidance on developing resilient AI-driven security systems, covering issues of model robustness, scalability, and resilience. It also explores techniques for defending against adversarial attacks and maintaining ongoing system adaptation.

Chapter 12: Case Studies in AI-Powered Cybersecurity Solutions

Presents real-world case studies across sectors like finance, healthcare, and government, demonstrating how AI has transformed cybersecurity in various industries. Each case study provides lessons learned and best practices for successful AI deployments.

Chapter 13: The Future of Cyber Intelligence: Trends and Emerging Technologies

Concludes the book with a forward-looking perspective on AI and cybersecurity. This chapter highlights emerging technologies such as quantum computing and edge AI, discussing their potential impact and the future challenges in the ongoing evolution of cyber intelligence.

About the Author

Aloïs Lavigne is a seasoned cybersecurity expert and AI strategist with over a decade of experience in the tech industry. His career spans cybersecurity consulting, machine learning research, and strategic development in cyber intelligence, making him a leading voice in the intersection of artificial intelligence and digital security.

Aloïs began his journey in cybersecurity as a passionate developer and soon moved into AI-driven security solutions, recognizing the power of machine learning in transforming traditional defense mechanisms. He has since worked with global organizations across finance, healthcare, and government sectors, helping them harness AI to safeguard critical data, predict cyber threats, and adapt to the rapidly evolving digital threat landscape. Aloïs's deep understanding of both AI technologies and cybersecurity fundamentals has enabled him to lead teams in designing and implementing scalable, resilient, and ethical AI security systems.

In addition to his industry work, Aloïs is an advocate for ethical AI in security, balancing technological innovation with privacy and fairness. He has presented at numerous conferences and written extensively on machine learning, cyber intelligence, and the future of AI in cybersecurity. Through this book, he aims to bridge the knowledge gap for both security professionals and technology enthusiasts, providing insights that are both technically rich and practically accessible.

When not working on cybersecurity challenges, Aloïs enjoys teaching and mentoring aspiring data scientists and cybersecurity analysts, nurturing the next generation of tech innovators. Cyber Intelligence: AI and Machine Learning Approaches to Security is his latest contribution to the field, offering a comprehensive guide for anyone looking to understand and apply AI in the fight against cyber threats.

1. Introduction to Cyber Intelligence and the Role of AI

Chapter 1, Introduction to Cyber Intelligence and the Role of AI, sets the stage for understanding how artificial intelligence (AI) and machine learning (ML) are transforming the cybersecurity landscape. In a world where cyber threats are increasingly sophisticated and dynamic, traditional security approaches are often too reactive, leaving gaps in defense. This chapter introduces the fundamentals of cyber intelligence, outlining how AI's ability to process vast data at speed and detect complex patterns can provide a proactive edge in threat detection, prevention, and response. Readers will gain an understanding of why AI has become essential in modern security strategies and explore key challenges and opportunities that come with integrating AI into cybersecurity frameworks.

1.1 The Evolution of Cyber Threats and Intelligence

The evolution of cyber threats and intelligence is a story of increasing complexity, sophistication, and scale, as digital technologies have advanced and become deeply embedded in every facet of modern life. Over the past few decades, cyber threats have transformed from simple, isolated attacks to intricate, large-scale operations capable of inflicting massive damage on individuals, organizations, and even nations. To effectively defend against these threats, the field of cyber intelligence has had to evolve in parallel, adopting new technologies, methods, and approaches, particularly artificial intelligence (AI) and machine learning (ML), to stay ahead of ever-more sophisticated adversaries.

The Early Days of Cyber Threats: Simple Malware and Viruses

In the early days of the internet, cyber threats were relatively simple and often driven by malicious individuals or hobbyist hackers. These initial cyber threats were primarily viruses and worms, such as the infamous "ILOVEYOU" virus in 2000 or the "Morris Worm" in 1988. These early forms of malware were often spread via email attachments or network vulnerabilities, exploiting weaknesses in computer systems and requiring only basic scripts or code to execute. The primary intent of these attacks was typically to cause disruption or damage, with little motivation beyond the challenge of bypassing security measures.

At this stage, cyber intelligence was primarily reactive—organizations relied on signature-based detection systems, antivirus software, and firewall protections to recognize known threats. These defense mechanisms were effective at identifying and neutralizing malware once it was recognized, but they lacked the capability to predict or mitigate new types of threats before they caused harm.

The Rise of Advanced Persistent Threats (APTs)

As technology evolved, so did the tactics, techniques, and procedures (TTPs) used by cybercriminals. In the early 2000s, the emergence of more sophisticated cyberattacks, particularly Advanced Persistent Threats (APTs), marked a major turning point in the evolution of cyber threats. APTs are complex, multi-stage attacks, often carried out by well-funded and highly skilled threat actors such as nation-states or criminal syndicates. Unlike the earlier, simpler forms of malware, APTs are designed to infiltrate systems quietly and remain undetected over long periods, often gathering sensitive information or carrying out espionage.

One of the most notable APTs was the "Stuxnet" worm discovered in 2010, which was specifically designed to sabotage Iran's nuclear program. Stuxnet was a highly sophisticated and targeted attack that used multiple zero-day vulnerabilities to infiltrate industrial control systems. It demonstrated that cyber threats had moved beyond the realm of traditional IT systems and into critical infrastructure, a trend that continues to grow today.

With the rise of APTs, traditional methods of threat detection became insufficient. Signature-based approaches could no longer keep up with the ever-evolving tactics employed by attackers. The need for more advanced, proactive security measures became clear, and this is when the concept of cyber intelligence began to take shape.

The Role of Cyber Intelligence

Cyber intelligence refers to the process of gathering, analyzing, and interpreting data related to cyber threats, with the goal of identifying and mitigating risks before they materialize. Unlike traditional cybersecurity measures, which are largely reactive, cyber intelligence seeks to be predictive, anticipating future threats based on trends, behaviors, and patterns identified through data analysis.

In the early 2010s, as cybercrime and cyber espionage grew more sophisticated, the need for cyber intelligence became increasingly apparent. Organizations realized that they needed a more comprehensive, strategic approach to cybersecurity—one that integrated not only technical defenses but also intelligence gathering and analysis. Threat intelligence feeds, vulnerability assessments, and attack surface monitoring became core components of this new approach to cybersecurity.

Cyber intelligence became particularly important as the frequency of data breaches, ransomware attacks, and distributed denial-of-service (DDoS) attacks soared. The growing prevalence of "hacktivism" (cyberattacks motivated by political or ideological beliefs) and cybercrime-for-profit further underscored the need for businesses to not only defend their networks but also anticipate and respond to increasingly complex threats.

The Advent of Artificial Intelligence and Machine Learning

The next major leap in the evolution of cyber threats and intelligence occurred with the advent of artificial intelligence (AI) and machine learning (ML). These technologies have revolutionized the way that cyber threats are detected, analyzed, and mitigated. AI and ML provide security professionals with the tools to move from reactive to proactive threat management, enabling them to identify emerging threats and even predict future attacks based on historical data.

AI and ML have become essential in identifying patterns in large volumes of data that would be impossible for human analysts to detect. By training machine learning models on vast datasets of historical attack data, organizations can develop systems that can autonomously detect anomalies and potential threats in real time. These models are constantly learning from new data, allowing them to adapt to emerging tactics and techniques.

For example, AI can be used in anomaly detection systems to spot deviations from normal user behavior or network traffic patterns, which may indicate an insider threat or a zero-day attack. Machine learning models can also be trained to identify malicious payloads in email attachments or detect phishing attempts based on patterns in the content or structure of emails. The combination of AI and ML has enabled cybersecurity systems to evolve from rule-based systems to dynamic, intelligent systems that can learn and adapt to new threats on their own.

Cyber Threats Today: A Global, Multifaceted Challenge

Today, cyber threats are more complex and pervasive than ever before. Cybercriminals, nation-states, hacktivists, and even corporate competitors engage in sophisticated cyberattacks that target not only individuals and organizations but entire nations and global infrastructures. The types of attacks have expanded to include ransomware attacks, supply chain attacks, data breaches, deepfake technologies, and cyber espionage operations, all of which can have catastrophic consequences for governments, businesses, and citizens alike.

Furthermore, as businesses and individuals increasingly rely on interconnected devices in the Internet of Things (IoT), critical infrastructure, and cloud computing, the attack surface has expanded exponentially. Cybersecurity is no longer confined to protecting on-premise systems but now includes securing remote workforces, cloud environments, and IoT ecosystems.

To combat these threats, the field of cyber intelligence has evolved into a multi-disciplinary, global effort that combines threat analysis, data science, machine learning, and human expertise. Cyber intelligence is no longer limited to analyzing single threats; it now involves analyzing entire ecosystems of potential attacks, gathering intelligence from a variety of sources (including open-source intelligence), and using advanced analytical techniques to predict and prevent cyber threats before they occur.

The evolution of cyber threats has moved from relatively simple, isolated attacks to complex, highly coordinated, and persistent campaigns targeting critical infrastructures, sensitive data, and individual privacy. As cyber threats have grown in sophistication, so too has the field of cyber intelligence. From traditional signature-based defense systems to the adoption of AI and machine learning, cyber intelligence has evolved to meet the challenges of a rapidly changing digital world.

As we look toward the future, the continued advancement of AI, machine learning, and other emerging technologies will be critical in staying one step ahead of cyber adversaries. The challenge now is not only to detect and respond to threats quickly but also to predict and prevent them using intelligent, adaptive systems. The dynamic nature of cyber threats requires ongoing innovation, collaboration, and investment in cyber intelligence to ensure a safer and more secure digital world.

1.2 Defining AI and Machine Learning in Cybersecurity

In the rapidly evolving landscape of cybersecurity, artificial intelligence (AI) and machine learning (ML) are playing an increasingly vital role in detecting, preventing, and responding to cyber threats. To understand the significance of these technologies in cybersecurity, it's essential to first define what AI and machine learning are and how they contribute to the security landscape.

What is Artificial Intelligence (AI)?

Artificial intelligence refers to the simulation of human intelligence in machines that are programmed to think, learn, and perform tasks typically requiring human intelligence. These tasks include problem-solving, decision-making, language understanding, vision, and even creativity. In cybersecurity, AI systems aim to replicate human cognitive functions to analyze vast amounts of data, detect anomalies, predict threats, and automatically respond to cyber incidents.

AI encompasses a broad range of technologies, but in the context of cybersecurity, the most important capabilities include:

Pattern Recognition: AI can identify patterns in large datasets, such as network traffic or system logs, and use those patterns to recognize potential security threats. This is particularly useful for detecting unusual behavior indicative of a cyberattack.

Automated Decision Making: AI can autonomously make decisions based on the data it processes, allowing security systems to act swiftly in response to emerging threats. For instance, AI can automatically block suspicious traffic or isolate an infected device to prevent the spread of malware.

Natural Language Processing (NLP): AI can understand and process human language, which is useful for analyzing textual data, such as emails, social media, or threat reports, to identify potential phishing attempts, misinformation, or malicious intent.

Predictive Analytics: By learning from historical data and identifying trends, AI can predict potential threats and vulnerabilities, helping organizations take preemptive actions to avoid attacks.

What is Machine Learning (ML)?

Machine learning, a subset of AI, refers to the ability of machines to automatically learn from data and improve their performance without being explicitly programmed. In other words, rather than following predefined rules, machine learning algorithms can learn from data and adjust their behavior accordingly. ML models "train" on vast amounts of data, identifying correlations, trends, and patterns that can be used to make predictions or decisions.

In cybersecurity, machine learning is particularly important because it enables systems to continuously improve their detection capabilities as they process more data. The key types of machine learning used in cybersecurity include:

Supervised Learning: In supervised learning, algorithms are trained on labeled data, where the input data is paired with the correct output. This type of learning is useful for tasks like spam email detection or identifying known malware signatures, where the system is trained to recognize specific patterns or behaviors based on historical data.

Unsupervised Learning: Unlike supervised learning, unsupervised learning deals with unlabeled data. The algorithm must find hidden patterns or groupings within the data on its own. In cybersecurity, this can be used for anomaly detection, where the system identifies unusual behavior (e.g., abnormal login times or unauthorized access) without being explicitly told what to look for.

Reinforcement Learning: In reinforcement learning, an algorithm learns by interacting with an environment and receiving feedback (rewards or penalties). It continuously adjusts its actions based on the feedback to achieve a specific goal. This approach can be used to develop adaptive security systems that evolve in response to new threats or attack patterns.

Deep Learning: Deep learning, a specialized form of machine learning, uses neural networks with multiple layers to process data in a hierarchical manner. Deep learning models excel at handling complex, high-dimensional data such as images or videos. In cybersecurity, deep learning can be used for sophisticated tasks like detecting zero-day vulnerabilities, malware classification, or identifying advanced persistent threats (APTs).

The Role of AI and ML in Cybersecurity

The application of AI and machine learning in cybersecurity brings numerous advantages over traditional security methods. Traditional security systems are largely rule-based, relying on pre-defined signatures to detect known threats. However, these systems struggle to identify new, unknown threats (zero-day attacks), especially as the volume, speed, and complexity of cyberattacks increase. AI and machine learning address these challenges in several ways:

Proactive Threat Detection and Prevention: AI-powered systems can analyze data in real-time and identify potential threats before they manifest into full-blown attacks. Machine learning algorithms can also predict future threats based on historical data, allowing organizations to take preventive measures. For instance, an AI system might detect an unusual pattern of data exfiltration, such as an employee downloading a large volume of sensitive files, and immediately block the action.

Anomaly Detection and Behavioral Analysis: One of the most powerful applications of AI and ML in cybersecurity is in the detection of anomalies—activities that deviate from the normal pattern of behavior. By monitoring network traffic, user activities, or system processes, AI systems can identify unusual behavior that might indicate a security breach. For example, if an employee suddenly accesses sensitive data they don't typically interact with, the AI system may flag this as a potential insider threat or a compromised account.

Improved Threat Intelligence: AI and machine learning can be used to analyze large volumes of threat data from various sources, such as threat feeds, dark web monitoring, or social media. By leveraging NLP and sentiment analysis, AI systems can quickly identify emerging threats, vulnerabilities, or attack trends. This ability to process and synthesize vast amounts of unstructured data can enhance threat intelligence capabilities and provide organizations with actionable insights to bolster their defenses.

Incident Response and Automation: AI can automate incident response tasks, reducing the workload on security teams and accelerating the response time to potential threats. For example, if an AI system detects an attack, it can automatically initiate predefined actions, such as isolating the affected system, blocking malicious traffic, or alerting the security team. Machine learning models can also be used to prioritize threats, enabling security teams to focus on the most critical incidents first.

Continuous Learning and Adaptation: Machine learning systems continuously learn and improve as they are exposed to more data. This ability to adapt to new threats makes AI-driven cybersecurity systems highly effective at identifying previously unknown attack vectors or evolving tactics. This continuous learning process is particularly important in the face of constantly changing cyber threat landscapes.

The Challenges of AI and ML in Cybersecurity

Despite their advantages, there are several challenges and limitations to the use of AI and machine learning in cybersecurity. For example, the training of machine learning models requires large, high-quality datasets, which may not always be available. Inaccurate or biased data can lead to poor model performance, resulting in false positives or missed detections. Additionally, adversaries are also aware of AI and ML's potential and may use adversarial techniques to manipulate or bypass AI-driven security systems, making it essential for cybersecurity teams to implement robust defenses against such attacks.

Moreover, while AI and ML can automate many security tasks, human expertise is still critical for interpreting complex situations and making strategic decisions. The best outcomes are often achieved when AI and machine learning are used to augment human capabilities, rather than replace them entirely.

AI and machine learning are transforming the field of cybersecurity by enabling systems to proactively detect, analyze, and respond to threats at a scale and speed that traditional methods cannot match. These technologies are becoming integral to modern cybersecurity strategies, helping organizations protect sensitive data, defend against sophisticated attacks, and adapt to an ever-changing digital landscape. However, as with any technology, the integration of AI and ML into cybersecurity must be approached with care, ensuring that systems are trained on accurate data, remain transparent, and are resilient to adversarial tactics. With the right balance, AI and machine learning hold the potential to revolutionize the way organizations defend against cyber threats, providing a crucial advantage in the ongoing battle for digital security.

1.3 Opportunities and Challenges in AI-Powered Security

Artificial intelligence (AI) and machine learning (ML) have emerged as transformative forces in cybersecurity, offering organizations an array of opportunities to strengthen their defenses against an increasingly complex and evolving threat landscape. These technologies promise to revolutionize how security teams detect, analyze, and respond to cyber threats. However, the integration of AI into cybersecurity also presents a host of challenges that must be addressed to ensure the effective and responsible application of these powerful tools.

Opportunities in AI-Powered Security

Proactive Threat Detection and Prevention

One of the most significant opportunities AI offers in cybersecurity is its ability to proactively detect and prevent threats before they materialize into full-blown attacks. Traditional security systems often rely on signature-based detection, identifying known threats by matching them to a database of predefined patterns. This approach, however, falls short in defending against new, unknown threats—referred to as zero-day attacks.

AI, particularly machine learning, addresses this issue by recognizing abnormal patterns and behaviors, even when they don't match any known signature. For example, by continuously monitoring network traffic, AI systems can identify unusual patterns, such as a sudden spike in data transfers or suspicious login behavior, that may indicate a data breach or insider threat. This proactive detection allows security teams to respond faster, often before the attack fully develops.

Anomaly Detection and Behavioral Analytics

AI-powered security systems excel in identifying anomalies and understanding the normal behavior of users and devices on a network. Machine learning algorithms can be trained to recognize the standard patterns of activity within an organization and then flag any deviations from this norm. For instance, if an employee suddenly accesses a large number of sensitive files they do not typically interact with, or if a user logs in from an unfamiliar geographic location, the system can automatically raise an alert for further investigation.

Behavioral analytics powered by AI can also help detect advanced threats, such as insider threats or phishing attacks, which may not follow typical attack patterns but still involve unusual activity. This continuous analysis of behavior at the individual, device, and network level can help reduce the risk of attacks and improve overall security posture.

Automated Incident Response

AI can significantly enhance the speed and efficiency of incident response through automation. When a threat is detected, AI systems can automatically execute predefined responses, such as isolating compromised systems, blocking malicious IP addresses, or containing malware. This automation not only helps reduce response times, preventing further damage, but also frees up security professionals to focus on higher-level decision-making tasks.

For example, AI-based systems can instantly quarantine affected devices in case of a ransomware attack, or cut off suspicious network traffic to prevent the spread of malware. Such automated responses can limit the damage from an attack while also preventing human error, which is common in high-pressure situations.

Improved Threat Intelligence and Threat Hunting

AI can enhance threat intelligence by processing vast amounts of data from various sources, including threat feeds, dark web monitoring, social media, and open-source intelligence (OSINT). Natural Language Processing (NLP) enables AI systems to analyze text-based data, such as threat reports and security blogs, to identify emerging threats, attack techniques, or vulnerabilities.

Additionally, AI can be used to improve threat hunting by continuously scanning data for potential indicators of compromise (IoCs) or known tactics, techniques, and procedures (TTPs) used by threat actors. Machine learning algorithms can analyze historical attack data to identify trends and predict future attack vectors, which helps security teams stay ahead of evolving threats.

Scalability and Efficiency in Handling Data

Cybersecurity today involves handling vast amounts of data—far more than any human analyst can process in a timely manner. AI and ML technologies, however, excel in processing and analyzing large volumes of data at high speeds, allowing security teams to gain insights in real-time. This ability to scale and analyze enormous datasets makes AI invaluable in environments with high data volumes, such as large enterprises, cloud infrastructures, and Internet of Things (IoT) ecosystems.

As cyberattacks become more complex and widespread, the need to manage, analyze, and respond to data quickly becomes even more critical. AI can help organizations manage this data overload, providing them with actionable intelligence faster and more efficiently than traditional systems.

Challenges in AI-Powered Security

Despite its many advantages, the integration of AI into cybersecurity presents several challenges that need to be overcome to maximize its potential. These challenges include technical limitations, adversarial risks, ethical considerations, and organizational concerns.

Data Quality and Availability

Machine learning and AI algorithms rely on vast amounts of high-quality data to function effectively. The success of AI-driven security systems is directly tied to the quality and volume of data they are trained on. However, many organizations struggle to gather sufficient, clean, and labeled data that AI models need to deliver accurate predictions and decisions.

In cybersecurity, poor-quality or incomplete data can lead to inaccurate conclusions, such as false positives or missed detections. For instance, if a machine learning model is trained on biased data or lacks sufficient diversity in the data it is trained on, it could incorrectly classify legitimate activities as threats or fail to identify true threats.

Adversarial Attacks on AI Systems

As AI and machine learning become more prevalent in cybersecurity, attackers are also developing methods to exploit vulnerabilities in AI systems. Adversarial attacks involve manipulating input data in such a way that it misleads or confuses AI models, causing them to misclassify threats or make incorrect decisions. For example, attackers may intentionally introduce slight modifications to data, such as tweaking network traffic patterns, to evade detection by an AI system.

Such attacks against AI-powered security systems are an emerging concern and require continuous efforts to design more robust, resilient models that can withstand adversarial manipulation. To mitigate this risk, security teams must implement techniques like adversarial training, which exposes AI systems to manipulated data during the training phase to make them more resistant to such attacks.

Lack of Transparency and Explainability

One of the significant hurdles with AI in cybersecurity is the issue of transparency and explainability. Many AI algorithms, particularly deep learning models, operate as "black boxes," meaning their decision-making processes are not easily understandable by humans. This lack of transparency can create difficulties for security teams when trying to understand why a particular decision was made or how a certain conclusion was reached.

In cybersecurity, where accountability and trust are essential, the inability to explain AI-driven decisions may raise concerns, particularly when false positives or mistakes occur. It is important for AI models to provide explanations or reasoning behind their actions so that security teams can effectively verify and act upon the decisions made by these systems.

Integration with Existing Security Infrastructure

Integrating AI into existing cybersecurity infrastructures can be a complex and costly process. Many organizations already have a range of security tools and systems in place, such as firewalls, intrusion detection systems (IDS), and antivirus software. Incorporating AI-powered solutions into these systems requires careful planning to ensure compatibility, as well as sufficient training and resources for security professionals.

Moreover, not all AI-powered security tools are designed to work together seamlessly, creating potential silos of information and making it harder for organizations to implement a unified security strategy. The integration of AI with legacy systems and the need for staff to learn how to use these advanced tools effectively remain significant challenges.

Ethical and Legal Implications

The use of AI in cybersecurity raises important ethical and legal concerns, particularly regarding privacy, surveillance, and bias. AI-powered systems often require access to sensitive data to function effectively, which raises questions about the responsible handling and protection of personal information. In addition, there is the potential for AI to be used for mass surveillance, monitoring users' every move, which could lead to violations of privacy and human rights.

Another concern is algorithmic bias, where AI models could inadvertently reinforce existing biases present in the data they are trained on. For example, an AI system that has been trained on biased data may be more likely to flag certain behaviors as suspicious based on demographic factors, leading to discrimination or unfair treatment of certain groups.

AI and machine learning offer tremendous opportunities to advance cybersecurity capabilities, providing organizations with the tools to detect and respond to threats faster and more effectively. These technologies enable proactive defense mechanisms, enhance threat intelligence, automate incident responses, and provide the scalability needed to handle vast amounts of data in real-time. However, challenges such as data quality, adversarial risks, lack of transparency, and integration with existing systems must be addressed to fully realize the potential of AI in cybersecurity. Additionally, ethical and legal considerations must be carefully managed to ensure that AI-powered security solutions are used responsibly and fairly. With the right approach, AI can help create a more resilient and adaptive cybersecurity framework capable of staying ahead of ever-evolving threats.

1.4 Case for AI: Why Traditional Methods Fall Short

As the digital world becomes increasingly interconnected and cyber threats become more sophisticated, organizations face a growing challenge in securing their networks, systems, and data. Traditional cybersecurity methods, which often rely on signature-based detection, rule-based systems, and manual processes, are struggling to keep up with the speed, volume, and complexity of modern cyberattacks. Artificial intelligence (AI) and machine learning (ML) offer a compelling alternative, providing capabilities that go beyond the limitations of traditional security measures. This section explores why AI-powered cybersecurity solutions are essential and how they outperform conventional methods in several key areas.

1. The Limitations of Signature-Based Detection

Signature-based detection is one of the oldest and most widely used methods in cybersecurity. It involves scanning files, programs, or network traffic for known patterns (or "signatures") of malicious code, such as viruses, worms, or malware. Signature-based systems rely on a database of predefined signatures that are continually updated to identify new threats. However, there are several critical drawbacks to this approach:

Inability to Detect Zero-Day Attacks: Signature-based detection can only identify threats that have already been cataloged in the signature database. It is ineffective against zero-day attacks—new vulnerabilities or malware strains that have not yet been discovered or documented. Hackers can exploit zero-day vulnerabilities before signatures are available, rendering traditional signature-based systems powerless against them.

High Dependency on Updates: Signature databases need constant updates to stay current with new threats. Cybercriminals, however, are constantly evolving their tactics to evade detection, and there can be significant delays in releasing new signatures. During this window, systems remain vulnerable to undetected threats.

False Positives: Signature-based systems often generate false positives, where legitimate files or network traffic are flagged as malicious due to their similarity to known threats. This results in wasted resources, increased workloads for security teams, and potential disruptions to normal business operations.

In contrast, AI and machine learning do not rely on predefined signatures. Instead, they can analyze patterns of behavior and detect anomalies, even if those patterns have never been seen before. By learning from large volumes of data and adapting to new threats, AI-driven systems offer a more flexible and proactive defense against evolving attacks.

2. Rule-Based Systems Are Inflexible and Reactive

Traditional rule-based systems are another cornerstone of many legacy cybersecurity infrastructures. These systems follow predefined rules or algorithms to detect known threats and enforce security policies. While rule-based systems can be effective for basic security functions (such as blocking certain types of traffic or enforcing access control), they are inherently limited in several ways:

Limited Scope of Detection: Rule-based systems are designed to detect specific, known threats. They lack the flexibility to detect new or complex attacks that do not match the defined rules. For instance, if an attacker employs a new technique to bypass a rule or uses a tactic that the system is not programmed to recognize, the rule-based system will fail to detect the attack.

Inability to Learn or Adapt: Rule-based systems are static by nature. They cannot learn from past incidents or adapt to evolving attack strategies. Every time a new attack method emerges, security teams must manually update the rules, which takes time and effort. During this lag, organizations remain vulnerable.

Excessive Human Intervention: Many rule-based systems require significant human oversight and intervention. Security teams must constantly monitor the system, analyze alerts, and manually tweak configurations to adjust to new conditions or threat landscapes. This dependency on human input can lead to delayed responses and mistakes, particularly in high-stress environments or when security teams are overburdened.

AI and machine learning systems, on the other hand, are designed to continuously learn and adapt as they process new data. These systems can identify new attack vectors without explicit human programming, making them far more effective in responding to rapidly changing threats. Machine learning algorithms can also prioritize alerts based on severity, allowing security teams to focus on the most critical incidents first, reducing the likelihood of alert fatigue and improving the speed of response.

3. Manual Processes Are Slow and Error-Prone

In traditional cybersecurity operations, much of the work is still manual, involving tasks such as threat analysis, log review, incident response, and vulnerability scanning. While security professionals are highly skilled, these processes are time-consuming and prone to human error, especially when dealing with large volumes of data.

Time Constraints: Cybersecurity teams often struggle to keep up with the sheer volume of security alerts and incidents. Traditional methods can't keep pace with the ever-increasing data generated by modern IT environments, such as cloud platforms, IoT devices, and big data systems. This leads to delayed responses and missed threats, which can result in significant damage to the organization.

Human Error: The complexity of modern cyber threats and the repetitive nature of many manual processes increases the likelihood of human error. A misconfigured security rule, overlooking a crucial piece of data, or misidentifying a threat can have severe consequences, including failed attacks or undetected breaches.

AI-powered systems can automate many of these manual tasks, reducing the risk of errors and speeding up incident response times. For example, AI can automatically scan and correlate data from various sources (e.g., network traffic, endpoint devices, and logs) in real-time, identifying patterns of attack without needing human intervention. This allows security professionals to focus on more strategic tasks and quickly address the most pressing issues.

4. Sophisticated Attacks Require More Than Heuristic Detection

Cyber attackers are becoming more sophisticated, employing advanced tactics, techniques, and procedures (TTPs) to evade detection. These methods often involve blending in with normal network traffic, exploiting vulnerabilities in zero-day software, or using social engineering tactics such as spear-phishing to manipulate users into granting access to systems.

Traditional security methods—whether based on signatures, rules, or heuristics—often struggle to keep up with these advanced tactics. Heuristic detection, which analyzes the behavior of files and programs to detect potential threats, can identify suspicious activity but still lacks the intelligence needed to recognize more subtle, evasive attacks. These systems might flag an attacker's initial movement but fail to recognize the sophisticated steps they take to hide their presence, such as lateral movement or privilege escalation.

AI and machine learning are well-suited to detecting sophisticated and evasive attacks because of their ability to analyze vast amounts of data and detect complex patterns in real-time. For example, an AI system can recognize the subtle behavioral signals of an attacker attempting to move laterally across a network or escalate privileges in ways that are not immediately obvious. By combining multiple data sources and continuously learning from new attack methods, AI systems can detect advanced persistent threats (APTs) and other complex attack strategies that traditional methods might miss.

5. The Need for Real-Time Threat Analysis

With the rise of high-speed cyberattacks, including distributed denial-of-service (DDoS) attacks, ransomware campaigns, and data breaches, cybersecurity systems must operate in real time. Traditional security systems, particularly those relying on signatures or static rules, are not always capable of responding swiftly enough to mitigate fast-moving threats.

Latency and Delay: Traditional systems often suffer from delays in threat detection and response, especially when analyzing large volumes of data. For instance, signature-based detection systems might take time to identify a new attack if the signature database has not yet been updated. By then, the damage may already be done.

Time-Sensitive Risks: Cyber threats are increasingly time-sensitive, with attacks such as ransomware demanding immediate action to prevent data loss or financial damage. Traditional methods may not be able to react quickly enough to limit damage in such cases.

AI-powered security systems, however, are designed to process data in real-time and identify threats with minimal latency. Machine learning models can continuously monitor network traffic and user behavior, providing instant alerts for any suspicious activities. In cases of active attacks, AI systems can quickly initiate automated responses, such as blocking malicious IP addresses or isolating infected systems, to contain the threat and prevent further damage.

While traditional cybersecurity methods, such as signature-based detection, rule-based systems, and manual processes, have served as the foundation of security operations for many years, they are increasingly inadequate in the face of evolving, sophisticated cyber threats. AI and machine learning offer several advantages over traditional methods, including the ability to detect zero-day attacks, adapt to new threats, reduce human error, and respond to incidents in real-time. As cyberattacks grow in complexity and scale, AI-powered security solutions will be essential in providing organizations with the tools they need to stay ahead of attackers and protect their digital assets. The case for AI in cybersecurity is clear: traditional methods are no longer sufficient to address the challenges of modern cyber defense.

2. Fundamentals of Machine Learning and AI in Cybersecurity

Chapter 2, Fundamentals of Machine Learning and AI in Cybersecurity, provides a foundational overview of the key machine learning and artificial intelligence concepts relevant to the cybersecurity field. This chapter walks readers through essential ML techniques—such as supervised, unsupervised, and reinforcement learning—and introduces the critical stages of data processing, feature engineering, and model evaluation that enable effective security applications. With a focus on how these techniques can be used to identify, analyze, and mitigate cyber threats, readers will gain a solid technical grounding to understand and apply AI solutions in various cybersecurity scenarios. This chapter also highlights popular tools and frameworks, offering readers a toolkit for building and experimenting with AI-driven security models.

2.1 Overview of Machine Learning Techniques

Machine learning (ML) is a subset of artificial intelligence (AI) that empowers systems to automatically learn and improve from experience without explicit programming. In cybersecurity, ML has gained immense importance due to its ability to detect patterns, identify anomalies, and predict emerging threats by analyzing vast amounts of data. In this section, we will provide an overview of the primary machine learning techniques used in cybersecurity and how they contribute to threat detection, defense strategies, and incident response.

Machine learning algorithms can be broadly categorized into three main types based on the learning process: supervised learning, unsupervised learning, and reinforcement learning. These approaches serve different purposes and can be applied to various aspects of cybersecurity.

1. Supervised Learning

Supervised learning is the most commonly used machine learning technique in cybersecurity. It involves training a model on labeled data—data that has both input features and a corresponding output label (e.g., "malicious" or "benign"). The goal of supervised learning is to enable the model to predict the correct output when exposed to new, unseen data based on patterns learned during training.

Use in Cybersecurity: In the context of cybersecurity, supervised learning algorithms are often employed for tasks such as malware classification, spam email detection, and intrusion detection. For example, a supervised learning model might be trained on a labeled dataset containing network traffic, where each data point is tagged as either "normal" or "malicious." Once trained, the model can classify new network traffic and detect malicious activities.

Common Algorithms:

- **Decision Trees**: These are used for classification and regression tasks. Decision trees work by splitting the data into subsets based on different attributes and using those splits to make predictions.
- **Support Vector Machines (SVM):** This technique is effective for binary classification tasks. It works by finding the hyperplane that best separates different classes in a dataset.
- **Logistic Regression**: Often used for binary classification problems, logistic regression models the probability of an instance belonging to a certain class.

Advantages: Supervised learning models are highly effective for tasks with clearly defined patterns and labeled data. Once trained, they can make accurate predictions and can be retrained with new data to improve performance.

Limitations: Supervised learning requires a large amount of labeled data, which can be costly and time-consuming to collect. Furthermore, it may struggle to detect novel, previously unseen attacks if the training data does not cover all potential attack scenarios.

2. Unsupervised Learning

Unlike supervised learning, unsupervised learning does not require labeled data. Instead, it seeks to identify hidden patterns or structures within the data. The goal of unsupervised learning is to group similar data points together or reduce the complexity of the data while retaining essential information.

Use in Cybersecurity: Unsupervised learning is particularly useful for anomaly detection and identifying new types of attacks. Since many cyberattacks exhibit anomalous behavior (e.g., unexpected traffic patterns or unusual login attempts), unsupervised learning can be used to identify these outliers without needing prior knowledge of specific attack patterns.

Common Algorithms:

- **K-Means Clustering**: A widely used clustering technique that groups data points into "k" clusters based on their similarity. This is often used for segmenting network traffic or grouping similar types of network behavior.
- **Hierarchical Clustering**: This technique builds a tree of clusters, where similar data points are progressively merged. It is helpful for visualizing data hierarchies and identifying patterns in cybersecurity data.
- **Principal Component Analysis (PCA):** A dimensionality reduction technique that simplifies large datasets by focusing on the most important features. It helps reduce the complexity of data, making it easier to analyze and identify anomalies.

Advantages: Unsupervised learning is ideal for detecting novel or previously unseen threats, as it does not rely on prior knowledge of what constitutes an attack. It can automatically detect deviations from normal patterns, which is essential for identifying sophisticated or zero-day attacks.

Limitations: Unsupervised learning models can sometimes be less accurate compared to supervised models because they do not have predefined labels to guide the learning process. Additionally, it can be challenging to evaluate the effectiveness of unsupervised models since the true nature of anomalies may not always be clear.

3. Reinforcement Learning

Reinforcement learning (RL) is a type of machine learning where an agent learns to make decisions by interacting with its environment and receiving feedback in the form of rewards or penalties. Unlike supervised and unsupervised learning, RL does not rely on data with labels or predefined patterns. Instead, it emphasizes trial and error, allowing the agent to learn optimal actions over time.

Use in Cybersecurity: In the context of cybersecurity, reinforcement learning is often applied to optimize security policies, enhance automated response systems, and adapt defense mechanisms based on feedback from previous actions. For example, RL can be used to train a security agent to respond to various types of attacks by adjusting firewall rules, dynamically blocking malicious IPs, or configuring network defenses based on threat levels.

Common Algorithms:

- **Q-Learning**: A popular reinforcement learning algorithm that enables agents to learn the optimal action to take in any given state by estimating the expected future rewards of possible actions.
- **Deep Q Networks (DQN):** An extension of Q-learning that incorporates deep neural networks to handle more complex environments and large state spaces, such as those found in cybersecurity.
- **Proximal Policy Optimization (PPO):** A more recent RL algorithm that improves upon Q-learning by optimizing the policy directly, making it more suitable for environments with high-dimensional action spaces.

Advantages: RL allows for highly dynamic and adaptive security measures. It can continuously improve its responses based on real-time data, which is particularly valuable in environments with rapidly evolving threats. RL-based systems can self-learn and optimize their defenses over time, leading to more efficient cybersecurity practices.

Limitations: Reinforcement learning requires a significant amount of data and time to train, particularly in complex environments like cybersecurity. Additionally, since RL agents learn by trial and error, there is a risk of introducing harmful actions or decisions during the learning phase. This makes RL less suitable for real-time or mission-critical security decisions unless carefully controlled.

4. Semi-Supervised Learning

Semi-supervised learning is a hybrid approach that combines elements of both supervised and unsupervised learning. In this method, a small amount of labeled data is used in conjunction with a larger set of unlabeled data to improve the learning process. This technique is valuable in scenarios where labeled data is scarce or expensive to obtain but there is an abundance of unlabeled data available.

Use in Cybersecurity: Semi-supervised learning can be applied in scenarios where labeling large volumes of security data (such as network traffic or log files) is impractical. It can help improve threat detection models by leveraging both labeled attack data and unlabeled network data to uncover patterns and detect anomalies more effectively.

Common Algorithms:

- **Label Propagation**: A technique where labels from a small set of labeled data points are propagated to similar, unlabeled data points based on their proximity or similarity in the feature space.

- **Self-Training**: A method where an initial model is trained using labeled data, and then it is used to label a large set of unlabeled data. The model is iteratively retrained with the newly labeled data.

Advantages: Semi-supervised learning offers a practical solution for cybersecurity teams dealing with a lack of labeled data. By combining labeled and unlabeled data, these models can still achieve high performance, making them an ideal choice for many real-world cybersecurity applications.

Limitations: The performance of semi-supervised learning depends heavily on the quality of the small labeled dataset and how well it generalizes to the larger pool of unlabeled data. Mislabeling can lead to incorrect predictions and inaccurate threat detection.

Machine learning techniques offer tremendous potential to enhance cybersecurity by automating the identification of threats, improving anomaly detection, and optimizing security responses. Supervised learning excels at classifying known threats, while unsupervised learning is ideal for detecting novel and unknown attacks. Reinforcement learning provides adaptive solutions for dynamic security environments, while semi-supervised learning bridges the gap between labeled and unlabeled data. By understanding the strengths and limitations of these machine learning approaches, cybersecurity professionals can implement the most suitable techniques to strengthen their defenses and stay ahead of increasingly sophisticated cyber threats.

2.2 Data Preparation and Feature Engineering for Security

In the realm of machine learning (ML) and artificial intelligence (AI) for cybersecurity, the quality of data used to train models is critical to the effectiveness of the resulting systems. Data preparation and feature engineering are foundational steps in any ML pipeline, as they help transform raw data into a format that is useful for training algorithms. In cybersecurity, the data typically involves large volumes of logs, network traffic, system events, and other security-related information. This data must be carefully processed to ensure that machine learning models can accurately identify threats and anomalies.

In this section, we will explore the essential processes of data preparation and feature engineering within the context of cybersecurity. These processes involve cleaning raw data, selecting relevant features, transforming data into a format suitable for machine learning, and ensuring that the data is balanced and represents real-world attack scenarios. Proper data preparation can be the difference between a model that delivers actionable insights and one that fails to detect threats or produces too many false positives.

1. Data Collection and Cleaning

Before any machine learning model can be trained, it is essential to gather and clean the data. In cybersecurity, data comes from various sources, including network traffic logs, firewall logs, intrusion detection system (IDS) alerts, system logs, and even user activity data. The key steps in data collection and cleaning for cybersecurity include:

Data Collection: The first step is to collect the relevant data from different sources. These could include:

- **Network Traffic Logs**: Information about incoming and outgoing network packets, connection requests, and communication patterns.
- **Firewall Logs**: Records of inbound and outbound traffic, including information about blocked and allowed connections.
- **IDS/IPS Alerts**: Data from intrusion detection and prevention systems that provide real-time alerts about potential security incidents.
- **System Logs**: Logs from operating systems, applications, and databases that provide information on events and behaviors.

Data Cleaning: Raw security data often comes with inconsistencies, missing values, and noise that must be cleaned before it can be used for machine learning. Key data cleaning steps include:

- **Handling Missing Values**: Missing data points can be filled with default values, or, in some cases, rows with missing values can be removed. Alternatively, imputation techniques can be used to estimate missing values based on other data.
- **Removing Redundancy**: Log data might contain duplicate entries or unnecessary information that does not add value to threat detection models. These should be filtered out.
- **Normalization**: Data normalization standardizes the range of features to ensure that no single feature dominates the learning process due to differences in scale. This is particularly important when working with numerical data that may vary widely (e.g., network traffic size versus user login attempts).
- **Dealing with Noise**: Security data often contains irrelevant or noisy entries, such as harmless network traffic. Noise reduction techniques, like smoothing or filtering,

can be applied to remove unimportant data points that could distort the model's predictions.

The cleaned dataset should be free of errors, missing values, and irrelevant information, ensuring that the model learns only from useful, high-quality data.

2. Feature Engineering in Cybersecurity

Feature engineering is the process of selecting, modifying, or creating new variables (features) from raw data that will help improve the performance of machine learning models. In cybersecurity, features might represent user behaviors, network activities, system events, or even patterns indicative of potential threats. The quality and relevance of features directly affect the model's ability to identify security incidents. Effective feature engineering involves domain expertise to ensure the right aspects of security data are captured.

Key aspects of feature engineering for cybersecurity include:

Selecting Relevant Features: Not all available data is useful for machine learning. The goal is to choose the most relevant and informative features that will allow the model to detect security threats. In cybersecurity, some important features might include:

- **Frequency of Access**: How often a user logs into a system or accesses a certain resource.
- **Source and Destination IP Address**: The IP addresses involved in communication can reveal suspicious or malicious activity if, for example, unusual geolocations or blacklisted IP addresses are involved.
- **Packet Size and Type**: Anomalies in network traffic, such as unusually large data packets or traffic with unusual patterns, may indicate a DDoS attack or data exfiltration.
- **Login Attempts**: Multiple failed login attempts or logins from unusual times or locations can indicate brute force attacks or account compromises.
- **System Calls and Process Behavior**: Unusual patterns in system calls or executable processes may be indicative of malware or suspicious activity.

Selecting the most relevant features can help the model focus on the aspects of data that truly indicate malicious activity, while ignoring irrelevant information that could introduce noise.

Creating New Features: Sometimes, raw data may need to be transformed or combined to create new, more insightful features. For example:

- **Time-Based Features**: You can extract time-related features such as the time of day, weekday vs. weekend, or time between login attempts to understand patterns related to attacks such as brute-force login attempts.
- **Aggregated Metrics**: Aggregating data over a specific time window (e.g., number of failed login attempts in the last hour or network traffic volume in the last 24 hours) can help detect outliers and abnormal activities.
- **Categorical and Numerical Features**: In cybersecurity, data can be a mix of both categorical (e.g., IP address categories, host names) and numerical features (e.g., traffic volume, session duration). ML algorithms require different techniques for handling each:

Encoding Categorical Features: Categorical data (such as protocol types or event types) must be converted into numerical form through techniques like one-hot encoding or label encoding.

- **Scaling Numerical Features**: Numerical features like packet size, response time, or system resource usage might require scaling (e.g., normalization or standardization) to bring all variables into a similar range.
- **Dimensionality Reduction**: In some cases, the number of features might be too large, making the model overfit or computationally expensive. Techniques such as Principal Component Analysis (PCA) can be used to reduce the dimensionality of the feature set while preserving the most significant variance, ensuring that only the most important features are used for model training.

3. Labeling the Data for Supervised Learning

In supervised learning, the model needs labeled data to learn the relationship between input features and the corresponding output labels. In the context of cybersecurity, this involves marking whether an event or data point is malicious or benign. Labeling can be done through:

- **Manual Labeling**: Experts manually categorize data as either normal or malicious, often using their expertise to identify and label cyberattacks, anomalies, or incidents.
- **Automated Labeling**: In certain cases, automated systems or rule-based algorithms can be used to generate labels based on known attack patterns, heuristics, or threat intelligence sources.

Accurate labeling is essential for training an effective supervised learning model. Incorrect labels or inconsistencies in labeling can lead to poor model performance or missed threats.

4. Handling Imbalanced Datasets

Cybersecurity datasets are often imbalanced, with a much larger number of normal events compared to malicious or suspicious ones. For example, in a dataset of network traffic logs, the vast majority of data points may represent legitimate user activity, with only a small percentage being attack attempts. Imbalanced datasets can lead to skewed models that are biased toward the majority class and fail to detect rare but critical threats. To address this issue, techniques such as:

- **Resampling**: This involves either oversampling the minority class (malicious events) or undersampling the majority class (normal events) to balance the dataset.
- **Synthetic Data Generation**: Techniques such as SMOTE (Synthetic Minority Over-sampling Technique) can generate synthetic samples of the minority class to help balance the dataset without losing valuable information from the majority class.
- **Cost-Sensitive Learning:** Adjusting the learning algorithm to penalize misclassifications of the minority class more heavily can help the model pay more attention to detecting rare threats.

Handling data imbalance is crucial to ensure that the model is not overly biased toward normal activities and remains effective at identifying malicious events, even when they are infrequent.

Data preparation and feature engineering are crucial steps in developing machine learning models for cybersecurity. Proper data cleaning, feature selection, and transformation ensure that the model can accurately identify threats and anomalies. In cybersecurity, the complexity and volume of data make these processes even more important, as the success of AI-driven security solutions depends on the quality of the data fed into them. By preparing the data thoughtfully, selecting the most relevant features, and addressing challenges such as imbalanced datasets, organizations can enhance the effectiveness of their machine learning models and improve their overall cybersecurity posture.

2.3 Evaluating Model Effectiveness in Cyber Contexts

Evaluating the effectiveness of machine learning (ML) models in cybersecurity is a critical step in ensuring that the systems in place can accurately detect, predict, and mitigate potential threats. Given the complexities of cybersecurity, where data is often noisy, imbalanced, and constantly evolving, evaluating model performance requires specialized metrics and methodologies to ensure that the machine learning models are both accurate and robust. Traditional evaluation methods, such as accuracy, are insufficient for cybersecurity contexts, where the costs of false positives (incorrectly flagging benign behavior as malicious) and false negatives (failing to detect actual attacks) can be severe.

This section will explore how to evaluate machine learning models effectively in cybersecurity, focusing on key evaluation metrics, techniques, and considerations specific to the domain. Proper evaluation ensures that the model can be deployed safely in real-world scenarios, accurately identifying malicious activities while minimizing the risk of missing critical threats or overwhelming security teams with too many false alerts.

1. Key Evaluation Metrics in Cybersecurity

In cybersecurity contexts, evaluating the performance of machine learning models goes beyond just measuring accuracy. Because security data is often highly imbalanced (with far more benign activities than malicious ones), more specialized evaluation metrics are required. Some of the most important metrics for evaluating the effectiveness of a model in cybersecurity are:

Confusion Matrix: The confusion matrix is the foundation for many other evaluation metrics. It is a table that compares the predicted labels to the actual labels, providing a breakdown of four possible outcomes:

- **True Positives (TP):** Correctly identified malicious activities.
- **True Negatives (TN):** Correctly identified benign activities.
- **False Positives (FP):** Incorrectly flagged benign activities as malicious.
- **False Negatives (FN):** Failed to detect actual malicious activities.

From the confusion matrix, several key metrics can be derived to assess the model's performance.

Precision: Precision measures the proportion of positive predictions (malicious activities) that are correct. It is calculated as:

$$Precision = \frac{TP}{TP + FP}$$

High precision means that when the model predicts an attack, it is likely to be correct. This is critical in reducing false positives in security alerts.

Recall (Sensitivity): Recall, or sensitivity, measures the proportion of actual positive instances (real threats) that are correctly identified. It is calculated as:

$$Recall = \frac{TP}{TP + FN}$$

A high recall ensures that the model is good at identifying true threats, even if it means producing some false positives along the way.

F1-Score: The F1-score is the harmonic mean of precision and recall, providing a balanced measure that considers both false positives and false negatives. It is particularly useful in cybersecurity, where both false positives and false negatives are costly. The formula is:

$$F1\text{-score} = 2 \times \frac{Precision \times Recall}{Precision + Recall}$$

The F1-score is useful when the data is imbalanced, as it balances the need for high precision with the importance of identifying all relevant threats.

Receiver Operating Characteristic (ROC) Curve and Area Under the Curve (AUC): The ROC curve plots the true positive rate (recall) against the false positive rate (FPR). The AUC score, which is the area under the ROC curve, is a single value that summarizes the model's ability to discriminate between positive (malicious) and negative (benign) classes. A higher AUC indicates better model performance, particularly when faced with an imbalanced dataset.

False Positive Rate (FPR) and False Discovery Rate (FDR): In cybersecurity, the cost of false positives can be high, leading to alert fatigue and wasted resources. The FPR is calculated as:

$$FPR = \frac{FP}{FP + TN}$$

The FDR measures the proportion of false positives among all predicted positives:

$$FDR = \frac{FP}{TP + FP}$$

A low FPR and FDR are crucial in ensuring that security teams do not waste time investigating benign activities.

2. Handling Imbalanced Datasets

In cybersecurity, datasets are often imbalanced, with a much larger proportion of benign activities compared to malicious activities (e.g., legitimate user actions versus attacks). This imbalance can skew model performance, as most models are inclined to predict the majority class (benign) and overlook the minority class (malicious).

Several techniques can be applied to address class imbalance:

Resampling: This technique involves either oversampling the minority class (e.g., artificially increasing the number of attack instances) or undersampling the majority class (reducing the number of benign instances). Techniques such as SMOTE (Synthetic Minority Over-sampling Technique) can be used to generate synthetic examples of the minority class, helping the model learn to detect attacks more effectively.

Cost-Sensitive Learning: In cost-sensitive learning, models are penalized more heavily for misclassifying the minority class (malicious activities). This approach ensures that the model prioritizes identifying threats and reduces the cost of false negatives.

Anomaly Detection: In some cases, particularly in unsupervised learning or when labeled data is scarce, the model can focus on detecting anomalies instead of classifying normal vs. malicious events. This approach relies on the assumption that attacks deviate from regular patterns of behavior, and models trained to detect anomalies can help detect novel or unseen threats.

3. Cross-Validation and Model Generalization

To evaluate how well a machine learning model generalizes to new, unseen data, cross-validation is essential. Cross-validation involves splitting the available dataset into multiple subsets (folds) and training the model on different combinations of training and testing sets. This helps assess whether the model can maintain high performance across diverse data points and under different conditions, which is crucial in dynamic and unpredictable cybersecurity environments.

K-Fold Cross-Validation: In k-fold cross-validation, the dataset is split into "k" equally sized folds. The model is trained on "k-1" folds and tested on the remaining fold. This process is repeated for each fold, ensuring that every data point is used for both training and testing.

Stratified Cross-Validation: In imbalanced datasets, stratified cross-validation ensures that the class distribution (e.g., the ratio of benign to malicious instances) is preserved in each fold. This prevents the model from being biased toward the majority class during training.

Holdout Validation: The dataset is split into two subsets, typically a training set (e.g., 80% of the data) and a testing set (e.g., 20%). The model is trained on the training set and evaluated on the testing set. While this approach is simpler, it can be prone to overfitting or underfitting depending on the dataset's size and variability.

4. Model Interpretability and Explainability

In cybersecurity, the interpretability and explainability of a model are vital for trust and accountability. Security professionals need to understand why a model flagged a certain behavior as malicious, especially in critical systems where human intervention may be required.

Model Interpretability: Some machine learning models, like decision trees or linear regression, are inherently interpretable, as their decisions can be traced through the feature space. Other complex models, such as deep learning models, are more difficult to interpret but can still be made interpretable through methods like feature importance analysis, decision visualization, and layer-wise relevance propagation (LRP).

Explainable AI (XAI): XAI aims to create models that not only perform well but also offer insights into their decision-making processes. In cybersecurity, this is important for gaining the trust of security teams and ensuring that automated systems can be audited and understood when investigating incidents.

5. Real-World Testing and Deployment

While evaluation metrics and validation techniques provide insights into model performance, real-world testing is essential to ensure that machine learning models perform well in live environments. Once a model is trained and validated, it should be deployed in a test environment where it can be monitored for performance over time. Continuous evaluation in real-world conditions helps identify areas for improvement, address evolving attack strategies, and refine the model as more data becomes available.

Evaluating the effectiveness of machine learning models in cybersecurity requires a deep understanding of both the technical aspects of the models and the unique challenges of the security domain. Standard metrics such as precision, recall, and F1-score, along with techniques like cross-validation, anomaly detection, and addressing class imbalance, ensure that machine learning models can effectively identify and respond to cyber threats. Moreover, model interpretability and real-world testing are crucial for ensuring the robustness, trustworthiness, and continual improvement of AI-driven cybersecurity systems. By thoroughly evaluating models, security teams can confidently deploy machine learning tools that enhance their ability to defend against ever-evolving cyber threats.

2.4 Introduction to Tools and Frameworks in Security ML

The field of cybersecurity has increasingly relied on machine learning (ML) to detect and mitigate threats. With its ability to analyze vast amounts of data, recognize patterns, and adapt to new attack techniques, ML is transforming the way organizations protect their networks, systems, and sensitive information. However, to successfully implement ML models for cybersecurity, practitioners need robust tools and frameworks that facilitate the development, deployment, and management of these models. In this section, we will explore the tools and frameworks commonly used in security-focused machine learning, examining their capabilities, features, and how they contribute to the effectiveness of AI-driven security systems.

1. Popular Machine Learning Libraries for Security

A variety of general-purpose machine learning libraries and frameworks are widely used in cybersecurity to train models for tasks such as anomaly detection, classification, and predictive analysis. These libraries provide powerful, pre-built algorithms and functionalities that save time and effort, making them essential tools in the cybersecurity AI toolkit.

Scikit-learn: Scikit-learn is one of the most popular Python libraries for machine learning. It is widely used for a variety of tasks, including classification, regression, clustering, and anomaly detection. With its simple and consistent API, Scikit-learn provides an accessible platform for building and evaluating ML models. It also supports various evaluation metrics, cross-validation techniques, and feature selection methods, making it useful for training cybersecurity models. For example, it is commonly used in intrusion detection systems (IDS) to detect abnormal patterns in network traffic.

TensorFlow and Keras: TensorFlow is a powerful open-source framework developed by Google that allows developers to build and deploy machine learning models. It supports deep learning and other advanced ML techniques, and it is commonly used in cybersecurity tasks that require complex neural networks and large-scale data processing. Keras, a high-level neural networks API, is built on top of TensorFlow and simplifies the creation of deep learning models. These frameworks are suitable for tasks like malware detection, network traffic analysis, and predictive modeling.

PyTorch: PyTorch is another deep learning framework that is gaining popularity due to its flexibility and ease of use. Developed by Facebook's AI Research lab, PyTorch allows for dynamic computation graphs, which makes it especially useful for research and rapid prototyping. In cybersecurity, PyTorch is often used for advanced applications such as malware classification, anomaly detection, and intrusion detection, particularly where deep learning techniques are involved.

XGBoost: XGBoost is a powerful and efficient implementation of gradient-boosted decision trees (GBDT), widely used for classification and regression tasks. In cybersecurity, XGBoost is often used for threat detection, phishing detection, and fraud detection due to its ability to handle imbalanced datasets and provide high performance with minimal feature engineering. Its speed and scalability make it a popular choice for real-time security applications.

LightGBM: LightGBM is another gradient-boosted framework that is highly efficient for large datasets. It is similar to XGBoost but tends to be faster and more scalable. LightGBM is particularly useful in cybersecurity for threat detection models that require high-speed processing and the ability to scale across large volumes of security event data.

2. Specialized Security-Focused Machine Learning Frameworks

In addition to general-purpose ML libraries, there are several frameworks specifically designed for use in cybersecurity applications. These tools incorporate domain-specific features and functionalities that make them particularly suited for threat detection, risk analysis, and incident response.

Splunk: Splunk is one of the most widely used platforms for searching, monitoring, and analyzing machine-generated big data. While not a machine learning library per se, Splunk integrates with various ML tools and frameworks to help organizations build custom threat detection models. With its ability to collect and analyze log data in real-time, Splunk is a powerful tool for security information and event management (SIEM) systems. It supports machine learning techniques for anomaly detection and predictive analytics, enabling security teams to detect suspicious activity as it occurs.

ELK Stack (Elasticsearch, Logstash, Kibana): The ELK Stack is a collection of open-source tools that help with the ingestion, processing, and visualization of data. Elasticsearch provides a scalable search engine for analyzing large datasets; Logstash is used to collect and transform data from various sources; and Kibana offers a powerful visualization layer. In the context of security, the ELK Stack is often used for log aggregation and real-time threat detection. Machine learning features, such as anomaly detection, can be added to the stack to automatically detect security issues in log data.

Kali Linux and Security Tools: Kali Linux is a Linux distribution widely used for penetration testing and security auditing. It comes pre-loaded with many cybersecurity tools that incorporate machine learning algorithms for tasks like vulnerability scanning, network monitoring, and malware analysis. Tools such as Snort (intrusion detection), OpenVAS (vulnerability scanning), and Suricata (network traffic analysis) can be used in conjunction with machine learning models to enhance their detection capabilities.

AI and ML-Based IDS/IPS: Traditional intrusion detection systems (IDS) and intrusion prevention systems (IPS) are being enhanced with machine learning techniques to improve their ability to detect advanced persistent threats (APTs) and zero-day exploits. Frameworks such as Bro/Zeek and Suricata can integrate ML algorithms to detect unusual patterns and behaviors in network traffic that traditional signature-based IDS/IPS may miss. These systems often leverage unsupervised learning, clustering, and anomaly detection techniques to identify previously unknown attack vectors.

3. Security-Specific Machine Learning Frameworks for Anomaly Detection

Anomaly detection plays a central role in the cybersecurity field, particularly in detecting network intrusions, fraud, and unusual system behaviors. Various tools and frameworks are specifically tailored for anomaly detection tasks:

AnomalyDetection (by Twitter): AnomalyDetection is a robust, open-source R package developed by Twitter for detecting anomalies in time series data. This framework is ideal for cybersecurity applications that involve network traffic monitoring, intrusion detection, or user behavior analytics. AnomalyDetection utilizes a combination of statistical models and machine learning techniques to detect outliers and anomalous patterns in time-series data, such as spikes in network traffic or sudden changes in login behavior.

Scikit-learn's Anomaly Detection Module: Scikit-learn also provides a variety of anomaly detection algorithms, such as Isolation Forest, One-Class SVM, and Local Outlier Factor. These methods can be applied to various cybersecurity tasks, including identifying network intrusions, detecting abnormal system behaviors, and recognizing unusual access patterns that could indicate a security breach.

DeepAnomaly: DeepAnomaly is a machine learning framework for anomaly detection based on deep learning models. By applying autoencoders and other deep learning architectures, DeepAnomaly can detect complex anomalies in large-scale datasets such as network logs, application traffic, or system performance metrics. This tool is particularly effective for detecting sophisticated attack techniques, including advanced persistent threats (APTs) and insider threats.

4. Integrating Machine Learning into Security Operations

Once machine learning models are trained, the next step is integrating them into existing security operations. Several frameworks and tools are designed to help with the deployment and continuous monitoring of ML-powered security systems.

Apache Kafka: Apache Kafka is a distributed streaming platform that is commonly used for real-time data ingestion in cybersecurity. Kafka allows for the continuous flow of log data, network traffic, and security event data, which can then be fed into machine learning models for real-time analysis and alerting. When integrated with other ML frameworks, Kafka can support real-time threat detection and incident response systems.

TensorFlow Serving: TensorFlow Serving is an open-source framework for serving machine learning models in production environments. It is widely used for deploying trained models and making them accessible for real-time predictions. In a cybersecurity context, TensorFlow Serving can be used to deploy ML-based threat detection models, enabling continuous monitoring and real-time threat identification.

Kubeflow: Kubeflow is an open-source Kubernetes-native platform designed for deploying and managing machine learning workflows. In the context of cybersecurity, Kubeflow can be used to deploy machine learning models at scale, orchestrating tasks like data collection, model training, and inference, and ensuring that security operations teams can respond to threats quickly.

Machine learning is transforming cybersecurity by providing advanced tools for threat detection, analysis, and response. To effectively build, deploy, and manage ML models for security, professionals need to leverage a diverse set of tools and frameworks. Popular machine learning libraries like TensorFlow, Scikit-learn, and PyTorch offer powerful algorithms for a range of security tasks, while specialized tools like Splunk, ELK Stack, and AI-powered IDS/IPS solutions help integrate these models into real-world environments. Furthermore, anomaly detection frameworks, real-time streaming platforms, and model-serving technologies are critical to ensuring that ML models are effective and scalable in production. By understanding and utilizing these tools, cybersecurity teams can enhance their ability to detect emerging threats, respond to incidents swiftly, and improve the overall security posture of their organization.

3. Threat Detection Using Machine Learning

Chapter 3, Threat Detection Using Machine Learning, delves into how machine learning algorithms are leveraged to identify and respond to cyber threats in real-time. This chapter examines the application of supervised and semi-supervised learning techniques in detecting malicious activity, such as malware, phishing, and network intrusions, and explains how these models are trained to recognize patterns indicative of threats. Readers will explore feature extraction methods that enhance model accuracy and learn strategies for minimizing false positives, a crucial aspect of effective threat detection. Through case studies, this chapter demonstrates real-world implementations of ML-based threat detection, providing insights into how organizations use these techniques to strengthen their defenses.

3.1 Supervised Learning Approaches in Threat Detection

Supervised learning is one of the most widely used machine learning (ML) techniques in the field of cybersecurity, particularly in threat detection. This approach relies on labeled datasets—where the input data is paired with the correct output (or label)—to train models that can predict outcomes for new, unseen data. In the context of cybersecurity, the labels usually represent the type of activity or event (such as benign or malicious), and the goal of the model is to learn the relationship between features of the data (such as network traffic, file properties, or user behavior) and the corresponding labels. Once trained, the model can classify new, incoming data as benign or malicious, or even predict the type of attack.

Supervised learning is particularly valuable in threat detection because it can automatically identify patterns, anomalies, and behaviors associated with security threats. By leveraging historical data of past cyberattacks, supervised learning models can be trained to detect similar attacks in real time. In this section, we will explore various supervised learning approaches, their applications in cybersecurity, and the specific steps involved in using them for threat detection.

1. Classification Algorithms in Threat Detection

In cybersecurity, the primary task of supervised learning is classification, which involves assigning a given input to one of several predefined categories or classes. Several classification algorithms are widely used for threat detection, each with its strengths, weaknesses, and applicability depending on the nature of the problem.

Decision Trees: Decision trees are a popular choice for threat detection due to their transparency and ease of interpretation. They work by recursively splitting the data based on feature values, forming a tree-like structure where each branch represents a decision based on a feature, and each leaf node represents a classification outcome (e.g., benign or malicious). Decision trees are particularly useful in scenarios where it is important to explain the model's decision-making process. In threat detection, decision trees can classify network traffic or user behaviors based on attributes like packet size, frequency, or system access patterns.

Random Forests: Random forests are an ensemble learning method that builds multiple decision trees and aggregates their outputs to make a final prediction. This approach improves upon individual decision trees by reducing the risk of overfitting and improving generalization. In threat detection, random forests are widely used to classify network intrusions, malware, and phishing attacks. They can handle large feature sets and provide robust performance even when the data is noisy or imbalanced.

Support Vector Machines (SVM): Support vector machines are another popular supervised learning algorithm, particularly effective in high-dimensional spaces. SVM works by finding the hyperplane that best separates data points of different classes (e.g., benign vs. malicious) in the feature space. It is well-suited for binary classification tasks, making it useful for detecting network intrusions or identifying malicious files. SVM is particularly effective when there is a clear margin of separation between classes, but it can struggle with very large datasets or when the data is highly imbalanced.

Logistic Regression: Logistic regression is a linear classification model used for binary classification problems, such as detecting malicious vs. benign behavior. It estimates the probability of a data point belonging to a particular class, making it easy to interpret and implement. Although logistic regression may not be as powerful as more complex models (like decision trees or random forests), it can serve as a simple yet effective method for identifying low-complexity threats or filtering out known benign activities in network traffic or system logs.

K-Nearest Neighbors (KNN): The KNN algorithm classifies data points based on the majority class of their k-nearest neighbors in the feature space. In threat detection, KNN is useful for identifying anomalous behaviors or outliers by comparing new data points to existing labeled examples. For instance, KNN can be applied to detect abnormal network traffic patterns that resemble those of past security incidents. KNN's simplicity and non-parametric nature make it useful for identifying relatively simple attacks, but it can struggle with large datasets or when there is high noise in the data.

2. Feature Engineering for Threat Detection

Supervised learning models depend on the quality and relevance of the features (input variables) used to train the model. In cybersecurity, feature engineering plays a critical role in determining the success of the model. Feature engineering involves selecting, modifying, and creating new features from raw data that can help the model make better predictions. Well-designed features allow the model to detect complex security patterns and make more accurate predictions.

Network Traffic Features: For network intrusion detection, features might include packet size, packet frequency, IP addresses, port numbers, or time-based attributes such as request frequency. These features can help the model identify suspicious patterns in the flow of network traffic, such as denial-of-service (DoS) attacks or data exfiltration.

User Behavior Features: In user behavior analytics (UBA), features may include the time of day a user logs in, the number of failed login attempts, or the number of files accessed. By analyzing user behavior, supervised learning models can detect potential insider threats, compromised accounts, or abnormal login patterns that may indicate an ongoing attack.

File Features: When detecting malicious files or malware, features might include file size, file type, file hashes, or metadata (e.g., file creation or modification dates). For example, supervised learning algorithms can identify files that match known signatures of malware, or flag files that exhibit unusual behaviors such as excessive file modifications.

Time-Series Features: Time-series features are essential for detecting attacks that unfold over time, such as advanced persistent threats (APTs). Features can include event timestamps, rates of specific actions (e.g., login attempts), or the time intervals between certain activities (e.g., login followed by a privilege escalation). By analyzing these patterns, models can identify emerging threats before they cause significant damage.

Feature selection and dimensionality reduction techniques, such as Principal Component Analysis (PCA) or mutual information, are also used to identify the most important features and reduce the complexity of the dataset. This can improve model performance, reduce overfitting, and make the model more interpretable.

3. Training the Model and Model Evaluation

Once the features are engineered and prepared, the next step is to train the model using the labeled data. The training process involves providing the model with input data along with the correct labels, allowing it to learn the relationship between the features and the target class (e.g., benign or malicious). After training, the model needs to be evaluated to ensure it can generalize well to new, unseen data.

Cross-Validation: Cross-validation, particularly k-fold cross-validation, is used to evaluate the performance of the model. In this process, the dataset is split into k subsets, and the model is trained and tested k times using different combinations of training and testing data. This ensures that the model is tested on multiple data splits, improving the reliability of the evaluation.

Evaluation Metrics: For threat detection, the typical evaluation metrics include accuracy, precision, recall, and F1-score. Precision and recall are particularly important in cybersecurity, as minimizing false positives (benign activities flagged as malicious) and false negatives (malicious activities missed) is crucial. Additionally, metrics such as the Area Under the Curve (AUC) of the Receiver Operating Characteristic (ROC) curve can be used to evaluate the model's discriminative ability.

4. Real-Time Threat Detection and Deployment

After training and evaluation, the final step is deploying the model into a live environment for real-time threat detection. In this stage, the model continuously receives new data and makes predictions about whether the data represents a legitimate or malicious activity. In cybersecurity, models need to be able to make fast, accurate predictions to minimize the impact of an attack.

Model Monitoring: Once deployed, the model's performance must be continuously monitored to ensure it remains effective. This involves tracking metrics such as prediction accuracy, false positives, and false negatives, and updating the model as new threats or attack vectors emerge.

Adversarial Testing: Models should also be tested against adversarial attacks, where attackers intentionally manipulate data to evade detection. For example, an adversary might attempt to modify network traffic patterns to avoid triggering an anomaly detection model. Adversarial testing helps ensure that the model can withstand and adapt to evolving attack tactics.

Supervised learning plays a pivotal role in modern threat detection systems by enabling machines to automatically identify and classify malicious activities based on historical labeled data. Commonly used algorithms such as decision trees, random forests, SVM, and logistic regression can be applied to a wide range of cybersecurity problems, from network intrusion detection to malware classification. Feature engineering is crucial in designing models that can capture the complexity of security threats, and proper training and evaluation techniques ensure the models are effective and accurate. By deploying and continuously monitoring these models in real-time, cybersecurity teams can improve their ability to detect and mitigate threats, enhancing overall system security.

3.2 Feature Extraction for Malicious Activity Detection

Feature extraction is a critical step in building effective machine learning models for malicious activity detection in cybersecurity. In essence, feature extraction involves transforming raw data into a set of meaningful attributes or features that a machine learning model can use to make predictions. These features capture the important characteristics of the data, allowing the model to distinguish between benign and malicious activities. By extracting the right features, security systems can more effectively identify suspicious behaviors, anomalies, and attacks, ranging from network intrusions to malware infections and phishing attempts.

This section explores the process of feature extraction for malicious activity detection, focusing on the types of features commonly used, techniques for extracting them, and how they contribute to enhancing the performance of machine learning models in detecting cyber threats.

1. Types of Features for Malicious Activity Detection

Malicious activity manifests in various forms, such as abnormal network traffic, unauthorized access attempts, or suspicious file behavior. Therefore, the features extracted must be able to represent these activities effectively. Below are some common types of features used in malicious activity detection:

Network Traffic Features: Network traffic is one of the most common data sources for detecting malicious activities like Distributed Denial of Service (DDoS) attacks, data exfiltration, or intrusion attempts. Features extracted from network traffic data include:

- **Packet size and packet frequency**: Large packets or a high frequency of requests can signal a DDoS attack.
- **Source and destination IP addresses**: Unusual connections from unfamiliar or blacklisted IPs could indicate a potential attack or intrusion.

- **Port numbers**: Malicious activities often involve uncommon ports or protocols.
- **Flow duration and flow size**: Abnormal flow characteristics, such as unusually long or large data transfers, can signal suspicious behavior.

System Call Features: System calls are low-level operations made by applications or the operating system, such as opening a file or accessing a network resource. Malicious software or attackers often trigger unusual patterns of system calls to exploit vulnerabilities.

- **Frequency and type of system calls**: Frequent calls to sensitive system resources, such as the registry or file system, may indicate malware attempting to escalate privileges or exfiltrate data.
- **Unusual patterns in system call sequences**: A sequence of system calls that deviates from typical application behavior can indicate malicious activity, such as a ransomware attack or privilege escalation.

File Features: Files on a system can exhibit behaviors that are indicative of malicious activity, particularly when dealing with malware or ransomware.

- **File attributes**: These include file size, file creation/modification times, file name, and extension. Files with suspicious attributes, such as executable files in unexpected directories, can signal an attack.
- **File hashes (MD5, SHA1, SHA256):** Hashes are unique identifiers for files. If a file hash matches known malicious software signatures, it can immediately be flagged as malicious.
- **File access patterns**: Files that are opened, modified, or encrypted at an unusually high rate could indicate a ransomware attack.

User Behavior Features: Detecting malicious activity often involves observing deviations from normal user behavior, which can be indicative of insider threats or compromised accounts.

- **Login frequency and timing**: Unusual login times, such as logins at odd hours or from unfamiliar locations, could suggest account compromise.
- **Access patterns**: Excessive access to sensitive files or systems could indicate that a user's credentials have been compromised or that an insider threat is present.
- **Failed login attempts**: Multiple failed login attempts followed by a successful login could indicate a brute-force attack or credential stuffing.

Anomaly Detection Features: These features focus on detecting deviations from baseline behavior, which is often an indicator of a malicious attack.

- **Statistical features**: The mean, variance, and skewness of various behavioral metrics, such as the number of files accessed or the rate of network requests, can help detect unusual activities.
- **Time-based features**: Time-related features such as the time between events, or the distribution of activities across time, are useful for detecting patterns such as APTs, which typically unfold over a long period.
- **Entropy and distribution analysis**: Features like entropy can help assess the unpredictability or randomness of activity, such as the randomness of IP addresses or file accesses, helping to spot unusual behaviors.

2. Techniques for Feature Extraction

Feature extraction methods are designed to transform raw, unstructured data into structured features that are more usable for machine learning models. In cybersecurity, where the data is often high-dimensional, heterogeneous, and sparse, feature extraction plays a key role in improving model accuracy and efficiency.

Manual Feature Extraction: In traditional machine learning models, feature extraction is performed manually, based on domain knowledge and expertise. Security professionals or data scientists use their understanding of cybersecurity threats to select relevant features. For example, they may choose specific network traffic metrics or system call patterns that are indicative of malicious behavior. While this approach allows for careful feature selection, it is often time-consuming and requires expertise.

Automated Feature Extraction: With the advent of deep learning and more sophisticated data processing tools, automated feature extraction techniques have emerged. These techniques use algorithms to automatically extract the most informative features from raw data, often using unsupervised learning methods. For example, unsupervised clustering algorithms like K-means or DBSCAN can identify groups of similar data points, which can then be analyzed to discover hidden patterns or anomalies in the data.

Deep Learning-based Feature Extraction: Deep learning methods, especially those using neural networks, can automatically learn hierarchical features from raw data. In cybersecurity, convolutional neural networks (CNNs) can be applied to network traffic data or file metadata to automatically extract patterns that traditional models may miss.

Recurrent neural networks (RNNs) can be used to model sequential data such as logs or system calls to detect long-term malicious behavior or attacks that unfold over time.

Feature Selection Techniques: After the initial feature extraction, the next challenge is determining which features are most relevant for training the machine learning model. Feature selection techniques help eliminate redundant or irrelevant features, thereby improving the model's performance and reducing its complexity. Common techniques for feature selection include:

- **Correlation-based feature selection**: This technique removes features that are highly correlated with others, as they do not contribute unique information.
- **Mutual information**: Measures the statistical dependency between features and the target variable, helping to identify the most informative features.
- **Recursive feature elimination (RFE):** This iterative process removes the least important features, one by one, until the optimal set of features is achieved.

Principal Component Analysis (PCA): PCA is a dimensionality reduction technique used to extract features that capture the most variance in the data. It transforms the original features into a smaller set of new features (principal components), which are linear combinations of the original features. PCA is especially useful in cybersecurity for reducing the size of high-dimensional datasets, such as those involved in network traffic analysis, without losing significant information.

3. Feature Engineering for Specific Threats

Different types of cyber threats require specific features to be extracted for optimal detection. Below are examples of feature extraction tailored to specific malicious activities:

Malware Detection: For detecting malware, key features might include file behavior (such as file system modifications or unusual file access patterns) and the file's metadata (name, size, hash). Dynamic analysis (observing the behavior of the file when executed) can provide additional features, such as network activity generated by the malware or system calls it makes.

Phishing Detection: In the case of phishing attacks, features extracted from email metadata (e.g., sender's email address, subject line, and URL patterns) and content (e.g., the presence of suspicious links, misspellings, or unusual attachments) can be used. Features based on network traffic patterns, such as DNS queries or response times, can also provide insight into phishing attempts, especially when URLs are linked to known malicious domains.

Intrusion Detection: For intrusion detection, features from system logs, authentication attempts, and network traffic are particularly valuable. Features like the frequency of login attempts, the location of incoming traffic, and the sequence of system calls can help detect brute-force attacks, privilege escalation attempts, or lateral movement within a network.

Denial-of-Service (DoS) Detection: In the case of DoS attacks, features extracted from network traffic data, such as packet rate, IP address anomalies, and port scanning activities, are essential for identifying the attack. Statistical features such as the number of requests made per unit of time, along with the source and destination of traffic, can help distinguish between normal and malicious activity.

4. Challenges in Feature Extraction for Malicious Activity Detection

Despite its importance, feature extraction is not without its challenges:

- **High Dimensionality**: Cybersecurity datasets often contain a vast number of features, which can make feature extraction and model training computationally expensive. Dimensionality reduction techniques like PCA or feature selection methods are essential in managing this complexity.
- **Imbalanced Data**: In many real-world cybersecurity datasets, malicious activity is much less common than benign activity, leading to class imbalance. This imbalance can bias machine learning models and make them more likely to classify normal activities as benign, missing actual threats. Techniques such as oversampling, undersampling, or using different evaluation metrics (e.g., F1-score) can help mitigate this problem.
- **Evolving Threats**: Cybersecurity threats are constantly evolving, and the features that were effective for detecting older attack types may no longer be as useful. Continuous monitoring, adaptation, and updating of feature extraction techniques are necessary to keep up with new and emerging threats.

Feature extraction is a vital component of building effective machine learning models for malicious activity detection. By extracting meaningful features from raw data, cybersecurity models can better identify patterns and anomalies indicative of security threats. As attackers evolve their techniques, so must the feature extraction methods used in detecting them. Advanced techniques, such as deep learning and automated feature selection, are helping to improve the effectiveness and efficiency of these detection systems. By focusing on extracting the most relevant and informative features, security professionals can leverage machine learning to build robust systems capable of defending against a wide range of cyberattacks.

3.3 Evaluating and Mitigating False Positives

In the context of cybersecurity and machine learning, false positives occur when a system incorrectly classifies legitimate behavior or activity as malicious. False positives are a significant challenge in threat detection because they can lead to unnecessary alarm, wasted resources, and system disruptions. They are especially problematic in environments where high accuracy and timely responses are critical, such as financial institutions, healthcare organizations, and government agencies.

In this section, we will discuss how to evaluate false positives in machine learning models used for threat detection and explore various strategies to mitigate them, thus improving the effectiveness and efficiency of cybersecurity systems.

1. The Impact of False Positives in Cybersecurity

False positives can have a number of negative consequences for cybersecurity operations, including:

Wasted Resources: When a system generates a false positive, security teams must allocate resources to investigate the event, which may result in wasted time and effort. This is especially problematic in large-scale systems with thousands or millions of alerts. If security analysts spend too much time investigating false alarms, they may miss real threats.

Alert Fatigue: As false positives accumulate, security teams can become overwhelmed by the volume of alerts. This phenomenon, known as "alert fatigue," can lead to desensitization to alerts and the potential for overlooking legitimate threats. The increasing frequency of false positives can impair an organization's ability to respond quickly to genuine security breaches.

Operational Disruption: In some cases, false positives may trigger responses that disrupt normal operations. For example, if a security system mistakenly flags benign user activity as malicious, it might lock out legitimate users or block essential services, affecting productivity and user experience.

Decreased Confidence in Detection Systems: Frequent false positives can undermine the confidence of security teams in the automated detection systems. If these systems are consistently over-sensitive and generate a large number of false alarms, security personnel may begin to ignore alerts or trust their own judgment over the system's outputs.

Thus, minimizing false positives is essential to ensuring the efficiency, reliability, and operational continuity of cybersecurity systems.

2. Evaluating False Positives

Evaluating false positives is critical for understanding their impact and determining how to reduce their frequency. Below are some key strategies and metrics used to evaluate false positives in the context of machine learning models for threat detection:

Confusion Matrix: A confusion matrix is a fundamental tool for evaluating the performance of classification models. It provides a detailed breakdown of the predictions made by the model, categorizing them into four groups:

- **True Positives (TP):** The number of times the model correctly identified a malicious activity as malicious.
- **False Positives (FP):** The number of times the model incorrectly flagged benign activity as malicious.
- **True Negatives (TN):** The number of times the model correctly identified benign activity as benign.
- **False Negatives (FN):** The number of times the model failed to detect malicious activity, classifying it as benign.

The false positive rate (FPR) can be calculated from the confusion matrix as:

$$FPR = \frac{FP}{FP + TN}$$

A low FPR is desirable, as it indicates that the model is effectively distinguishing between malicious and benign activities without generating too many false alarms.

Precision and Recall: Two other important evaluation metrics are precision and recall, which provide more nuanced insights into how well the model is performing in terms of both false positives and false negatives.

Precision measures the proportion of true positives among all the instances that the model identified as malicious. It is given by:

$$Precision = \frac{TP}{TP + FP}$$

High precision indicates that the model is making fewer false positives, but it may come at the cost of reduced recall (i.e., missing more real threats).

Recall (or sensitivity) measures the proportion of true positives among all actual malicious instances. It is given by:

$$Recall = \frac{TP}{TP + FN}$$

High recall ensures that fewer attacks go undetected but may lead to more false positives. The trade-off between precision and recall needs to be carefully managed depending on the use case and threat landscape.

F1-Score: The F1-score is the harmonic mean of precision and recall, offering a balanced evaluation metric when both false positives and false negatives are important:

$$F1 = 2 \times \frac{Precision \times Recall}{Precision + Recall}$$

The F1-score provides a single number that reflects both the precision and recall of the model, making it useful when trying to find a balance between minimizing false positives and false negatives.

Receiver Operating Characteristic (ROC) Curve and Area Under the Curve (AUC): The ROC curve plots the true positive rate (recall) against the false positive rate (FPR) for various threshold values. The area under the ROC curve (AUC) quantifies the overall ability of the model to discriminate between malicious and benign activities. A higher AUC value generally indicates better model performance in terms of minimizing false positives and false negatives.

3. Mitigating False Positives

Once false positives are evaluated, steps must be taken to mitigate their occurrence. Below are several approaches and strategies to reduce the rate of false positives in threat detection systems:

Threshold Tuning: Machine learning models often rely on a threshold to classify an event as malicious or benign. For example, a model may output a probability score for a given event being malicious, and if this probability exceeds a certain threshold, the event is flagged as an attack. By adjusting this threshold, security teams can control the trade-off between false positives and false negatives. Lowering the threshold may catch more malicious activity but increase false positives, while raising it can reduce false positives but potentially miss some attacks. Fine-tuning the threshold based on the specific context of the system or the severity of attacks is a critical step in balancing model performance.

Class Imbalance Handling: In many real-world scenarios, the data used to train models is imbalanced, with far more benign events than malicious ones. This imbalance can cause models to be overly sensitive to benign data and thus increase false positives. Techniques such as oversampling the minority class (malicious activity) or undersampling the majority class (benign activity) can help address this issue. Additionally, using algorithms designed to handle imbalanced data, such as SMOTE (Synthetic Minority Over-sampling Technique), can improve the model's ability to distinguish between malicious and benign activities.

Ensemble Methods: Ensemble methods, such as Random Forests or Gradient Boosting Machines, combine multiple models to improve prediction accuracy. These techniques aggregate predictions from several base models, which reduces the likelihood of false positives by averaging out errors. In the case of security detection, ensemble methods can be particularly effective in minimizing false positives while maintaining high recall.

Feature Selection and Engineering: Proper feature selection and engineering are essential for reducing false positives. By selecting relevant features that are highly indicative of malicious behavior, models are less likely to produce false positives from benign activities. Feature engineering techniques, such as Principal Component Analysis (PCA) or mutual information, can help identify the most important features and discard irrelevant or redundant ones, which improves the model's ability to discriminate between malicious and benign data.

Contextual Analysis: Incorporating context into the detection process can significantly reduce false positives. For example, a network traffic anomaly that occurs at a certain time of day may be entirely normal for some users but suspicious for others. By analyzing user behavior patterns, geography, and device usage, models can take context into account when making predictions. Machine learning models that incorporate contextual features—such as the time of day, user history, and the typical behavior of network traffic—can more accurately distinguish between legitimate and malicious activities.

Continuous Monitoring and Feedback: False positives should be continuously monitored and reviewed by security analysts. As the system processes new data, it should also learn from the feedback provided by analysts. Using active learning or human-in-the-loop approaches, where analysts validate or correct the model's predictions, can help the system improve over time, reducing the rate of false positives.

Explainability and Interpretability: Providing explanations for why a model classifies an activity as malicious can help analysts better understand and verify the model's decision-making process. Explainable AI (XAI) techniques, such as LIME (Local Interpretable Model-agnostic Explanations) or SHAP (Shapley Additive Explanations), can provide insights into which features contributed to a particular prediction. By understanding the reasoning behind the model's decisions, security analysts can more easily filter out false positives and focus on real threats.

False positives present a significant challenge for machine learning-based threat detection systems in cybersecurity. While these systems are essential for identifying and mitigating attacks, high rates of false positives can overwhelm security teams, waste resources, and create operational inefficiencies. By evaluating false positives using metrics like confusion matrices, precision, recall, and AUC, and by employing strategies such as threshold tuning, class imbalance handling, and ensemble methods, organizations can minimize false alarms and improve the performance of their cybersecurity systems. Additionally, continuous monitoring, contextual analysis, and explainability techniques can further refine detection models and reduce the occurrence of false positives over time. Ultimately, the goal is to create a robust and reliable cybersecurity system that can accurately detect malicious activity while minimizing disruptions caused by false positives.

3.4 Case Studies in Machine Learning-Based Threat Detection

Machine learning-based threat detection systems have been increasingly deployed across various industries to identify and mitigate cyber threats in real time. These systems leverage the power of advanced algorithms to analyze vast amounts of data, recognize patterns, and make predictions about potential threats, enabling faster and more accurate threat responses. However, deploying machine learning models in a real-world context can present unique challenges. This section explores several case studies that highlight the practical application of machine learning in cybersecurity threat detection, focusing on the results, challenges, and lessons learned from each example.

1. Case Study: Network Intrusion Detection System (NIDS) in a Financial Institution

Background: A major financial institution deployed a machine learning-based network intrusion detection system (NIDS) to safeguard its network against unauthorized access, DDoS (Distributed Denial of Service) attacks, and other network-based threats. The bank had a large volume of network traffic to monitor and required a solution that could automatically detect anomalies and unauthorized activities in real time.

Solution: The institution implemented a machine learning approach using supervised learning techniques. They used labeled network traffic data to train a model that could classify network activity as benign or malicious. Features such as IP addresses, port numbers, packet sizes, protocol types, and communication patterns were extracted and fed into the model. The system was designed to continuously learn from new data and improve its detection accuracy over time.

Results: The machine learning model was able to detect multiple types of network intrusions that traditional signature-based detection methods had missed, such as zero-day attacks and DDoS attacks that were masked by legitimate traffic. The system successfully flagged unusual patterns, such as abnormal traffic from specific geographic regions or spikes in traffic volume, that were indicative of an attack.

Impact: The financial institution saw a significant reduction in response times to attacks and improved its ability to block malicious traffic in real-time, protecting sensitive customer data and financial assets.

Challenges:

- **False positives**: Despite the improved detection rates, the system generated a high volume of false positives, particularly during periods of network maintenance or large traffic spikes. The security team had to adjust thresholds and apply more sophisticated feature selection techniques to address this issue.

- **Data imbalance**: As the institution processed large amounts of benign network traffic, the machine learning model faced challenges with class imbalance (more benign traffic than malicious). This made it harder for the model to accurately detect rare attacks, which required the use of techniques like oversampling or anomaly detection algorithms to improve performance.
- **Lessons Learned**: The key takeaway was the importance of continuous model training and the need for human-in-the-loop systems to refine model predictions, especially when it comes to reducing false positives and dealing with changing network traffic patterns.

2. Case Study: Malware Detection with Deep Learning at a Technology Company

Background: A leading technology company specializing in software development faced increasing threats from malware attacks, including ransomware and trojans, targeting both its internal network and customer-facing applications. Traditional antivirus software was not sufficient to detect new and evolving malware variants.

Solution: The company decided to implement a deep learning-based solution for malware detection. The system used a convolutional neural network (CNN) to analyze binary executable files, system behavior, and network activity. Features such as file hashes, file structures, system calls, and execution patterns were extracted from suspected files and used as input to the neural network. The goal was to detect new, unknown malware by learning from a vast dataset of both malicious and benign software samples.

Results: The deep learning model demonstrated superior performance compared to traditional malware detection methods. It was able to identify previously unseen malware, even those using novel obfuscation techniques. By training on large datasets, the model continuously improved its ability to detect malware variants by recognizing new behavioral patterns, such as unusual system calls or atypical file modifications.

Impact: The company's security team was able to block malware attacks in real-time and prevent the spread of ransomware across their network. The machine learning system also helped to reduce the reliance on manually updating virus signature databases, which is common in traditional antivirus solutions.

Challenges:

- **Data privacy and quality**: Obtaining a large and diverse set of malware samples for training was challenging, as many malicious files were not publicly available.

Ensuring the quality and representativeness of the training data was essential for the model's success.
- **Adversarial attacks**: As the model became more successful at detecting malware, attackers began using adversarial techniques to modify malicious files in ways that could bypass the detection system. The company had to continuously update the model and incorporate techniques to make the system more resilient to adversarial attacks.
- **Lessons Learned**: The case study highlighted the power of deep learning in detecting novel and previously unseen malware. However, it also underscored the need for continual training and adaptation, as well as the importance of monitoring for adversarial tactics that can circumvent detection methods.

3. Case Study: Phishing Email Detection in a Global E-Commerce Company

Background: A global e-commerce company, with millions of customers worldwide, was facing a surge in phishing attacks targeting its users. These phishing attacks included fraudulent emails designed to steal customer credentials and payment information. The company needed a system that could automatically detect and block phishing emails before they reached customers' inboxes.

Solution: The company implemented a machine learning-based phishing detection system that analyzed the content of incoming emails, including subject lines, sender information, embedded URLs, and email body text. Natural Language Processing (NLP) techniques were used to process the email content and extract features, such as the use of suspicious phrases, unusual sender addresses, and links to known malicious websites. A supervised machine learning model, trained on labeled phishing and legitimate emails, was deployed to classify incoming emails as phishing or not.

Results: The machine learning model successfully identified phishing emails with high accuracy, reducing the number of phishing attacks that reached customers. It also flagged emails with suspicious characteristics, such as deceptive subject lines or requests for sensitive information. The system helped prevent significant financial losses and brand reputation damage by stopping phishing attempts before they could trick users.

Impact: The e-commerce company saw a noticeable decrease in customer complaints related to phishing and fraud. Additionally, the model improved over time as more labeled data was collected and processed, allowing it to detect even more sophisticated phishing attempts.

Challenges:

- **Evolving attack techniques**: Attackers frequently altered the content and format of phishing emails to bypass detection systems. For example, they began using obfuscation techniques such as replacing characters in URLs to evade detection.
- **False positives**: Some legitimate emails, such as those from new or unusual senders, were incorrectly flagged as phishing. The company had to adjust the model's thresholds and incorporate user feedback to fine-tune the system.
- **Lessons Learned**: The case study demonstrated the value of using NLP and machine learning for detecting phishing emails. However, it also highlighted the importance of continuously updating models and utilizing feedback loops to reduce false positives and adapt to new phishing tactics.

4. Case Study: Insider Threat Detection in a Healthcare Organization

Background: A large healthcare organization, with a vast amount of sensitive patient data, was concerned about potential insider threats. These threats could come from employees accessing patient records without authorization or misusing their access privileges for malicious purposes. The organization needed a way to detect suspicious behavior patterns that could indicate insider threats.

Solution: The organization used machine learning to analyze user behavior and detect anomalies. They implemented a system that monitored access logs, file interactions, and login patterns. The system extracted features like the frequency and timing of data access, the type of data accessed, and deviations from normal user behavior. Unsupervised anomaly detection algorithms were used to detect outliers in user behavior that could signal malicious activity or policy violations.

Results: The machine learning system was able to identify several potential insider threats, such as employees accessing records outside their usual scope of work or downloading large amounts of sensitive data. The system flagged these behaviors for further investigation by security teams.

Impact: The healthcare organization was able to detect and prevent unauthorized access to sensitive patient information, ensuring compliance with regulations such as HIPAA (Health Insurance Portability and Accountability Act). It also helped to reduce the risk of data breaches or malicious data theft by insiders.

Challenges:

- **Data privacy concerns**: Monitoring user behavior to detect potential insider threats raised privacy concerns, particularly regarding the collection and analysis of employee activity logs. The organization had to ensure compliance with privacy regulations.
- **False positives**: The system flagged legitimate activities, such as authorized users accessing data for research or administrative purposes, as suspicious. Fine-tuning the model and using contextual information helped reduce false positives.
- **Lessons Learned**: This case study highlighted the effectiveness of machine learning in detecting insider threats by analyzing user behavior. It also emphasized the importance of balancing security measures with employee privacy and the need for continuous model refinement to reduce false positives.

Machine learning-based threat detection systems have proven to be highly effective in a range of cybersecurity use cases, from detecting network intrusions to preventing phishing attacks and identifying insider threats. Each of the case studies discussed in this section demonstrates the power of machine learning in improving detection accuracy, minimizing response times, and reducing human error in security operations. However, as with any technological solution, challenges such as false positives, evolving attack strategies, and data privacy concerns remain. By learning from these case studies, organizations can implement machine learning-based systems that are robust, adaptable, and capable of providing real-time protection against a wide variety of cyber threats.

4. Anomaly Detection and Behavioral Analysis

Chapter 4, Anomaly Detection and Behavioral Analysis, explores how machine learning techniques identify unusual patterns and behaviors that may indicate potential security threats. Focusing on unsupervised learning and clustering methods, this chapter explains how anomaly detection models are trained to recognize deviations from normal behavior, helping to uncover previously unknown threats like insider attacks or advanced persistent threats (APTs). Readers will also learn about behavioral analysis, where user and network activity patterns are profiled to distinguish between typical and suspicious actions. This chapter provides insights into implementing and fine-tuning these models for accurate real-time detection, highlighting their critical role in preemptive cybersecurity strategies.

4.1 Unsupervised Learning Techniques for Anomaly Detection

Anomaly detection is a critical component of modern cybersecurity systems, particularly for identifying novel or previously unseen threats. Unlike supervised learning, where the model is trained on labeled data (i.e., data that has been explicitly categorized as malicious or benign), unsupervised learning operates without the need for labeled data. This makes it highly suitable for detecting anomalies or outliers in scenarios where attack patterns are not known in advance, such as in zero-day attacks, new malware variants, or insider threats.

In cybersecurity, unsupervised anomaly detection methods aim to identify data points or behaviors that deviate significantly from what is considered normal within a given environment. Since attackers often employ tactics designed to evade detection by conventional signature-based methods, the ability to recognize abnormal patterns is crucial for catching new and sophisticated threats.

This section discusses some of the key unsupervised learning techniques used for anomaly detection in cybersecurity, highlighting their strengths, limitations, and practical applications.

1. Clustering-Based Anomaly Detection

One of the most common unsupervised learning techniques for anomaly detection is clustering, which groups similar data points together based on shared features or attributes. Data points that do not fit well into any cluster can be considered anomalous. The most widely used clustering algorithms for anomaly detection include:

K-Means Clustering: K-means is a popular clustering algorithm that groups data points into K distinct clusters by minimizing the variance within each cluster. In the context of anomaly detection, data points that are far from the centroids (the mean position of a cluster) can be flagged as potential anomalies. The distance metric, typically Euclidean distance, is used to measure how far a point lies from the nearest cluster centroid.

Strengths:

- Efficient and scalable for large datasets.
- Can handle a variety of features, such as numerical or categorical data.

Limitations:

- Requires prior knowledge of the number of clusters (K), which may not always be known in cybersecurity applications.
- Sensitive to the initial placement of centroids, which may affect the quality of clustering.

DBSCAN (Density-Based Spatial Clustering of Applications with Noise): Unlike K-means, which assumes that clusters are spherical and of similar size, DBSCAN is density-based and can identify clusters of arbitrary shape. DBSCAN defines clusters as regions of high density separated by regions of low density, and it labels data points in sparse regions as outliers (anomalies). This makes DBSCAN particularly well-suited for detecting anomalies in datasets with irregular cluster shapes.

Strengths:

- Does not require the number of clusters to be specified upfront.
- Handles noise and outliers more effectively by designating sparse points as anomalies.

Limitations:

- Sensitive to the choice of the radius (ε) and the minimum number of points (MinPts) parameters, which may require tuning.

- May struggle with clusters of varying densities.

By identifying outliers in the data, clustering-based anomaly detection can help detect unusual patterns of network traffic, file access, or system behavior that could indicate a cyberattack or breach.

2. Isolation Forest

The Isolation Forest algorithm is a tree-based method that isolates anomalies instead of profiling normal data. The key idea is that anomalies are easier to isolate than normal data points because they are few and different from the rest of the data. The algorithm constructs an ensemble of decision trees and uses random partitioning to isolate individual data points. Points that require fewer splits to isolate are more likely to be anomalies.

Strengths:

- Efficient and well-suited for high-dimensional datasets, such as network traffic data or system logs.
- Scalable and capable of handling large datasets quickly.
- Less sensitive to the dimensionality of the data compared to some other techniques.

Limitations:

- May not perform well if the dataset contains complex relationships between features or if anomalies are highly subtle.
- The performance depends on the quality of the feature set used.

Use Case: In cybersecurity, Isolation Forest can be used to detect unusual patterns in user access logs or application behavior, such as unauthorized access to sensitive files or abnormal data requests that could indicate a breach or insider threat.

3. Autoencoders (Deep Learning for Anomaly Detection)

Autoencoders are a type of artificial neural network used for unsupervised learning tasks, including anomaly detection. The network is trained to compress data into a lower-dimensional representation (encoding) and then reconstruct it back to its original form (decoding). The model learns the normal patterns in the data by minimizing the reconstruction error. Data points that result in a high reconstruction error (i.e., the model fails to recreate them accurately) are considered anomalies.

Strengths:

- Capable of learning complex, non-linear patterns in data.
- Useful for high-dimensional data, such as images, network traffic logs, or behavioral patterns in large datasets.
- Can be trained without labeled data and generalizes well to new, unseen anomalies.

Limitations:

- Requires a large amount of data to train effectively.
- The choice of model architecture and hyperparameters can significantly impact performance.
- May not perform as well on small or highly imbalanced datasets.

Use Case: In cybersecurity, autoencoders are often applied to network traffic data or endpoint behavior analysis. They are particularly effective in detecting zero-day attacks or insider threats that do not match known patterns but exhibit unusual characteristics.

4. One-Class SVM (Support Vector Machine)

One-Class Support Vector Machine (SVM) is an algorithm designed specifically for anomaly detection in unsupervised settings. One-Class SVM works by learning a boundary that encloses most of the data points in a high-dimensional space. The model identifies outliers as points that lie outside this boundary. One-Class SVM is particularly effective in cases where the majority of the data is normal, and only a few data points are anomalous.

Strengths:

- Well-suited for high-dimensional data, such as user activity logs, system performance metrics, or intrusion detection data.
- Can perform well even in cases where anomalies are sparse and difficult to distinguish from normal data.

Limitations:

- May struggle when the data is not well-separated, or when anomalies lie near the decision boundary.
- Sensitive to the choice of kernel and regularization parameters, which may require careful tuning.

Use Case: One-Class SVM is commonly used in detecting fraudulent activities or security breaches where malicious behavior deviates significantly from typical user or system behavior. It is especially useful in areas like intrusion detection or detecting unsolicited access to systems that don't match historical patterns.

5. Statistical Methods

Statistical anomaly detection techniques rely on modeling the statistical properties of data and flagging points that deviate from expected behavior. These techniques assume that normal data follows a certain distribution, such as Gaussian (normal) distribution, and that anomalies can be detected by identifying data points that fall far from the mean (or other statistical measures like variance).

Gaussian Mixture Models (GMM): A probabilistic model that assumes data points are generated from a mixture of several Gaussian distributions. Anomalies are detected by looking for data points that have low likelihoods of belonging to any of the Gaussian components.

Z-Score Analysis: A simple statistical method where anomalies are flagged if their values deviate significantly from the mean (i.e., if their Z-score is above a certain threshold).

Strengths:

- Simple and intuitive to implement.
- Effective for detecting anomalies in data that follows a well-known statistical distribution.

Limitations:

- Assumes that normal data follows a specific distribution, which may not always be the case in complex or dynamic environments.
- May not perform well in cases where the data exhibits complex, non-linear relationships.

Use Case: Statistical anomaly detection is often used in monitoring system performance, such as CPU usage, network bandwidth, or storage utilization. A significant deviation from the expected values (based on historical data) could indicate an abnormal event like a DDoS attack, system malfunction, or unauthorized system access.

Unsupervised learning techniques for anomaly detection provide powerful tools for identifying previously unknown or emerging threats in cybersecurity. By leveraging algorithms like clustering, Isolation Forests, autoencoders, One-Class SVM, and statistical methods, organizations can build systems capable of detecting deviations from normal behavior, which is critical for spotting sophisticated attacks that bypass traditional signature-based detection methods.

Each technique has its strengths and challenges, and the choice of method often depends on the specific characteristics of the data being analyzed and the type of anomaly being targeted. By understanding the strengths and limitations of these unsupervised methods, security professionals can better utilize them to enhance threat detection and response capabilities in their cybersecurity infrastructure.

4.2 Profiling and Modeling User Behavior

In modern cybersecurity, the behavior of users within an organization's network or system provides crucial insights into potential threats, especially insider threats, fraud, or compromised accounts. Profiling and modeling user behavior is an essential approach to detect deviations that could indicate malicious activity. This process involves analyzing and understanding what "normal" user behavior looks like in order to identify abnormal behavior patterns that could be indicative of a cyberattack, data breach, or other security incidents.

By profiling users and modeling their behavior over time, cybersecurity systems can leverage data to detect anomalies that deviate from established patterns. These techniques are particularly useful in scenarios such as unauthorized access, privilege escalation, phishing attacks, or insider threats. This section explores how user behavior profiling and modeling work in the context of cybersecurity, with an emphasis on methods, technologies, and practical applications.

1. The Concept of User Behavior Analytics (UBA)

User Behavior Analytics (UBA) refers to the process of applying data analytics to monitor, analyze, and understand user behavior within an organization's network. It involves gathering data from various sources, such as network logs, authentication logs, application usage, and system interactions, and using it to create a baseline of normal activity for each user or group of users. Once a baseline is established, UBA systems can detect deviations that may signify suspicious or anomalous activities.

UBA is based on the assumption that malicious behavior often deviates from the norm, making it easier to spot potential threats through anomaly detection. For example, if an employee suddenly accesses a large number of sensitive files that they would not normally need for their job role, this could indicate a breach, misuse of privileges, or an insider threat.

Key Components of UBA:

- **Data Collection**: Collecting logs and data points from systems such as user activity logs, network traffic, authentication requests, file access, and application use.
- **Baseline Creation**: Building a statistical or machine learning model that represents normal user behavior based on historical data.
- **Anomaly Detection**: Identifying deviations from the baseline that could indicate suspicious behavior.
- **Alert Generation**: Triggering alerts when abnormal behavior is detected, prompting further investigation.

2. Feature Engineering for User Behavior Modeling

The foundation of any successful user behavior profiling system is the selection and extraction of relevant features that can effectively represent user activity. Features represent the characteristics of a user's behavior and serve as input for machine learning models, anomaly detection algorithms, or statistical methods. The choice of features is crucial in ensuring that the system can distinguish between normal variations in behavior and true malicious activity.

Common features used for profiling user behavior include:

- **Login Patterns**: Frequency and timing of logins, such as whether a user logs in at unusual times or from uncommon locations.
- **Data Access Patterns**: Which files or databases a user accesses, how often they access them, and the volume of data being retrieved.

- **Application Usage**: The types of applications a user interacts with, how frequently, and the way they use those applications (e.g., commands entered in a system, search queries, etc.).
- **Network Activity**: The amount of traffic generated by a user, including web browsing, remote connections, and communications with external IPs or devices.
- **File and System Modifications**: Whether a user modifies system configurations, downloads files, or makes other administrative changes.
- **Geographic Location**: The locations from which users log in (e.g., detecting logins from foreign countries or unexpected IP addresses).

Feature Engineering Considerations:

- **Contextualization**: Understanding the context of the activity is critical. For instance, a user accessing a large number of files may be normal for an administrator, but suspicious for a regular employee. Thus, user roles and specific job requirements should inform feature selection.
- **Normalization**: It's essential to normalize data to account for variations in user behavior that occur due to role, department, or other factors. For example, salespeople may frequently access customer data, while accountants typically access financial records.
- **Granularity**: Feature granularity matters in behavioral modeling. Fine-grained data, such as individual keystrokes, mouse movements, or file timestamps, might reveal subtle signs of malicious intent.

3. Behavioral Clustering and Profiling

Once user data is collected and relevant features are extracted, the next step is to group users based on their similar behaviors. Clustering techniques can help to identify groups of users who exhibit similar activity patterns, enabling security teams to create profiles for each group. Clustering is typically used in unsupervised learning settings, where the system groups users without predefined labels.

Common clustering algorithms used in behavior profiling include:

- **K-Means Clustering**: A popular method for partitioning users into clusters based on their behavioral features. Each cluster represents a group of users with similar patterns, such as access times, file usage, or network activity.
- **DBSCAN (Density-Based Spatial Clustering of Applications with Noise)**: This method groups users based on density, meaning it can handle irregular or

overlapping user behavior patterns and identify outliers (anomalies) more effectively.
- **Hierarchical Clustering**: This approach creates a hierarchy of clusters, allowing for more flexible grouping and easy identification of subgroups within larger clusters of users with similar behaviors.

Benefits of Behavioral Clustering:

- **Role-Based Profiling**: Clustering can be used to create profiles based on the role or department of users. For example, sales representatives may form one cluster, while IT administrators may form another, each with distinct behavior patterns.
- **Anomaly Detection**: By understanding the typical behavior of each cluster, security systems can more easily detect when an individual's behavior deviates significantly from the group norm, such as an admin accessing unusual files outside their role.

Challenges:

- **Dynamic Behavior**: Users' behavior can change over time due to factors such as new responsibilities, promotions, or changes in work patterns. This makes it challenging to maintain accurate profiles.
- **Contextual Anomalies**: Some deviations in behavior might be legitimate (e.g., a user needing to access a file they normally wouldn't because of a specific project), so clustering systems need to account for contextual changes.

4. Machine Learning Models for User Behavior

Machine learning models can play a significant role in the accurate profiling and modeling of user behavior. The advantage of using machine learning is that it can learn and adapt over time, improving its ability to detect anomalies and adjust to changing user patterns. Various machine learning models can be employed to build user behavior profiles:

Supervised Learning: In cases where labeled data is available (e.g., known instances of malicious activity or user breaches), supervised models such as decision trees, support vector machines (SVMs), and random forests can be trained to classify user behavior as either normal or suspicious.

Unsupervised Learning: For situations where labeled data is not available, unsupervised techniques like clustering, Isolation Forest, and autoencoders (discussed earlier) can detect anomalies by comparing current behavior to established profiles.

Reinforcement Learning: This is an emerging area for anomaly detection, where the system continuously learns from interactions and rewards based on the detection of malicious behavior. For instance, the system could reward itself when it successfully identifies a threat or anomaly without raising false alarms.

Advantages:

- **Adaptability**: Machine learning models can evolve over time as they are exposed to new data, adapting to changes in user behavior.
- **Scalability**: These models are capable of handling large datasets, such as log data from thousands or millions of users, without requiring manual rule updates.

Challenges:

- **Data Quality**: Machine learning models require high-quality, clean data for training. If the data is noisy or incomplete, the model's accuracy can be compromised.
- **False Positives**: Incorrectly flagging legitimate activities as anomalous is a common challenge. Continuous model tuning and human-in-the-loop verification are often needed.

5. Detecting Insider Threats with Behavioral Profiling

One of the most critical applications of user behavior profiling is the detection of insider threats—malicious activities carried out by trusted individuals within the organization. Behavioral profiling helps identify suspicious patterns, such as:

- Unusual login times or locations (e.g., an employee logging in from an unfamiliar country).
- Access to sensitive files outside of the user's job role or unusual file download volumes.
- Excessive or unauthorized system changes, such as modifying security settings or transferring large volumes of data.
- By comparing the current behavior of users to their historical profile and the profiles of similar users, security systems can flag potential insider threats early, before the damage escalates.

Profiling and modeling user behavior are powerful tools in the cybersecurity arsenal, particularly for detecting anomalies that could indicate malicious activity. By capturing normal behavioral patterns and using unsupervised learning techniques, organizations can create accurate models of user behavior and detect deviations that may represent a threat. These methods are critical for identifying insider threats, fraud, or account compromises and can significantly enhance an organization's ability to respond to emerging security incidents.

However, building and maintaining effective user behavior models requires careful consideration of feature selection, data quality, and ongoing model refinement. As user behavior constantly evolves, profiling systems must be adaptable and capable of identifying not only well-known attack vectors but also novel threats.

4.3 Real-Time Analysis for Intrusion Detection

In the rapidly evolving landscape of cybersecurity, real-time analysis for intrusion detection is a critical component of modern security operations. Traditional intrusion detection systems (IDS) often struggle to keep up with the fast-paced nature of cyber threats, where attacks can unfold in seconds or minutes. As a result, real-time detection methods powered by advanced technologies such as machine learning, artificial intelligence (AI), and big data analytics have become indispensable for identifying and mitigating security breaches as they happen.

Real-time intrusion detection involves monitoring network traffic, system activities, and user behaviors to identify suspicious or malicious actions in real-time, enabling organizations to respond to threats before significant damage occurs. By leveraging continuous data streams and applying advanced algorithms for immediate analysis, real-time intrusion detection systems (IDS) can help prevent data breaches, unauthorized access, and various types of cyberattacks such as denial-of-service (DoS), malware propagation, and insider threats.

This section explores how real-time analysis is applied in intrusion detection, focusing on the underlying techniques, technologies, and the role of artificial intelligence and machine learning in enhancing detection accuracy and response speed.

1. Real-Time Data Collection and Monitoring

The foundation of any effective real-time intrusion detection system is continuous data collection and monitoring. In order to detect intrusions as they occur, systems need access to data from multiple sources, including network traffic, system logs, authentication logs, application interactions, and user behaviors. This data provides the raw material for identifying anomalies and security breaches in real-time.

Common sources of data for real-time monitoring include:

- **Network Traffic**: Monitoring packets, sessions, and connections in real time to detect signs of network-based attacks like Distributed Denial-of-Service (DDoS), SQL injection, or man-in-the-middle attacks.
- **Host Activity Logs**: Logs from endpoints, including workstations, servers, and IoT devices, which help detect unusual system activities such as unauthorized access or changes to system files.
- **User Authentication Data**: Monitoring login attempts, multi-factor authentication (MFA) logs, and session tracking to identify credential stuffing, brute-force attacks, or unauthorized access.
- **Application Logs**: Real-time monitoring of applications and services to identify suspicious patterns of usage or command execution that could signal an intrusion attempt.

By collecting data from diverse sources, security teams can gain a comprehensive view of activity across their network, making it easier to detect malicious actions in their earliest stages.

2. Techniques for Real-Time Intrusion Detection

Real-time intrusion detection systems (IDS) rely on several key techniques to analyze incoming data and identify potential threats. These techniques can be broadly classified into two categories: signature-based detection and anomaly-based detection. In recent years, the integration of machine learning and AI has enhanced the effectiveness of these methods, enabling more dynamic and adaptive intrusion detection.

2.1 Signature-Based Detection

Signature-based detection is a traditional method that relies on predefined patterns or "signatures" of known threats. It works by comparing incoming data against a database of known attack signatures or patterns of malicious behavior. When a match is found, an alert is triggered, indicating that a known intrusion has occurred.

Strengths:

- **High accuracy for known threats**: Signature-based detection is highly effective at detecting known threats, such as viruses, malware, or known attack vectors.
- **Fast detection**: The comparison of data to known signatures is fast, enabling real-time detection.

Limitations:

- **Ineffective against new or unknown threats**: Signature-based methods fail to detect new attack methods or zero-day vulnerabilities, as these do not have predefined signatures.
- **Constant updates required**: Signature databases must be regularly updated to keep up with new threats, making the system reliant on timely updates.

2.2 Anomaly-Based Detection

Anomaly-based detection focuses on identifying deviations from established norms or baselines of "normal" behavior. By continuously monitoring network activity, user behavior, and system operations, the IDS creates a model of normal activity. If a deviation from this baseline occurs—such as an unexpected login location, abnormal data transfer rates, or unusual application behavior—the system flags it as potentially malicious.

Strengths:

- **Detects unknown threats**: Anomaly-based detection is capable of detecting new, previously unseen threats because it does not rely on predefined signatures. This makes it useful for identifying novel or sophisticated attacks like zero-day exploits or insider threats.
- **Adaptability**: Anomaly detection can adapt over time as the system learns and refines what constitutes normal behavior in a given environment.

Limitations:

- **False positives**: Anomaly-based systems can generate false positives, especially if the model of normal behavior is not well-defined. For example, if a user performs a legitimate action that deviates slightly from their usual behavior, the system might flag it as suspicious.
- **Training and tuning**: The system requires training on baseline data, which can be time-consuming and complex, especially in dynamic environments where user behavior or network traffic frequently changes.

2.3 Hybrid Systems: Combining Signature and Anomaly Detection

Many modern real-time IDS solutions combine both signature-based and anomaly-based detection to leverage the strengths of both methods while minimizing their weaknesses. A hybrid approach allows systems to quickly detect known threats through signature matching while also identifying new or unusual attack patterns through anomaly detection.

For example, when an anomaly is detected, the system may cross-reference it with known attack signatures to assess whether it matches a known threat. If no match is found, the anomaly can be flagged for further analysis by security analysts or subjected to more advanced detection techniques, such as machine learning.

Strengths:

- **Comprehensive detection**: The hybrid approach provides a more holistic security solution, detecting both known and unknown threats.
- **Reduced false positives**: By combining both methods, the system can reduce the likelihood of flagging legitimate behavior as suspicious.

Limitations:

- **Complexity**: Hybrid systems can be more complex to set up and manage, requiring more resources for configuration, maintenance, and monitoring.

3. Machine Learning and AI in Real-Time Intrusion Detection

Machine learning and artificial intelligence have revolutionized the field of real-time intrusion detection by enhancing the ability of IDS systems to identify complex and previously unknown threats. Rather than relying on predefined rules or signatures, machine learning models can analyze vast amounts of data in real time and learn to recognize subtle patterns that might indicate an intrusion.

3.1 Supervised Learning Models

In a supervised learning approach, the machine learning model is trained using labeled data, where known instances of normal and malicious activity are provided. The model learns to classify new data based on this training. Common supervised learning algorithms for intrusion detection include decision trees, support vector machines (SVM), and random forests.

Strengths:

- **Accurate threat classification**: Supervised models can provide high accuracy in classifying known attack types.
- **Continuous learning**: The model can continuously be updated with new labeled data to improve detection accuracy.

Limitations:

- **Data labeling requirements**: Labeled data is often difficult to obtain, and the model's performance depends on the quality and diversity of the training data.

3.2 Unsupervised Learning Models

Unsupervised learning models, such as clustering algorithms and autoencoders, are trained on unlabeled data, making them suitable for detecting unknown or zero-day attacks. These models learn the inherent structure in the data and flag instances that deviate significantly from normal behavior.

Strengths:

- **Detection of unknown threats**: Unsupervised learning can detect new and previously unseen attack patterns.
- **Reduced reliance on labeled data**: These models do not require manually labeled data, making them more adaptable.

Limitations:

- **Higher false positives**: Unsupervised models are more prone to false positives, especially if the definition of "normal" behavior is not well-established.

3.3 Deep Learning for Intrusion Detection

Deep learning techniques, particularly neural networks, are increasingly being applied in real-time intrusion detection due to their ability to process large and complex datasets with minimal feature engineering. Deep learning models, such as Convolutional Neural Networks (CNNs) and Recurrent Neural Networks (RNNs), can automatically extract meaningful features from raw data, making them highly effective for intrusion detection.

Strengths:

- **Automatic feature extraction**: Deep learning models can automatically learn the most relevant features from raw data, reducing the need for manual feature engineering.
- **High accuracy and scalability**: Deep learning models excel at detecting complex attack patterns and are capable of processing vast amounts of data in real-time.

Limitations:

- **Resource-intensive**: Training deep learning models requires significant computational resources and time.
- **Black-box nature**: Deep learning models are often viewed as "black boxes," making it difficult to interpret or understand how they reach their conclusions.

4. Real-Time Incident Response

Once an intrusion is detected in real-time, the system must respond swiftly to minimize the damage. Automated incident response plays a crucial role in this process, leveraging predefined workflows and playbooks to take immediate actions, such as blocking malicious IP addresses, isolating compromised systems, or alerting security personnel.

Key Actions in Incident Response:

- **Automatic blocking or isolation**: Real-time IDS systems can take immediate actions, such as blocking IP addresses associated with a malicious actor or quarantining compromised devices.
- **Alert generation**: Security teams are notified instantly, allowing them to investigate and take corrective action.
- **Root cause analysis**: Real-time systems often provide detailed logs and context to help security teams understand the attack's origin and scope.

Real-time analysis for intrusion detection is vital for defending against modern cyberattacks, especially those that unfold rapidly or target unknown vulnerabilities. By combining data collection, machine learning, anomaly detection, and real-time incident response, organizations can detect and mitigate threats before they escalate into major breaches. As cyber threats continue to evolve, the ability to analyze data in real-time will remain crucial for maintaining a strong defense and ensuring proactive protection against emerging security risks.

4.4 Tuning and Optimizing Anomaly Detection Systems

Anomaly detection is a powerful method for identifying unusual patterns in data that may indicate a cyber threat, but its effectiveness relies heavily on proper tuning and optimization. Anomaly detection systems, particularly those powered by machine learning and artificial intelligence, must be finely tuned to ensure they can differentiate between legitimate deviations and true malicious activity. Without the correct configuration, these systems can either miss threats or generate an overwhelming number of false positives, both of which undermine their utility in a security context.

This section delves into the importance of tuning and optimizing anomaly detection systems for maximum accuracy and efficiency. It explores the challenges faced when fine-tuning such systems and offers practical strategies for improving their performance, as well as maintaining their effectiveness over time.

1. Understanding the Need for Tuning

Anomaly detection systems are typically trained to identify deviations from an established "normal" baseline of behavior. However, defining what constitutes "normal" is complex and can vary significantly depending on the environment, user activity, and even time of day. A system that is too rigid or overly sensitive might generate false alarms, flagging benign activities (e.g., a system administrator accessing a server) as suspicious. On the other hand, a system that is too lenient might fail to detect actual threats (e.g., a hacker mimicking legitimate behavior).

Tuning is necessary because real-world environments are dynamic. User behavior evolves over time, network traffic fluctuates, and new devices or services are added. Furthermore, attackers often try to blend into normal operations, making it harder to spot malicious activity. Proper tuning of the detection model ensures that the system can adjust to changes in normal behavior while maintaining a high detection rate for real threats.

2. Key Considerations in Tuning Anomaly Detection Systems

There are several factors to consider when tuning an anomaly detection system. These considerations impact how the system performs, the number of false positives it generates, and its ability to detect novel or evolving attacks.

2.1 Feature Selection and Engineering

The choice of features—essentially the data points that represent user or system behavior—is fundamental in shaping how well an anomaly detection system can differentiate between normal and abnormal activity. Selecting relevant features requires a deep understanding of the environment, the types of threats to be detected, and the nature of normal operations.

Considerations for Feature Selection:

- **Relevance**: Features should directly correlate with the behaviors you are trying to monitor. For example, login time, data access patterns, and unusual file transfers might be more relevant than general system uptime.
- **Dimensionality**: Using too many features can lead to a "curse of dimensionality," where the system becomes overly complex and computationally expensive. Feature reduction techniques such as Principal Component Analysis (PCA) or t-Distributed Stochastic Neighbor Embedding (t-SNE) can help by reducing the number of features without losing critical information.
- **Correlation**: Highly correlated features should be avoided, as they provide redundant information that can degrade model performance. Feature selection techniques like mutual information or feature importance can help identify the most significant features.
- **Behavioral Context**: Some anomalies may be specific to certain contexts (e.g., an unusual login pattern during a security update may not be anomalous), so features must be selected with these variables in mind.

2.2 Baseline Normal Behavior

Creating an accurate baseline of normal behavior is essential for anomaly detection systems. The baseline represents the "expected" patterns of user or system activity, and the system flags deviations from this baseline as potential anomalies.

Challenges in Baseline Creation:

- **Dynamic Environments**: User behavior and system activity change over time. For instance, remote work or seasonal fluctuations in business activity may alter the baseline, requiring continuous adjustments.
- **Granularity of the Baseline**: A system might be too sensitive if the baseline is set at a very granular level (e.g., monitoring behavior on a per-minute or per-second basis). Conversely, a baseline that's too broad might miss subtle deviations indicative of an attack.

Strategies for Baseline Tuning:

- **Rolling Windows**: Using a rolling window to continuously update the baseline based on recent data can help account for seasonal or short-term changes in behavior.
- **Dynamic Thresholding**: Instead of applying a static threshold for anomaly detection, dynamic thresholds that adapt to changing activity levels can offer a more flexible and accurate approach.
- **Adaptive Baseline Models**: Machine learning models like autoencoders or k-means clustering can adjust baselines automatically, learning from new data as it arrives. This helps in identifying evolving behaviors and adapting to changes in system usage.

2.3 Threshold Selection

Once a baseline of normal behavior is defined, setting appropriate thresholds for detecting anomalies is a critical aspect of system tuning. A threshold is the point at which the system flags a behavior as anomalous. If the threshold is set too low, the system may generate an excessive number of false positives, while a threshold that's too high could result in missed detections of true threats.

Considerations for Threshold Tuning:

- **False Positives vs. Missed Detections**: There is often a trade-off between minimizing false positives and detecting true threats. Security teams need to decide what is more critical for their environment—either to minimize disruption from false alarms or to ensure that no malicious activities go undetected.
- **Environmental Sensitivity**: In highly sensitive environments, such as financial institutions or government agencies, a lower threshold may be acceptable in exchange for heightened security. In less sensitive environments, higher thresholds may be used to reduce the volume of alerts.
- **Sliding Thresholds**: Some systems use sliding thresholds, which adjust based on factors such as time of day, the user's typical behavior, or the severity of the detected anomaly.

2.4 Real-Time Feedback and Retraining

Real-time feedback and continuous retraining of the system are essential for maintaining its accuracy and adapting to new types of attacks. In dynamic environments, threat actors often employ techniques to evade detection, making it necessary for the system to continuously improve its models.

Approaches to Real-Time Feedback:

- **Human-in-the-loop**: Security analysts can provide feedback on the system's performance by reviewing false positives and false negatives. This feedback can be incorporated into the model to fine-tune its accuracy.
- **Online Learning**: Online learning algorithms update the model incrementally as new data arrives, making them ideal for adapting to changing behavior and threat landscapes in real time.
- **Model Retraining**: Periodic retraining of machine learning models is essential for incorporating new data, ensuring the system stays relevant and accurate in identifying new threats or adapting to shifting baseline behavior.

3. Addressing False Positives and False Negatives

False positives (incorrectly identifying normal behavior as anomalous) and false negatives (failing to identify a true attack) are common challenges in anomaly detection systems. Balancing these two types of errors is a key element of tuning an anomaly detection system.

- **Minimizing False Positives**: To reduce false positives, consider adjusting the system's sensitivity, refining feature selection, or incorporating additional contextual information (e.g., role-based access controls or time-of-day patterns). False positives may also be reduced by applying post-processing techniques, such as filtering or correlating events across different data sources.
- **Minimizing False Negatives**: To minimize false negatives, adjust thresholds and incorporate more sophisticated anomaly detection techniques, such as deep learning, that can detect subtle signs of suspicious activity.

4. Testing and Validation

Before deploying an anomaly detection system in a production environment, it's essential to thoroughly test and validate it. This process involves simulating both normal and malicious activities to assess the system's accuracy and performance.

Key Testing Strategies:

- **Cross-Validation**: Use cross-validation techniques to assess how well the model generalizes to unseen data and performs in different scenarios.
- **Simulated Attacks**: Simulate various attack types, such as brute-force attempts, privilege escalation, or data exfiltration, to evaluate how effectively the system can detect these activities in real-time.

Tuning and optimizing an anomaly detection system is a critical task for ensuring its reliability, accuracy, and efficiency in real-time cybersecurity operations. From feature selection and baseline creation to threshold adjustment and real-time feedback, each aspect plays a crucial role in ensuring that the system can detect legitimate threats while minimizing false positives. Through ongoing tuning, continuous training, and regular evaluation, anomaly detection systems can evolve to meet the demands of a changing threat landscape, providing timely alerts and helping security teams mitigate risks before they escalate into full-blown incidents.

5. Natural Language Processing for Threat Intelligence

Chapter 5, Natural Language Processing for Threat Intelligence, explores the powerful role of Natural Language Processing (NLP) in extracting actionable insights from unstructured text data, such as threat reports, social media posts, blogs, and other open-source intelligence (OSINT). This chapter introduces the core NLP techniques used in cybersecurity, including text classification, entity recognition, and sentiment analysis, to identify and assess emerging threats. Readers will discover how NLP helps automate the processing of large volumes of threat data, enabling quicker identification of relevant patterns and trends. By the end of this chapter, readers will understand how NLP can enhance threat intelligence gathering, improve situational awareness, and support proactive defense mechanisms.

5.1 Fundamentals of NLP for Security Applications

Natural Language Processing (NLP) has become a pivotal tool in cybersecurity, enabling systems to understand, interpret, and derive actionable insights from human language. In a world where vast amounts of unstructured data are generated daily—ranging from emails and social media posts to security logs and threat reports—NLP allows security professionals to analyze, categorize, and act upon text-based information in ways that were once unimaginable.

NLP plays an essential role in enhancing various aspects of cybersecurity, particularly in threat intelligence, malware analysis, and incident response. By bridging the gap between raw text data and structured insights, NLP empowers security systems to sift through enormous amounts of textual data, identify emerging threats, and facilitate a more proactive approach to security.

This section introduces the fundamental concepts of NLP and its application within the context of cybersecurity, focusing on how it enhances threat detection, vulnerability assessment, and risk management through text and language processing.

1. Understanding Natural Language Processing

At its core, Natural Language Processing (NLP) is a field of artificial intelligence (AI) that enables computers to process and analyze human language. NLP combines computational linguistics, machine learning, and statistical models to understand and generate text or speech that humans can understand.

In cybersecurity, NLP's primary goal is to convert unstructured, complex textual data into structured insights that machines can understand. This is important because much of the information used in security operations is in the form of text—be it written reports, user activity logs, email communications, or social media posts related to cyber threats.

Some key NLP tasks relevant to cybersecurity include:

- **Tokenization**: Breaking down text into smaller units, such as words or phrases, to understand its structure.
- **Named Entity Recognition (NER)**: Identifying and classifying entities such as organizations, countries, dates, or specific threats (e.g., malware names) from unstructured text.
- **Part-of-Speech Tagging**: Determining the grammatical structure of a sentence to understand how words relate to each other.
- **Sentiment Analysis**: Evaluating the sentiment of a piece of text (positive, negative, neutral) to identify emotional tone, which can be useful for detecting phishing attempts or fraudulent activity.
- **Text Classification**: Categorizing text into predefined categories (e.g., identifying whether an email is a phishing attempt, a spam message, or a legitimate communication).

2. The Role of NLP in Cyber Threat Intelligence

Threat intelligence involves gathering, analyzing, and acting on information about potential or active cyber threats to an organization. Traditionally, threat intelligence relies heavily on human analysts to sift through vast amounts of textual data (e.g., reports, emails, forum posts) to identify indicators of compromise (IOCs) or emerging attack patterns. NLP significantly accelerates this process by automating much of the analysis.

Key Applications of NLP in Threat Intelligence:

- **Automated Threat Report Analysis**: NLP can be used to analyze threat intelligence feeds, security blogs, and research papers to extract and categorize key information such as new malware families, attack techniques, and vulnerable systems. This helps security teams stay informed about the latest threats without manually reviewing each report.

- **Threat Actor Profiling**: By analyzing communication patterns and narratives from cybercriminal forums, darknet sites, or leaked documents, NLP helps identify potential threat actors and understand their tactics, techniques, and procedures (TTPs). This enables proactive defense strategies.
- **Event Correlation**: NLP allows for the automatic correlation of unstructured text from different sources (e.g., alerts, logs, emails) to detect patterns of malicious activity. For instance, NLP can detect the mention of a known exploit or malware in various communication channels and link them to an ongoing attack.

3. NLP in Malware Analysis and Detection

One of the most critical applications of NLP in cybersecurity is in malware analysis. Many forms of malware are designed to evade traditional detection systems by obfuscating their code or communicating with command-and-control servers through encrypted channels. However, NLP can play a significant role in analyzing malware-related text and improving detection capabilities.

Malware-Related NLP Applications:

- **Automated Analysis of Malware Descriptions**: Researchers often release detailed reports and descriptions of new malware strains, which are often published in text form. NLP tools can automatically parse and extract key attributes, such as malware names, attack vectors, and indicators of compromise (IOCs), which are vital for identifying and mitigating new threats.
- **Static and Dynamic Analysis of Malware Behavior**: In addition to analyzing static malware descriptions, NLP can be applied to dynamic behavioral data collected during malware execution (e.g., logs, command logs, and interactions with files or processes). NLP can help identify patterns or keywords that suggest malicious behavior, assisting analysts in building more comprehensive threat models.
- **Phishing Detection**: Phishing emails often contain specific linguistic cues, such as urgency, spoofed sender addresses, and subtle social engineering techniques. NLP can be used to analyze email content, subject lines, and metadata to automatically classify and detect phishing attempts.

4. NLP for Incident Response and Security Operations

In the context of incident response, time is critical, and cybersecurity professionals need to quickly process and respond to any emerging security incidents. NLP helps by automating the extraction of key data from various sources, such as alerts, logs, or communication threads, enabling faster decision-making.

Key Uses of NLP in Incident Response:

- **Incident Triage**: Security operations teams are often inundated with large volumes of alerts and logs. NLP techniques can be used to triage and prioritize incidents based on severity, urgency, and context, helping analysts focus on the most critical threats first. NLP can also filter out non-critical alerts or repetitive patterns, improving efficiency.
- **Log Analysis**: System and network logs are key sources of information during a security incident. By using NLP to process these logs, organizations can identify unusual patterns, track potential intrusion indicators, and correlate events across different systems to understand the scope of the breach.
- **Automated Report Generation**: After an incident, organizations must often generate detailed reports to communicate findings, remediation steps, and lessons learned. NLP can help by automating the generation of such reports based on incident logs, attack timelines, and other relevant data, reducing the time spent on documentation and improving response efficiency.

5. Challenges and Limitations of NLP in Security

While NLP offers significant advantages in the realm of cybersecurity, there are challenges that must be addressed to maximize its effectiveness:

- **Ambiguity in Language**: Natural language is often ambiguous, and identifying the meaning of words in different contexts can be difficult. For example, the word "attack" could refer to a cyberattack, a military strike, or even an aggressive comment in a discussion forum. Disambiguating such terms requires sophisticated models that can understand the context of the data.
- **Language Variations**: Textual data can come in many languages, dialects, or technical jargon, making it difficult for NLP systems to process all data uniformly. NLP systems need to be adapted to handle these variations, which may involve specialized training data or models.
- **Data Quality**: NLP algorithms rely on large amounts of high-quality, labeled data to train models effectively. In cybersecurity, acquiring sufficient labeled data can be challenging, especially for detecting new or evolving threats.
- **Computational Resources**: Advanced NLP techniques, such as deep learning-based models (e.g., transformer models like BERT and GPT), require substantial

computational power and large datasets to train. This may be a limiting factor for some organizations.

NLP is an invaluable tool for enhancing the effectiveness of cybersecurity measures, especially in areas such as threat intelligence, malware analysis, and incident response. By enabling the automated extraction and analysis of insights from vast amounts of unstructured textual data, NLP allows security professionals to identify and mitigate cyber threats more efficiently. However, its challenges—ranging from ambiguity and data quality issues to the need for specialized resources—must be addressed to maximize its impact in the field of cybersecurity. With continued advancements in AI and machine learning, the future of NLP in cybersecurity holds immense potential to revolutionize the way we detect and respond to cyber threats.

5.2 Processing and Classifying Unstructured Threat Data

In the world of cybersecurity, vast amounts of unstructured data are generated every day—ranging from emails, social media posts, and web traffic to system logs, security alerts, and threat intelligence feeds. This unstructured data often holds critical information about emerging threats, vulnerabilities, and attack techniques. However, the challenge lies in processing and classifying this unstructured data to extract meaningful and actionable insights that can guide security teams in defending against cyberattacks.

Unstructured data is typically in the form of raw text, which lacks the clear organization found in structured data such as databases or spreadsheets. While structured data can be easily analyzed using conventional tools and models, unstructured data presents a more complex challenge. Fortunately, with the advancements in Natural Language Processing (NLP) and machine learning (ML), organizations can now better process, classify, and analyze unstructured threat data to identify emerging threats, vulnerabilities, and attack trends in real time.

This section focuses on the methods and techniques used to process and classify unstructured threat data within the context of cybersecurity. We will explore how organizations can apply NLP and ML models to detect malicious activities, prioritize security risks, and ultimately improve incident response.

1. Challenges in Processing Unstructured Threat Data

Unstructured threat data comes in a variety of forms—text-based threat reports, emails, security logs, chat logs, news articles, social media posts, and more. The primary challenge is that this data is not organized in any predetermined format, making it difficult to extract relevant information and insights without sophisticated processing techniques.

Some key challenges in processing unstructured threat data include:

- **Volume**: The sheer volume of unstructured data can overwhelm security systems. Threat intelligence feeds, security logs, and social media platforms generate vast amounts of data every day. Manual analysis is impractical, and automating the process requires robust systems that can handle large-scale data efficiently.
- **Diversity**: Unstructured data is highly diverse, with different formats (e.g., emails, blog posts, forum discussions) and varied content (e.g., technical jargon, informal language, slang, abbreviations). This diversity makes it difficult for traditional systems to process and analyze data effectively.
- **Ambiguity**: Human language is inherently ambiguous, which can pose a significant challenge for NLP and ML models. Words or phrases may have different meanings based on context, and attackers may intentionally use obfuscation tactics to evade detection.
- **Relevance**: Not all unstructured data is relevant to a given security context. For example, social media chatter about a security breach might include both valuable information and irrelevant opinions or discussions. Identifying which data points are worth analyzing requires precise classification.

To address these challenges, it is essential to apply NLP techniques that can efficiently process and classify the data, providing useful insights that security teams can act upon.

2. Processing Unstructured Threat Data Using NLP

The first step in processing unstructured data is to transform it into a format that machine learning algorithms can understand. NLP techniques play a crucial role in this process by breaking down text, extracting key features, and preparing the data for analysis.

Key NLP techniques for processing unstructured threat data include:

Tokenization: The process of dividing text into smaller, manageable pieces—usually words or phrases (tokens). Tokenization is essential for further text analysis as it helps to identify individual components, such as usernames, IP addresses, or keywords related to security threats.

Part-of-Speech Tagging: This technique involves identifying the grammatical structure of a sentence by labeling each word as a noun, verb, adjective, etc. In the context of threat intelligence, part-of-speech tagging can help determine relationships between entities (e.g., which user initiated an attack or which system is affected).

Named Entity Recognition (NER): NER is a key technique in which NLP models identify and classify named entities such as organizations, IP addresses, software, and vulnerabilities mentioned in the text. For example, NER can extract the names of malware families, vulnerable systems, or indicators of compromise (IOCs) from security reports or threat intelligence feeds.

Sentiment Analysis: Although sentiment analysis is often used in social media monitoring, it can also be valuable in cybersecurity. For example, analyzing the tone of a discussion on cybercrime forums can help identify shifts in threat actors' tactics, techniques, and procedures (TTPs). Negative or aggressive language may indicate a heightened level of malicious intent.

Topic Modeling: Topic modeling is a method used to discover the themes or topics in a large corpus of text. In threat data analysis, topic modeling can help categorize threat reports, analyze security blogs, and cluster related incidents. By identifying emerging topics in threat intelligence, security teams can track trends and gain early warnings about new attack methods.

Once unstructured data is processed, it can be classified and analyzed using machine learning techniques to detect, categorize, and respond to cybersecurity threats.

3. Classifying Unstructured Threat Data

Once the unstructured threat data is processed, it needs to be classified into categories that are useful for security analysis. Classification models use labeled datasets to learn how to assign new data to predefined categories, such as "malware," "phishing," "vulnerability," or "intrusion."

Several machine learning algorithms can be applied to classify threat data, including:

Supervised Learning: In supervised learning, a model is trained on a labeled dataset where each piece of text is already classified into a specific category (e.g., phishing email, malware report). The model learns the patterns and features that correspond to each category and can then predict the category of new, unseen text data. Algorithms like Logistic Regression, Support Vector Machines (SVMs), and Random Forests are commonly used in text classification tasks.

Unsupervised Learning: In the case of unlabeled data, unsupervised learning methods such as clustering (e.g., K-means clustering) can be used to group similar pieces of data. For instance, similar threat reports or logs can be clustered together based on their content, and the model can identify potential relationships between different attacks. Unsupervised learning techniques are particularly useful when the types of threats are unknown or when threat categories need to be dynamically updated.

Deep Learning: More complex deep learning models, particularly Recurrent Neural Networks (RNNs) and Transformer-based models (e.g., BERT), are increasingly used in threat classification tasks. These models are designed to capture the sequential nature of language and can be trained on large datasets of unstructured threat data. Deep learning models have demonstrated success in classifying threats with higher accuracy than traditional methods, especially when dealing with large, high-dimensional data.

Text Similarity and Matching: For threat data such as vulnerability reports or security blogs, text similarity measures can help identify related pieces of information. For example, comparing newly discovered vulnerabilities with previously known ones can help identify patterns in attacks or predict how an attacker might exploit a particular vulnerability.

Once the data is classified, organizations can filter, prioritize, and escalate relevant threats based on their classification, helping analysts focus on the most urgent or high-risk incidents.

4. Practical Use Cases of Processing and Classifying Threat Data

Threat Intelligence Feeds: Threat intelligence providers often release large amounts of data, such as reports detailing the latest attack trends, malware descriptions, and IOCs. NLP can be used to process these reports and classify them into categories (e.g., "new malware," "vulnerability exploit," "phishing attempt"). This enables security teams to quickly assess the relevance of the threat information and take appropriate actions.

Social Media Monitoring: Cybercriminals often discuss new attack methods, share exploits, or leak data on social media platforms, dark web forums, and other online communities. NLP techniques like sentiment analysis, NER, and topic modeling can be applied to these conversations to detect early warning signs of cyberattacks, social engineering campaigns, or data breaches.

Email and Phishing Detection: Emails are one of the most common vectors for cyberattacks, especially phishing. NLP models can be trained to identify phishing emails by analyzing common linguistic patterns—such as urgency, requests for sensitive information, or spoofed sender addresses—and classifying them as malicious.

Security Logs and Event Correlation: Security logs are a vital source of unstructured threat data. By applying NLP to these logs, organizations can classify suspicious activities, correlate events across different systems, and prioritize incidents based on severity. For example, NLP can identify log entries that indicate a potential data breach or system compromise, flagging them for further investigation.

Processing and classifying unstructured threat data is essential for extracting meaningful insights that can guide security operations. Through the use of NLP and machine learning, organizations can automate the analysis of vast amounts of text-based data, identify emerging threats, and prioritize security risks effectively. While challenges such as data volume, diversity, and ambiguity exist, advances in NLP models and machine learning techniques are making it increasingly feasible to handle unstructured threat data in real-time. As cybersecurity continues to rely more heavily on automated systems, the ability to classify and act upon unstructured data will be a critical factor in preventing and mitigating cyberattacks.

5.3 Sentiment and Context Analysis in Threat Intelligence

In the field of cybersecurity, threat intelligence involves gathering, analyzing, and acting upon data related to potential or ongoing cyber threats. Traditional threat intelligence often focuses on detecting technical indicators, such as IP addresses, malware signatures, or file hashes. However, in recent years, there has been growing recognition of the value of non-technical, textual data. Cybercriminals, hacktivists, and threat actors frequently communicate their intentions, tactics, and tools through social media platforms, forums, dark web marketplaces, and other online venues. Therefore, analyzing the sentiment and context of such communications can provide critical insights into the nature and potential impact of an attack.

Sentiment analysis and context analysis are Natural Language Processing (NLP) techniques that focus on understanding the tone, emotions, and intent behind textual data. These techniques are particularly valuable in threat intelligence as they help security professionals understand the motivations and urgency of cyberattacks, predict the behavior of threat actors, and identify emerging threats before they escalate.

This section explores the importance of sentiment and context analysis in threat intelligence, how these techniques work, and the specific ways in which they contribute to more effective cybersecurity strategies.

1. Understanding Sentiment Analysis in Cybersecurity

Sentiment analysis refers to the use of NLP techniques to identify and extract subjective information from text, particularly the emotional tone or sentiment expressed in the text. In the context of cybersecurity, sentiment analysis can help analyze written communications—such as emails, social media posts, forum discussions, and dark web chatter—to detect signs of malicious intent, urgency, or aggression.

The main goal of sentiment analysis is to determine whether the sentiment behind a piece of text is positive, negative, or neutral, and then further classify it into more granular categories like anger, fear, confidence, or hostility. Sentiment analysis provides security teams with insights into the nature of the threat, helping them prioritize their responses based on the emotional context of the threat.

For example:

- **Positive Sentiment**: May indicate benign or legitimate discussions, such as an announcement of a vulnerability patch or a discussion on best practices for security.
- **Negative Sentiment**: Could reveal aggressive actions, cyberattacks, or the intention to exploit a vulnerability.
- **Hostile or Aggressive Sentiment**: May suggest imminent threat actor activity, such as a cybercriminal boasting about a new exploit, planning a data breach, or advertising malware for sale.

By monitoring and analyzing sentiment in real time, security teams can gain early warning signs of potential attacks, detect insider threats, or identify social engineering tactics that may be employed by attackers.

Applications of Sentiment Analysis in Threat Intelligence:

- **Social Media Monitoring**: Cybercriminals and hacktivist groups often use platforms like Twitter, Telegram, and Reddit to discuss new vulnerabilities, threats, or attacks. By analyzing the sentiment of these discussions, security teams can gauge the mood of potential threat actors and assess whether an attack is imminent or in preparation.

- **Dark Web Monitoring**: The dark web is a hotspot for illegal activities, including the sale of exploits, stolen data, and malware. Analyzing the sentiment of discussions on these forums can give cybersecurity professionals a sense of the urgency or level of sophistication of the threat. If the sentiment shifts to a more hostile or aggressive tone, it may indicate a new wave of cyberattacks or a high-priority threat.
- **Phishing and Social Engineering**: Sentiment analysis is particularly valuable in detecting phishing attempts and social engineering tactics. Phishing emails or scam messages often rely on urgency or manipulation to coerce victims into taking quick action. A sentiment analysis of the email content can highlight signs of urgency, which may signal a potential phishing attack.

2. Context Analysis: Understanding the Bigger Picture

While sentiment analysis provides valuable insights into the emotional tone of textual data, context analysis helps place that sentiment in the proper context. In threat intelligence, context analysis involves understanding the circumstances surrounding a piece of data, the source of the information, and the relationships between entities mentioned in the text. It also considers the broader situation—such as geopolitical events, industry-specific risks, or historical attack patterns—that may influence or provide meaning to the threat intelligence.

Context analysis is crucial because cyber threats are rarely isolated events; they are often part of larger campaigns or incidents. Contextualizing a threat provides a more comprehensive view of the situation, helping security teams understand the threat's origins, potential targets, and likely next steps.

For instance:

- **Threat Actor Motivation**: If a threat actor's message mentions a specific political event, it could indicate that the attack is politically motivated (e.g., hacktivist groups targeting government agencies). Context analysis helps analysts interpret whether a specific attack is part of a broader social or political movement.
- **Linking Threats to Vulnerabilities**: If a threat intelligence report mentions a specific software vulnerability, understanding the context—such as the version of the software in use, previous attacks exploiting similar vulnerabilities, and the current threat landscape—can help prioritize the response and patching efforts.
- **Geopolitical Influence**: Threats often align with geopolitical events, such as military conflicts, trade disputes, or protests. Context analysis helps security teams

interpret how current events might influence cyberattack patterns or elevate the risk of attacks in certain regions.

Key Techniques in Context Analysis:

- **Entity Recognition**: Context analysis relies on identifying key entities in the text—such as individuals, organizations, countries, or software systems—and linking them to other known data sources to understand the full scope of the threat.
- **Topic Modeling**: Topic modeling algorithms can identify the primary themes of a discussion. In threat intelligence, this technique can help security teams understand whether an emerging topic is related to cyberattacks, such as new malware, data breaches, or vulnerabilities.
- **Event Correlation**: By correlating unstructured text data with structured data (e.g., system logs, vulnerability databases, threat feeds), security analysts can gain a better understanding of how specific events are connected. This can help identify attack trends, detect coordinated campaigns, and prioritize response efforts.

3. Combining Sentiment and Context for Better Threat Detection

While sentiment and context analysis can be powerful individually, their combined use significantly enhances threat detection capabilities. By examining both the tone of a communication and its broader context, security teams can better predict the intent, scale, and potential impact of a threat.

For example, suppose sentiment analysis detects that an online forum discussion has taken a hostile turn, and context analysis reveals that the discussion is centered on a new zero-day vulnerability. In this case, the combination of negative sentiment and contextual understanding of the vulnerability enables security teams to take immediate action—such as patching systems or increasing monitoring for signs of exploitation.

Likewise, when monitoring dark web chatter about a specific attack campaign, sentiment analysis might flag an urgent tone (indicating that an attack is imminent), while context analysis could reveal that the attackers are targeting a particular industry or organization. This combined insight allows for a targeted, more effective defense strategy.

4. Practical Use Cases for Sentiment and Context Analysis in Threat Intelligence

Cybercrime Forums: Cybercriminals often use online forums to exchange tools, tactics, and malware. Sentiment and context analysis can help identify conversations about new attack techniques, the sale of exploits, or the planning of attacks. A sudden spike in hostile sentiment or discussions about high-profile targets may indicate a significant attack is in the works.

Malware Analysis: Analyzing the sentiment and context of malware-related discussions in the cybersecurity community (e.g., in blogs or threat reports) can help security teams assess whether the malware is evolving, being used in a targeted campaign, or linked to known threat actors.

Emerging Threats: Sentiment and context analysis can help identify trends in emerging threats. For instance, security teams might notice that there is a growing sense of urgency in discussions around a new vulnerability. Combining this sentiment with context—such as whether the vulnerability is associated with widely used software—can help prioritize defensive measures.

Incident Response: During a cyberattack, sentiment and context analysis can help incident responders understand the scale of the attack. If attackers are using aggressive language and discussing specific targets in real-time, it can help responders anticipate the next steps in the attack and take swift action.

Sentiment and context analysis are powerful tools in the field of threat intelligence, helping cybersecurity professionals detect malicious intent, assess the urgency of threats, and gain a deeper understanding of threat actor motivations. By analyzing the emotional tone of communications and understanding the broader context in which they occur, organizations can improve their ability to predict and respond to cyberattacks before they cause significant damage. The integration of sentiment and context analysis into threat intelligence platforms not only enhances real-time threat detection but also provides more actionable insights that can guide decision-making and prioritize resources in an increasingly complex and dynamic cybersecurity landscape.

5.4 Leveraging Open-Source Intelligence (OSINT) with NLP

In the world of cybersecurity, Open-Source Intelligence (OSINT) refers to publicly available data that can be collected, analyzed, and used for threat intelligence purposes. OSINT plays a crucial role in helping security teams identify, track, and mitigate cyber threats by providing insights into potential vulnerabilities, attack patterns, and emerging threats. The sources of OSINT include a wide array of publicly accessible information, such as social media platforms, forums, blogs, websites, news outlets, and even dark web data. This data, when properly analyzed, can offer valuable clues about the tactics, techniques, and procedures (TTPs) used by cybercriminals and state-sponsored threat actors.

However, analyzing the vast amount of unstructured data available through OSINT can be a daunting task without the right tools and methodologies. This is where Natural Language Processing (NLP) becomes indispensable. NLP, a branch of artificial intelligence (AI) focused on the interaction between computers and human language, is designed to help machines interpret, analyze, and generate human language. By applying NLP techniques to OSINT, security teams can efficiently extract meaningful insights from large datasets, enabling them to identify threats, track adversary activities, and stay ahead of emerging security risks.

This section explores how NLP can be leveraged to enhance the effectiveness of OSINT in cybersecurity, focusing on key techniques, applications, and benefits.

1. The Role of OSINT in Cybersecurity

Before diving into how NLP can enhance OSINT, it is essential to understand the role of OSINT in cybersecurity. OSINT has become an indispensable tool for identifying potential threats and mitigating risks, as it provides valuable intelligence on both external and internal threats. OSINT can be divided into several categories, including:

Social Media and Public Communications: Monitoring social media platforms (such as Twitter, Facebook, LinkedIn) allows security teams to track emerging threats, such as discussions about new exploits, hacking techniques, or vulnerabilities. Threat actors may also use social media to leak stolen data, advertise malware, or communicate with other members of a hacker group.

Dark Web Monitoring: The dark web is home to illicit activities, including the sale of malware, stolen credentials, and other hacking tools. By tracking dark web marketplaces and forums, security teams can identify indicators of compromise (IOCs), such as new malware or the sale of zero-day exploits.

Public Databases and Security Bulletins: Many organizations, vendors, and government agencies release public advisories about vulnerabilities, data breaches, or security incidents. OSINT from these sources helps track the latest security threats and prioritize responses to newly discovered vulnerabilities.

Threat Intelligence Feeds: Security vendors and research institutions often provide OSINT in the form of threat intelligence feeds, which include information on the latest malware variants, phishing campaigns, attack trends, and more. These feeds can be used to update defense systems and improve threat detection capabilities.

While OSINT is valuable on its own, extracting actionable insights from massive amounts of unstructured data is often challenging. This is where NLP comes into play, as it enables security analysts to automate and streamline the process of transforming raw data into structured, usable intelligence.

2. How NLP Enhances OSINT Analysis

NLP is a powerful tool for processing and analyzing unstructured textual data. By applying NLP techniques to OSINT, security teams can efficiently categorize, extract, and interpret critical information from various data sources, which significantly improves the speed and accuracy of threat detection. Here are some of the ways NLP enhances OSINT analysis:

a. Text Classification and Categorization

One of the primary tasks in OSINT analysis is classifying the vast amount of textual data into relevant categories. For example, content from a cybercrime forum could be classified into different threat categories, such as malware discussions, phishing schemes, or data leaks. NLP algorithms, such as support vector machines (SVM) or deep learning models, can automatically classify text data based on pre-defined categories. By categorizing the information, security analysts can quickly filter out irrelevant content and focus on the most pertinent threats.

b. Named Entity Recognition (NER)

Named Entity Recognition (NER) is a key NLP technique used to identify and classify named entities within unstructured text. These entities can include organizations, individuals, geographical locations, IP addresses, domain names, malware names, and other relevant identifiers. For example, if a hacker group mentions a specific vulnerability or a targeted organization in a forum post, NER algorithms can extract these entities and highlight them as potential indicators of an attack.

By using NER to identify key entities, security teams can map out the relationships between different actors and objects, helping to build a clearer picture of the threat landscape. NER can also be used to track specific threat actors and their tactics, techniques, and procedures (TTPs), making it easier to recognize recurring patterns or ongoing campaigns.

c. Sentiment Analysis

As discussed earlier, sentiment analysis involves determining the emotional tone of a piece of text—whether it's positive, negative, or neutral. In the context of OSINT, sentiment analysis can be used to gauge the mood of online discussions related to cyber threats. For example, aggressive or hostile language in dark web forums may indicate imminent attack plans, while discussions about vulnerabilities with urgency in tone could signal an active exploit.

By combining sentiment analysis with other NLP techniques, security teams can prioritize threats that appear to be more urgent or more dangerous. This allows analysts to focus on high-priority threats and reduce the likelihood of missing significant developments in real-time.

d. Topic Modeling

Topic modeling is another essential NLP technique used in OSINT to discover hidden topics or themes within large sets of documents or text data. It allows security analysts to automatically group similar pieces of content based on shared themes, even when there is no explicit labeling or predefined categorization.

For example, when analyzing threat intelligence reports, forum posts, or blog articles, topic modeling can identify recurring themes related to specific types of attacks (e.g., ransomware campaigns, phishing attacks, or DDoS threats). By uncovering emerging topics, security teams can stay ahead of evolving threats and ensure that they are prepared for new attack vectors that may otherwise go unnoticed.

e. Trend Detection and Emerging Threats

NLP can be instrumental in detecting trends and emerging threats within the OSINT ecosystem. By analyzing historical and real-time data from various sources, NLP algorithms can identify shifts in the types of threats being discussed or the tactics being employed by cybercriminals. For example, if the frequency of discussions about a particular exploit increases in forums or social media, it could indicate that the exploit is gaining traction and may soon be used in widespread attacks.

Trend detection can help security teams proactively defend against emerging threats, providing insights into which vulnerabilities need to be patched or which attack vectors need closer monitoring.

3. Practical Applications of NLP for OSINT in Cybersecurity

The integration of NLP with OSINT opens up numerous possibilities for enhancing cybersecurity defenses. Here are some practical applications where NLP can be effectively used:

a. Monitoring Social Media for Threats

Social media platforms, such as Twitter, Reddit, and Telegram, are often used by hackers to communicate and share information about vulnerabilities, tools, and attack techniques. By using NLP to monitor social media in real time, security teams can quickly detect discussions about new threats or attack campaigns. Sentiment analysis can help determine the urgency of the situation, while NER can identify references to specific organizations, malware, or exploits.

b. Dark Web and Deep Web Analysis

The dark web is notorious for being a hub for cybercriminal activity, including the sale of stolen data, malware, and hacking tools. NLP can be used to monitor dark web forums and marketplaces for discussions related to cybercrime activities. By applying text classification, sentiment analysis, and topic modeling, security teams can identify potential threats and take early action to mitigate risks.

c. Vulnerability and Patch Management

By processing OSINT from public sources such as security advisories, vendor bulletins, and industry reports, NLP can help identify vulnerabilities that are actively being discussed or exploited. It can also highlight newly discovered vulnerabilities that need immediate attention, enabling organizations to prioritize patching and updating their systems to mitigate risks.

d. Threat Actor Profiling and Attribution

NLP can assist in profiling threat actors by analyzing their language, behaviors, and tactics as revealed in online communications. By examining their patterns of speech, preferred tools, and target organizations, analysts can develop profiles of threat actors and potentially attribute attacks to specific groups or individuals. This is particularly useful for organizations that want to understand their adversaries better and anticipate future threats.

4. Challenges and Limitations of NLP in OSINT

Despite the power of NLP in OSINT analysis, there are some challenges and limitations that need to be considered:

- **Data Quality**: OSINT data is often noisy and may contain irrelevant or misleading information. The accuracy of NLP models depends heavily on the quality of the input data, so ensuring that the data is clean and relevant is critical.
- **Multilingual Data**: Many OSINT sources, particularly on the dark web, operate in multiple languages. NLP models need to be capable of handling multilingual text and understanding cultural differences in language use.
- **Context and Ambiguity**: Human language is complex, and NLP models sometimes struggle with ambiguity, sarcasm, or the changing context of threat discussions. Incorporating context-aware models and continuous earning is essential for improving the accuracy of analysis.

Leveraging Open-Source Intelligence (OSINT) with Natural Language Processing (NLP) has revolutionized threat intelligence in cybersecurity. By applying advanced NLP techniques to analyze vast amounts of unstructured data, security teams can extract valuable insights from publicly available sources, including social media, forums, blogs, and dark web discussions. NLP enhances OSINT by enabling efficient classification, entity recognition, sentiment analysis, and trend detection, which ultimately improves the accuracy and speed of threat detection and mitigation. As cyber threats continue to evolve, the integration of NLP with OSINT will play an increasingly critical role in helping organizations stay one step ahead of adversaries.

6. Predictive Analytics in Cybersecurity

Chapter 6, Predictive Analytics in Cybersecurity, focuses on the application of predictive modeling techniques to anticipate and prevent cyber threats before they occur. This chapter explains how machine learning algorithms analyze historical data to identify risk patterns, vulnerabilities, and potential attack vectors, allowing organizations to predict and prioritize future threats. Readers will learn about risk scoring systems, anomaly detection models, and attack trend forecasting, which help organizations stay one step ahead of cyber adversaries. Through case studies and practical examples, this chapter demonstrates how predictive analytics enhances proactive defense strategies, enabling organizations to take preventive measures rather than just reacting to incidents.

6.1 Principles of Predictive Modeling in Cybersecurity

Predictive modeling in cybersecurity refers to the use of historical data, statistical algorithms, and machine learning techniques to forecast future events, behaviors, or outcomes. It plays a crucial role in identifying potential threats before they happen, allowing security teams to proactively defend against cyberattacks and mitigate risks. By applying predictive models to security data, organizations can anticipate and respond to emerging threats more efficiently and effectively.

Predictive modeling helps security teams shift from a reactive to a proactive stance by identifying patterns, trends, and behaviors that signal the likelihood of an impending attack or security incident. Whether it's forecasting the probability of a cyberattack, predicting which systems are most vulnerable, or identifying anomalous behavior that may indicate malicious activity, predictive modeling provides the intelligence needed to anticipate and prevent security breaches.

This section explores the core principles of predictive modeling in cybersecurity, covering the key concepts, methodologies, and applications that make it a powerful tool for enhancing security operations.

1. Understanding Predictive Modeling in Cybersecurity

At its core, predictive modeling uses historical data to predict future events. In the context of cybersecurity, this involves analyzing past incidents, attack patterns, and system behaviors to anticipate potential vulnerabilities, attack vectors, or the likelihood of a cyberattack occurring. Predictive models aim to identify high-risk situations or behaviors before they lead to a breach or other security incidents.

Key principles of predictive modeling in cybersecurity include:

Data-Driven Insights: Predictive models are built on data—usually historical data from past security incidents, network traffic, system logs, or threat intelligence feeds. This data is used to train machine learning models to detect patterns and trends that may predict future outcomes.

Risk Assessment: Predictive modeling helps assess the likelihood of a threat materializing based on the available data. It identifies potential risks, assigns probabilities to these risks, and helps prioritize security efforts to focus on high-likelihood threats.

Continuous Learning: Predictive models in cybersecurity are dynamic and adaptive, meaning they evolve as new data becomes available. As threat landscapes change, so too must the models. Continuous learning is a key element in ensuring the predictive model remains relevant and effective in an ever-evolving cyber threat environment.

2. Key Components of Predictive Modeling

Predictive modeling relies on several key components to be effective in cybersecurity contexts. These components include data, algorithms, models, and evaluation metrics.

a. Data Collection and Preprocessing

The first step in any predictive modeling task is data collection. For predictive cybersecurity models, the data typically comes from various sources, such as:

- **Network traffic logs**: Information about incoming and outgoing traffic, including the source and destination of packets, timestamps, and protocols used.
- **System logs**: Logs from firewalls, intrusion detection systems (IDS), antivirus software, and endpoint protection tools.
- **Threat intelligence feeds**: Public or commercial feeds that provide information about ongoing threats, vulnerabilities, and attack campaigns.
- **User behavior**: Data on how users typically interact with systems, networks, or applications, which helps identify anomalies in behavior.
- **Historical attack data**: Past incidents, such as malware outbreaks, data breaches, or attempted intrusions, that help security teams learn from previous attack patterns.

Once data is collected, it must be preprocessed to ensure it's clean and usable. This involves:

- **Removing noise**: Filtering out irrelevant or extraneous data that doesn't contribute to predictive modeling.
- **Handling missing data**: Filling in or dealing with missing data points that could affect the accuracy of the model.
- **Normalization**: Scaling data so that it fits into a consistent range, ensuring that features are comparable and the model performs well.

b. Feature Selection and Engineering

Feature selection and engineering are critical for building effective predictive models. Features are the variables that are used as inputs into the model to make predictions. In cybersecurity, features could include:

- **IP addresses**: To track unusual connections or identify potential command-and-control (C2) traffic.
- **Port numbers**: To identify unusual or unauthorized network activity.
- **File signatures**: To detect malware based on its unique fingerprint.
- **Login behavior**: To flag unusual login attempts, such as those occurring at odd times or from unknown locations.

Feature engineering refers to the process of transforming raw data into meaningful input variables that help the model make accurate predictions. This could involve aggregating data, creating new features (e.g., calculating the number of failed login attempts over time), or deriving higher-level features from raw data to improve the model's performance.

c. Algorithm Selection

The choice of algorithm is a fundamental aspect of predictive modeling. Different algorithms have varying strengths and weaknesses depending on the nature of the problem, the data, and the required output. In cybersecurity, common machine learning algorithms used for predictive modeling include:

- **Regression models**: Used to predict continuous outcomes, such as the likelihood of a system being compromised.
- **Classification models**: Used to categorize data into distinct classes or categories. For example, predicting whether a certain user behavior is "normal" or "malicious."

- **Decision trees and Random Forests**: Widely used for classification and regression tasks, especially when interpreting complex relationships in the data is important.
- **Neural networks**: Particularly effective for recognizing patterns in large datasets and identifying subtle threats.
- **Support Vector Machines (SVMs)**: Used for binary classification, such as identifying whether a given activity is benign or suspicious.

Each algorithm has trade-offs in terms of performance, interpretability, and computational cost. In cybersecurity, it's essential to strike a balance between predictive accuracy and real-time performance.

d. Model Evaluation and Validation

Once a predictive model is built, it must be evaluated to ensure it accurately predicts future events and performs well on unseen data. Common evaluation metrics for predictive models in cybersecurity include:

- **Accuracy**: The percentage of correct predictions made by the model.
- **Precision**: The proportion of true positive predictions (correctly identifying a threat) to all positive predictions made by the model.
- **Recall (Sensitivity):** The proportion of true positive predictions to all actual positives in the dataset (how well the model detects actual threats).
- **F1-Score**: A harmonic mean of precision and recall, providing a balance between the two metrics.
- **Area under the ROC Curve (AUC-ROC):** A performance measurement for classification models that evaluates the trade-off between true positive and false positive rates.

To avoid overfitting, where a model performs well on the training data but poorly on new data, techniques such as cross-validation and regularization are applied to ensure that the model generalizes well to unseen data.

3. Applications of Predictive Modeling in Cybersecurity

Predictive modeling in cybersecurity can be applied in various domains to identify and mitigate risks proactively. Some of the most common applications include:

a. Intrusion Detection Systems (IDS)

Predictive models can enhance traditional Intrusion Detection Systems (IDS) by helping detect novel threats that may not have known signatures. By predicting potential attacks based on patterns and behaviors in network traffic, predictive models can identify threats in real time, often before they cause any damage.

b. Malware Detection and Classification

Machine learning algorithms can predict whether a file or program is benign or malicious based on its features (e.g., size, structure, behavior). Predictive models can also classify malware types, helping security teams understand the nature of an attack and respond effectively.

c. Phishing Detection

Predictive models can identify phishing attempts by analyzing patterns in email content, sender behavior, and recipient interaction. By predicting the likelihood that an email is a phishing attempt, security teams can proactively filter out malicious messages before they reach users.

d. Vulnerability Management

Predictive models can help assess which systems, applications, or vulnerabilities are most likely to be targeted by attackers, allowing security teams to prioritize patching efforts and remediate the most critical vulnerabilities before they are exploited.

e. Insider Threat Detection

Predictive modeling can be used to spot potential insider threats by analyzing employee behaviors, such as access patterns, file transfers, and communications. If these behaviors deviate from the norm, predictive models can flag them as potential threats, helping organizations detect malicious or negligent insider actions early.

4. Challenges in Predictive Modeling for Cybersecurity

While predictive modeling offers numerous benefits, there are also challenges that must be addressed:

- **Data Quality and Availability**: The accuracy of predictive models depends heavily on the quality and completeness of the data. In cybersecurity, this means access to reliable, comprehensive data is critical.

- **Dynamic Nature of Threats**: Cyber threats are constantly evolving, which makes it challenging for models to stay current. Regular retraining and updates are necessary to ensure that predictive models continue to detect emerging threats.
- **False Positives and Negatives**: One of the ongoing challenges in predictive modeling is minimizing false positives (benign activities flagged as threats) and false negatives (threats missed by the model). Balancing these is critical for maintaining trust in predictive models.

Predictive modeling in cybersecurity is a powerful tool that enables organizations to forecast potential risks and identify emerging threats before they materialize. By using historical data, statistical algorithms, and machine learning techniques, security teams can anticipate attacks, detect anomalies, and prioritize responses effectively. While challenges remain, the continuous development of predictive models can help strengthen defenses, improve threat detection, and enhance overall cybersecurity resilience.

6.2 Risk Scoring and Vulnerability Prediction Models

Risk scoring and vulnerability prediction models play a pivotal role in cybersecurity by helping organizations assess the potential impact of cyber threats and prioritize their mitigation efforts. These models use machine learning and statistical techniques to analyze data about vulnerabilities, system configurations, and threat intelligence, and generate risk scores that reflect the likelihood and severity of an attack. By identifying and quantifying risks, cybersecurity teams can more effectively allocate resources, focusing on the areas most vulnerable to exploitation and those that could result in significant damage to an organization.

In this section, we will explore the principles behind risk scoring and vulnerability prediction models, their components, and how they can be applied to enhance the security posture of an organization. We'll also address the key challenges in developing and utilizing these models for effective risk management.

1. Understanding Risk Scoring in Cybersecurity

Risk scoring is a process used to assign a numerical value or score to potential security risks based on their likelihood and impact. The goal of risk scoring is to provide a standardized way to prioritize and address the various risks that an organization faces. A high-risk score typically indicates that the vulnerability or threat has a high likelihood of exploitation or could result in severe consequences, such as data breaches, financial loss, or reputational damage.

Risk scoring models often incorporate several factors to generate a comprehensive risk assessment, including:

- **Threat Likelihood**: The probability that a threat will exploit a given vulnerability. This is often determined by evaluating the frequency of similar attacks in the past and the current threat landscape.
- **Vulnerability Severity**: The potential impact of an attack, should it occur. This is often based on the severity of the vulnerability, such as whether it could lead to a complete system compromise or partial exposure of sensitive data.
- **Exploitability**: How easy it is for an attacker to exploit a given vulnerability. Factors such as whether the vulnerability can be exploited remotely, whether special privileges are required, and the availability of exploit code influence this aspect.
- **Asset Value**: The importance of the affected asset, whether it's a critical system, sensitive data, or an application vital to business operations. High-value assets, when compromised, generally lead to more significant losses.

The risk score is typically calculated by multiplying these factors or using weighted formulas that reflect the relative importance of each factor. This score can then be used to prioritize remediation efforts, with high-risk vulnerabilities receiving immediate attention and lower-risk issues being addressed in due course.

a. Common Risk Scoring Models

Several standardized frameworks are widely used to assign risk scores to vulnerabilities in cybersecurity:

CVSS (Common Vulnerability Scoring System): The CVSS is a widely adopted risk-scoring model developed by the Forum of Incident Response and Security Teams (FIRST). It provides a numerical score between 0 and 10 that reflects the severity of a vulnerability. The CVSS score is calculated based on several factors, including the complexity of exploiting the vulnerability, the availability of fixes or workarounds, and the potential impact on confidentiality, integrity, and availability.

Risk Matrix: A risk matrix assigns risk scores based on a combination of the likelihood and impact of a threat. The risk matrix can visually display risk levels, helping security teams quickly identify and assess critical vulnerabilities. It typically uses a two-axis grid with one axis representing likelihood and the other representing impact, with each cell corresponding to a risk score.

Quantitative Models: In some advanced cases, machine learning-based models can be employed to assess and predict risks using historical data, system configurations, and real-time threat intelligence. These models can analyze vast amounts of data to predict potential risks and assign dynamic risk scores based on current conditions.

2. Vulnerability Prediction Models in Cybersecurity

Vulnerability prediction models use machine learning techniques to identify and forecast which vulnerabilities are most likely to be exploited by attackers. These models predict which vulnerabilities, within a given system or network, pose the greatest risk based on historical data, system configurations, network characteristics, and external threat intelligence.

By analyzing past vulnerability data, attack patterns, and environmental factors, vulnerability prediction models can offer several benefits:

Proactive Risk Management: Vulnerability prediction models help organizations identify and address security weaknesses before they are exploited in an attack. Rather than waiting for a vulnerability to be actively exploited or reported by researchers, predictive models offer early warning signs, enabling proactive mitigation.

Resource Optimization: These models assist organizations in prioritizing their resources by focusing on the vulnerabilities that present the most significant risks, rather than attempting to patch everything indiscriminately. This allows security teams to allocate resources more effectively.

Predicting Exploit Trends: By analyzing trends in how vulnerabilities are exploited (e.g., whether certain vulnerabilities are more commonly targeted during specific times or in certain industries), prediction models can forecast future exploitations and help organizations prepare for emerging threats.

a. Machine Learning for Vulnerability Prediction

Vulnerability prediction models often rely on machine learning algorithms to process historical vulnerability data and other relevant factors (e.g., asset value, system configuration, threat intelligence) to predict which vulnerabilities are most likely to be exploited. Some common machine learning techniques used for vulnerability prediction include:

Classification Algorithms: Algorithms like Decision Trees, Random Forests, and Support Vector Machines (SVMs) can classify vulnerabilities into categories, such as "high-risk" or "low-risk," based on features extracted from the vulnerability data. These algorithms can be trained on historical data of vulnerabilities that were exploited in the past, enabling them to identify patterns and predict future exploitations.

Regression Models: Regression models can be used to predict continuous risk scores for vulnerabilities, helping security teams assess the severity of each vulnerability. These models might predict, for example, the financial or operational impact of an exploit, providing valuable insights into the business implications of vulnerabilities.

Clustering and Anomaly Detection: These techniques are useful for discovering unknown vulnerabilities that may be outliers or anomalies in the data. By detecting unusual behavior patterns or system configurations that deviate from the norm, clustering algorithms can identify potentially risky vulnerabilities that haven't been previously flagged.

b. Key Features Used in Vulnerability Prediction Models

Vulnerability prediction models typically consider a wide variety of features to evaluate which vulnerabilities pose the greatest risk. Some key features include:

- **Vulnerability Age**: Older vulnerabilities may have already been widely exploited, while newer vulnerabilities may still be under active exploitation.
- **Patch Availability**: The availability of patches or mitigations for a vulnerability significantly impacts its risk level. Unpatched vulnerabilities or those with no available fix are often high-risk.
- **Public Exploit Availability**: Vulnerabilities with known public exploits or "exploit kits" available to attackers are considered more dangerous.
- **Asset Sensitivity**: The importance of the system or asset affected by the vulnerability—critical infrastructure or sensitive data systems are higher priority for mitigation.
- **Attack Surface**: The more exposure a vulnerability has to potential attackers (e.g., externally facing services), the higher the likelihood it will be targeted.

3. Challenges in Risk Scoring and Vulnerability Prediction

Despite the significant potential of risk scoring and vulnerability prediction models, there are several challenges associated with their implementation and use:

Data Quality and Completeness: Accurate risk scores and vulnerability predictions depend heavily on the availability of high-quality, up-to-date data. Incomplete or inconsistent data can lead to inaccurate assessments and poor decision-making.

Evolving Threat Landscape: Cyber threats are continuously evolving, and attackers often exploit new vulnerabilities in creative and unforeseen ways. As a result, models must be updated regularly with new data to reflect changes in the threat landscape and ensure their predictions remain accurate.

False Positives and Negatives: Both risk scoring and vulnerability prediction models are susceptible to false positives (incorrectly marking a low-risk vulnerability as high risk) and false negatives (failing to flag a high-risk vulnerability). Striking the right balance between minimizing these errors is a key challenge in applying these models effectively.

Contextual Factors: While risk scoring models consider technical factors (e.g., vulnerability severity, exploitability), they may not always account for the broader business context, such as how a particular vulnerability aligns with an organization's threat model or risk appetite.

Risk scoring and vulnerability prediction models provide valuable tools for proactively identifying and addressing cybersecurity risks. These models enable organizations to prioritize their security efforts, identify emerging vulnerabilities, and allocate resources efficiently. By combining machine learning with traditional cybersecurity principles, organizations can enhance their defenses and stay one step ahead of attackers. However, challenges remain, particularly in ensuring data quality and minimizing false positives and negatives, and these models must be continuously updated to remain effective in the face of an evolving cyber threat landscape.

6.3 Forecasting Threat Trends and Attack Patterns

Forecasting threat trends and attack patterns is a crucial aspect of modern cybersecurity. It allows organizations to anticipate future threats, enabling them to implement preventive measures before attacks can materialize. By identifying emerging attack vectors and understanding the tactics, techniques, and procedures (TTPs) used by cyber adversaries, security teams can proactively protect critical assets, detect early warning signs, and strengthen their defenses.

In this section, we will explore the principles and techniques behind forecasting threat trends and attack patterns. We will also discuss the various data sources and machine learning methods employed to predict future cyber threats and provide actionable insights for security teams. Understanding how to forecast these trends can empower organizations to be more adaptive, responsive, and resilient in the face of ever-evolving cyber threats.

1. Understanding Threat Forecasting in Cybersecurity

Threat forecasting involves the use of historical data, machine learning algorithms, threat intelligence, and statistical methods to predict future attack trends, behaviors, and the likelihood of specific cyber threats. Unlike traditional reactive approaches, threat forecasting allows organizations to take a proactive stance by anticipating attacks and adjusting their defense strategies accordingly. The goal is to identify emerging threats, predict their potential impact, and prepare defenses in advance to minimize damage.

Threat forecasting is a complex process, requiring the analysis of a wide array of data sources to identify patterns, correlate events, and identify vulnerabilities in a timely manner. By understanding the patterns of past attacks, security teams can forecast potential future attack methods, as well as predict the types of assets or industries that may be targeted.

2. Key Components of Threat Forecasting

Effective forecasting of cyber threats involves several key components:

a. Historical Attack Data

Historical attack data is essential for predicting future threats. By analyzing past incidents, security professionals can identify trends, including the types of vulnerabilities exploited, attack methods used, and the characteristics of the systems targeted. This historical data can come from various sources, such as security logs, breach reports, or threat intelligence platforms. Understanding the attacker's behaviors and motives, as well as their common targets, provides valuable context for making accurate predictions about future attacks.

Key considerations include:

- **Frequency of attack types**: Analyzing the frequency of different attack types (e.g., ransomware, phishing, DDoS, insider threats) over time can help determine which threats are more likely to recur.

- **Exploited vulnerabilities**: Reviewing which vulnerabilities were most commonly targeted can highlight patterns in attacker behavior and the security gaps they are attempting to exploit.
- **Sector-specific trends**: Certain industries may be more prone to specific types of attacks. For instance, healthcare may be targeted more for sensitive data breaches, while financial institutions may be more likely to face fraud or financial theft.

b. Threat Intelligence

Threat intelligence provides actionable insights into current and evolving cyber threats. This intelligence is gathered from a variety of sources, including security vendors, government organizations, security communities, and dark web monitoring services. Threat intelligence feeds contain information about ongoing or emerging threats, indicators of compromise (IOCs), attack campaigns, and the tactics used by threat actors.

Threat intelligence plays a key role in threat forecasting by:

- **Identifying emerging threats**: It helps detect the early stages of new attack techniques or tools being adopted by adversaries.
- **Providing early warning signs**: Threat intelligence feeds can offer real-time alerts about attacks that are in progress, allowing organizations to respond quickly and limit the damage.
- **Detecting attack patterns**: By examining the behavior of threat actors over time, threat intelligence can reveal patterns that suggest new attack trends or strategies that adversaries are adopting.

c. Machine Learning and AI Models

Machine learning and AI are increasingly being applied to threat forecasting, allowing security teams to automate the process of detecting patterns in vast amounts of data. These models can analyze large datasets in real-time, detect anomalies, and provide predictions about future threats based on historical patterns. The advantage of using machine learning for threat forecasting is its ability to continuously learn from new data and improve predictions as more information becomes available.

Key machine learning techniques used in threat forecasting include:

- **Supervised Learning**: Algorithms are trained on labeled data (historical attack data), enabling them to classify future events as benign or malicious. These models can be used to predict attack likelihoods based on past data.
- **Unsupervised Learning**: In unsupervised learning, the model is not given labeled data but instead tries to identify patterns and anomalies on its own. This is particularly useful for detecting previously unknown threats that do not have predefined labels.
- **Time Series Forecasting**: This approach uses historical time-based data to predict future occurrences of attacks. Time series models, such as ARIMA (AutoRegressive Integrated Moving Average) or LSTM (Long Short-Term Memory) networks, can be used to forecast attack frequency or the likelihood of specific threats over time.

d. Threat Actor Profiling

Understanding the motivations, techniques, and behavior of threat actors is essential for forecasting their next move. This process involves building profiles of threat actors based on their previous actions, goals, and attack patterns. Threat actors can include hackers, cybercriminal organizations, nation-state actors, hacktivists, or insider threats, each with distinct goals and methods.

By analyzing threat actor profiles, organizations can:

- **Identify potential targets**: Understanding which organizations or sectors are typically targeted by specific threat actors can help predict where future attacks may occur.
- **Predict attack strategies**: Knowing how certain adversaries operate allows organizations to anticipate their tactics. For example, if a certain group frequently uses spear-phishing as their entry point, organizations can focus on improving email security in anticipation of similar attacks.
- **Recognize signature tactics**: Certain adversaries may exhibit signature behaviors, such as a preference for specific attack vectors (e.g., DDoS, social engineering) or the use of specific malware families. These traits can be used to predict future attacks and mitigate risks.

3. Applications of Forecasting Threat Trends and Attack Patterns

Forecasting threat trends and attack patterns has numerous practical applications in cybersecurity. These applications help organizations better prepare for and respond to emerging threats:

a. Proactive Defense and Risk Mitigation

By forecasting potential attack trends, organizations can strengthen their defenses ahead of time. This may involve patching vulnerabilities that are likely to be targeted, upgrading security systems to detect specific attack techniques, or reallocating resources to protect high-value assets. Proactive defense based on forecasted threats can significantly reduce the likelihood of a successful attack.

b. Incident Response Planning

Threat forecasting is essential in creating effective incident response plans. By anticipating potential attack scenarios, organizations can develop response strategies for various types of cyber incidents. For example, if the forecasting models predict an uptick in ransomware attacks, the incident response team can be trained to respond specifically to ransomware incidents, ensuring a faster, more coordinated response.

c. Vulnerability Management

Forecasting helps prioritize vulnerabilities based on the predicted likelihood of exploitation. If the models forecast that certain vulnerabilities will be targeted more frequently in the coming months, security teams can prioritize patching those vulnerabilities to mitigate the risk of a breach.

d. Threat Intelligence Sharing

Forecasting threat trends also facilitates collaboration between organizations, sectors, and countries. By sharing predictive insights and threat intelligence, organizations can enhance their overall security posture and stay ahead of emerging attacks. Collaboration allows for a more comprehensive understanding of global threat trends and fosters collective defense.

4. Challenges in Forecasting Threat Trends and Attack Patterns

While forecasting provides many advantages, there are also challenges associated with it:

- **Data Quality and Availability**: Threat forecasting relies heavily on accurate, high-quality data. Incomplete, outdated, or low-quality data can undermine the accuracy of predictions.

- **Dynamic and Evolving Threats**: Cyber threats are constantly changing, and new attack vectors are often introduced faster than they can be detected. This rapid evolution can make it challenging to accurately predict threats.
- **False Positives and Uncertainty**: Predictive models can sometimes generate false positives or inaccurate predictions. The complexity of forecasting future attacks often means there is a degree of uncertainty, which security teams must account for when planning defenses.

Forecasting threat trends and attack patterns is an essential part of a proactive cybersecurity strategy. By leveraging historical data, machine learning, threat intelligence, and threat actor profiling, organizations can anticipate future attacks, mitigate risks, and strengthen their defenses before an attack occurs. While there are challenges in implementing effective forecasting models, their ability to provide early warnings and actionable insights makes them invaluable for staying ahead of cybercriminals and protecting critical assets. With continuous refinement and integration of new data, threat forecasting will remain a cornerstone of modern cybersecurity operations.

6.4 Case Studies: Proactive Defense Through Predictive Analytics

Predictive analytics is a powerful tool in the realm of cybersecurity, enabling organizations to forecast potential threats and attacks before they materialize. By analyzing historical data, identifying patterns, and using machine learning models, predictive analytics can help organizations move from a reactive security posture to a more proactive one. This shift allows for more effective risk mitigation, faster response times, and a reduced likelihood of successful cyberattacks.

In this section, we will explore several case studies that demonstrate how predictive analytics has been effectively applied to cybersecurity. These real-world examples highlight the tangible benefits of using predictive techniques to anticipate cyber threats, enhance defenses, and protect sensitive data from malicious actors.

1. Case Study 1: Predicting and Preventing Ransomware Attacks

Ransomware attacks, in which attackers encrypt a victim's data and demand a ransom for its release, have become one of the most prominent and damaging cyber threats. In response, one large financial institution implemented a predictive analytics model to combat this rising risk. By leveraging machine learning algorithms to analyze historical attack data, the organization was able to identify patterns that typically preceded ransomware attacks.

a. The Challenge

The financial institution was dealing with a high volume of attempted ransomware attacks, most of which went undetected until they had already infiltrated the network. Traditional detection methods, such as signature-based antivirus systems, were no longer sufficient to identify new and sophisticated ransomware variants that could evade these defenses.

b. Solution

The organization employed a predictive analytics model that analyzed behavioral patterns associated with previous ransomware incidents, such as unusual file access behavior, abnormal encryption attempts, and anomalous network traffic patterns. The model utilized historical data from various sources, including endpoint activity logs, network traffic analysis, and external threat intelligence feeds.

Machine learning models, including supervised learning techniques, were trained to detect early indicators of ransomware activity. Once the model was deployed, it started flagging potential ransomware infections in their early stages, based on detected anomalies and deviations from normal system behavior.

c. Outcome

The financial institution was able to detect and thwart ransomware attacks much earlier in the attack lifecycle. The predictive analytics model identified threats before the malware had a chance to encrypt data, allowing the organization to intervene promptly. Additionally, the system flagged suspicious behaviors across different endpoints, enabling the security team to block the attack vector before it could spread.

As a result, the organization significantly reduced the number of successful ransomware attacks, lowered operational downtime, and avoided costly data breaches and ransom payments. The proactive defense approach saved both time and resources, demonstrating the efficacy of predictive analytics in preventing ransomware.

2. Case Study 2: Predicting Insider Threats in a Tech Company

Insider threats, where individuals with authorized access to systems misuse their privileges to compromise security, are a growing concern for many organizations, especially in industries handling sensitive intellectual property. A major tech company was struggling with detecting and mitigating insider threats that were often difficult to identify through traditional monitoring methods.

a. The Challenge

Traditional monitoring systems focused on detecting external threats but failed to capture suspicious behaviors from insiders. For instance, unauthorized data access or unusual file transfers by an employee could easily go unnoticed because of the trust placed in internal personnel.

b. Solution

The tech company turned to predictive analytics to enhance its ability to detect insider threats. By using machine learning models to analyze historical data on employee behavior, access patterns, and data usage, the company created a model to identify deviations from typical behavior.

Using unsupervised learning techniques, the model created baselines for normal behavior across different departments and individuals, considering factors like login times, frequency of file accesses, and the types of data employees were working with. The model also incorporated external factors such as company-wide changes, employee turnover, and the likelihood of disgruntlement or malicious intent.

Predictive models were applied to identify potential red flags—such as an employee suddenly accessing large amounts of sensitive data or transferring files to unauthorized devices or external systems. The system could raise alerts when such deviations occurred, prompting further investigation.

c. Outcome

The tech company was able to detect several potential insider threats before they led to any significant damage. For instance, the model flagged a senior employee who, after experiencing a personal conflict, began downloading sensitive company files in an unusually short period. The predictive system identified this activity as anomalous, and security teams were able to intervene early, preventing the unauthorized transfer of intellectual property.

Overall, predictive analytics helped the tech company reduce the risk of data exfiltration, improve employee monitoring, and enforce stricter access controls. By catching potential insider threats early, the company prevented financial loss and reputational damage, illustrating the value of predictive analytics in detecting internal vulnerabilities.

3. Case Study 3: Enhancing Phishing Attack Detection with Predictive Analytics

Phishing attacks, where attackers trick users into divulging sensitive information such as login credentials, have become a persistent and effective method for cybercriminals. A major telecommunications provider sought to enhance its phishing detection capabilities by incorporating predictive analytics into its security infrastructure.

a. The Challenge

While phishing attacks were frequent, the company's existing email filtering system had a high rate of false positives, flagging legitimate emails as malicious and hindering employee productivity. Traditional email filtering systems struggled to accurately distinguish between legitimate and fraudulent messages, especially when attackers used more sophisticated techniques, such as spear-phishing, to target specific employees.

b. Solution

The company implemented a predictive analytics solution that focused on analyzing the content and metadata of incoming emails. Using machine learning models, the company created an intelligent email filtering system capable of distinguishing between phishing emails and legitimate messages based on characteristics such as language patterns, sender reputation, email header analysis, and historical attack trends.

The predictive model analyzed patterns in previous phishing campaigns, such as common words, phrases, and red flags, and learned to spot emerging phishing techniques that traditional systems might miss. For instance, it detected when emails were crafted to appear as though they were coming from an internal system but contained minor discrepancies, such as incorrect sender addresses or unusual attachments.

c. Outcome

The predictive analytics model significantly improved the company's ability to detect phishing emails with higher accuracy. It drastically reduced false positives, allowing employees to focus on legitimate communications without worrying about unnecessary email blocks. Additionally, the system identified new phishing strategies and provided early warnings about targeted spear-phishing campaigns aimed at specific departments or high-level executives.

By preventing phishing attempts from successfully reaching end-users, the company reduced the risk of credential theft, data breaches, and ransomware infections. This case study highlights how predictive analytics can evolve traditional defenses and better prepare organizations for increasingly sophisticated social engineering attacks.

4. Case Study 4: Predicting Distributed Denial of Service (DDoS) Attacks

DDoS attacks, in which malicious actors flood a target system with an overwhelming amount of traffic to render it unusable, are among the most disruptive cyberattacks. A large e-commerce company that experienced frequent DDoS attacks sought to implement a proactive defense mechanism to reduce the impact of these attacks.

a. The Challenge

The company faced a persistent challenge in identifying DDoS attacks early enough to mitigate their impact. Once the attacks began, they typically overwhelmed the infrastructure before the security team had a chance to respond. As a result, the company suffered from significant downtime during major sales events, leading to loss of revenue and customer trust.

b. Solution

The company used predictive analytics to forecast the likelihood of a DDoS attack before it could occur. By analyzing historical DDoS attack data, the company identified key indicators of impending attacks, such as unusual spikes in traffic from specific geographic regions, increased query rates, and anomalous DNS requests. These patterns were input into a machine learning model that predicted the likelihood of a DDoS attack based on real-time traffic analysis.

The predictive model incorporated a variety of data sources, including network traffic logs, previous DDoS attempts, and external threat intelligence feeds that indicated increased attack activity in the wider cybersecurity landscape.

c. Outcome

By using predictive analytics, the e-commerce company was able to detect and mitigate DDoS attacks before they caused significant disruptions. The system raised alerts when early signs of a DDoS attack appeared, allowing the company's security team to implement countermeasures such as traffic redirection, IP filtering, or the activation of cloud-based DDoS protection services.

The proactive defense approach helped the company maintain uptime during critical sales events, safeguard customer transactions, and reduce operational costs associated with DDoS disruptions. This case study highlights the potential of predictive analytics in mitigating the impact of high-volume, disruptive attacks like DDoS.

These case studies demonstrate the power of predictive analytics in transforming cybersecurity from a reactive to a proactive discipline. By leveraging historical data, machine learning models, and real-time threat intelligence, organizations can forecast potential cyber threats, identify vulnerabilities, and take action before attacks can cause significant damage. Predictive analytics not only improves the accuracy and efficiency of threat detection but also enhances the overall resilience of an organization's cybersecurity infrastructure. As cyber threats continue to evolve, the use of predictive analytics will be critical in staying one step ahead of attackers and ensuring the security of sensitive data and systems.

7. AI-Driven Security Automation and Incident Response

Chapter 7, AI-Driven Security Automation and Incident Response, explores how artificial intelligence is revolutionizing the speed and effectiveness of cybersecurity operations through automation. This chapter covers the integration of AI into Security Orchestration, Automation, and Response (SOAR) systems, enabling the automated detection, analysis, and mitigation of cyber threats. Readers will learn how AI-driven tools can autonomously trigger responses to incidents, reducing human intervention and accelerating the time to resolution. The chapter also addresses the balance between human expertise and machine efficiency in incident response, and how AI can support decision-making during critical security events. With real-world examples, this chapter highlights how AI is transforming the way security teams manage and respond to cyber incidents.

7.1 Overview of Security Orchestration, Automation, and Response (SOAR)

Security Orchestration, Automation, and Response (SOAR) is a crucial advancement in the cybersecurity field, designed to help organizations streamline and optimize their security operations. SOAR platforms integrate various security tools, processes, and data sources to enable faster and more effective threat response. By combining orchestration, automation, and response, SOAR not only improves the efficiency of security operations but also helps reduce human error, accelerate incident response times, and enhance overall security posture.

As cyber threats continue to evolve in complexity and frequency, traditional methods of manual threat detection and incident response can no longer keep up with the scale and speed required. SOAR systems address these challenges by automating repetitive tasks, orchestrating the flow of information across disparate security technologies, and providing a centralized platform for managing and responding to security incidents.

In this section, we will explore the core components of SOAR, its benefits, and how it is transforming the way organizations handle security incidents. We will also discuss the relationship between SOAR and other key technologies, such as Security Information and Event Management (SIEM) and Threat Intelligence Platforms (TIPs), and examine how SOAR helps security teams enhance their ability to detect, analyze, and respond to threats more effectively.

1. What is SOAR?

SOAR refers to a set of technologies designed to improve the efficiency and effectiveness of security operations by automating tasks, integrating tools, and orchestrating security workflows. The core components of SOAR include:

Orchestration: This refers to the process of integrating different security tools, systems, and data sources to ensure they work together seamlessly. Orchestration helps ensure that security data flows correctly across various platforms, enabling them to complement each other rather than operate in isolation.

Automation: Automation involves using predefined workflows and scripts to perform repetitive tasks and processes without human intervention. In cybersecurity, this includes tasks such as triaging alerts, correlating data, and executing response actions like blocking malicious IP addresses or isolating infected endpoints.

Response: The response component enables organizations to react to security incidents in a timely and effective manner. SOAR platforms can trigger responses based on pre-established rules or manual intervention, helping security teams mitigate threats quickly and efficiently.

Together, orchestration, automation, and response enable a more agile, scalable, and proactive security operation. SOAR helps security teams handle a higher volume of alerts and incidents without getting overwhelmed, and allows them to focus on higher-priority tasks and more complex threats.

2. Key Benefits of SOAR

Implementing SOAR can provide organizations with numerous benefits, including:

a. Faster Incident Response

One of the primary advantages of SOAR is the ability to accelerate incident response. By automating routine tasks like alert triage, data enrichment, and preliminary analysis, SOAR platforms help security teams respond to threats much more quickly. This speed is critical in limiting the damage caused by security breaches and reducing response times from hours to minutes or even seconds.

b. Reduction of Human Error

Human error is a significant factor in many security incidents, whether it's misinterpreting an alert, overlooking a critical event, or performing a task incorrectly. SOAR platforms help reduce the risk of human error by automating repetitive processes, ensuring that security tasks are completed accurately and consistently every time. By removing manual intervention in mundane tasks, SOAR allows analysts to focus on more complex or strategic activities.

c. Improved Efficiency and Productivity

SOAR platforms improve the overall efficiency of security operations by automating routine tasks, allowing security teams to handle more incidents with fewer resources. By streamlining workflows, security operations centers (SOCs) can process a higher volume of alerts and incidents without increasing staffing requirements. Automation can help security analysts focus on tasks that require expertise, such as threat hunting or investigation, rather than repetitive actions that can be handled by machines.

d. Better Collaboration Across Teams

SOAR facilitates collaboration by providing a centralized platform where teams can share information and coordinate responses. Security, IT, and compliance teams can work together more efficiently, as SOAR provides a unified interface to track incidents, manage workflows, and share findings. The ability to orchestrate cross-team workflows ensures that everyone involved in the response process is aligned and can take action swiftly.

e. Consistent and Repeatable Workflows

By defining predefined workflows, SOAR ensures that response procedures are consistent and repeatable. This consistency helps organizations respond to similar threats in the same way every time, eliminating confusion or inconsistencies in handling incidents. Moreover, this repeatability allows security teams to continuously improve their incident response protocols based on lessons learned from previous incidents.

f. Enhanced Visibility and Reporting

SOAR platforms provide detailed reporting and dashboards, offering enhanced visibility into security operations. These reports give organizations insights into their security posture, including key metrics such as the time to detection, time to response, and the number of incidents handled. This visibility helps security leaders assess the effectiveness of their security operations and identify areas for improvement.

3. Components and Capabilities of SOAR

To better understand the full scope of SOAR, it's helpful to look at its individual components and how they contribute to a more efficient security response.

a. Security Orchestration

Orchestration in SOAR involves integrating various security technologies, such as Security Information and Event Management (SIEM) systems, endpoint protection platforms, firewalls, intrusion detection systems (IDS), and threat intelligence platforms (TIPs), among others. This integration ensures that data flows seamlessly between different tools and provides security teams with a unified view of security events.

For example, if an alert is triggered by a SIEM system, an orchestration layer can automatically pull additional context from threat intelligence feeds or endpoint security tools, enriching the alert with more detailed information. This context helps security analysts understand the nature of the threat and how to respond effectively.

b. Automation

Automation is the core of SOAR, allowing organizations to reduce the time spent on manual tasks and improve response efficiency. Automated tasks may include:

- **Alert triage**: Automatically categorizing and prioritizing alerts based on predefined rules.
- **Data enrichment**: Automatically pulling in context from external threat intelligence sources, such as IP reputation databases, vulnerability databases, and global threat feeds.
- **Incident containment**: Triggering automated actions like blocking IP addresses, isolating endpoints, or revoking user access during an active attack.

Automating these tasks not only saves time but also ensures consistent actions are taken, minimizing the risk of oversight and errors.

c. Incident Response

Incident response is the ultimate goal of a SOAR platform. SOAR allows security teams to respond to incidents by automating initial response actions (such as isolating a compromised system or blocking a malicious IP address) and guiding analysts through further investigation or remediation tasks. These workflows can be predefined or customized based on the type of incident. The platform can also help analysts manage the entire lifecycle of an incident—from detection and investigation to resolution and reporting.

The response phase also involves real-time collaboration among different security teams, such as incident response, forensic analysis, and threat intelligence teams, enabling more efficient handling of complex security incidents.

4. SOAR vs. Other Security Technologies

SOAR is often compared to related technologies like SIEM (Security Information and Event Management) and TIP (Threat Intelligence Platforms), as these systems are also central to modern security operations.

SIEM: SIEM systems aggregate and analyze log data from various sources to detect security incidents. While SIEM provides insights into potential security threats, it often requires manual intervention to investigate and respond. SOAR builds on SIEM by automating responses and orchestrating workflows across tools.

TIP: TIPs provide threat intelligence feeds, helping security teams understand the nature of cyber threats. SOAR platforms can integrate TIPs to automatically incorporate threat intelligence into their workflows, enhancing the response to known or emerging threats.

SOAR adds value by providing automation and orchestration, bridging the gap between detection and response, and improving the efficiency of security operations overall.

Security Orchestration, Automation, and Response (SOAR) is a transformative technology that enables organizations to manage and respond to security incidents more effectively. By orchestrating workflows, automating routine tasks, and providing a unified response platform, SOAR helps security teams stay ahead of cyber threats and improve their operational efficiency. In an era of ever-increasing cybersecurity threats, SOAR empowers organizations to respond faster, reduce human error, and handle a greater volume of incidents, all while maintaining a strong security posture.

7.2 Building Automated Incident Response Pipelines

Building automated incident response pipelines is a crucial step in improving an organization's ability to efficiently detect, mitigate, and recover from cybersecurity threats.

Incident response pipelines, when automated, help security teams handle a high volume of alerts and incidents with minimal human intervention, ensuring a faster, more consistent, and effective response. An automated pipeline integrates various security tools, processes, and technologies into a cohesive workflow, enabling the rapid detection, analysis, and resolution of incidents.

In this section, we will discuss the core components of an automated incident response pipeline, best practices for building such pipelines, and how automation enhances the efficiency and effectiveness of security operations. We will also explore real-world examples of automated incident response in action and the tools required to set up these pipelines.

1. Core Components of an Automated Incident Response Pipeline

To create a successful automated incident response pipeline, organizations must integrate several critical components to ensure seamless operations. These components work together to ensure that security incidents are detected, analyzed, and responded to promptly and effectively.

a. Data Collection and Integration

The first step in building an automated incident response pipeline is the collection of relevant data. This includes gathering logs, alerts, network traffic data, endpoint information, and threat intelligence feeds. Automated pipelines must integrate various data sources such as Security Information and Event Management (SIEM) systems, firewalls, Intrusion Detection Systems (IDS), Endpoint Detection and Response (EDR) tools, and external threat intelligence platforms (TIPs).

- **SIEM Systems**: These aggregate and correlate data from different sources, providing a centralized view of potential security incidents.
- **Endpoint Detection**: EDR tools provide valuable information on endpoint activity, such as file changes, processes, and network connections, which can be critical for detecting breaches.
- **Threat Intelligence**: TIPs provide external context, like information on emerging threats, known bad IPs, malware hashes, and attack techniques.

Automating the flow of data from these sources ensures that security teams have access to timely, relevant information without the need for manual data collection.

b. Alert and Incident Triage

Once data has been collected, the next step in the pipeline is triaging alerts to prioritize them based on severity and relevance. Manual triage can be time-consuming and error-prone, particularly when dealing with a large number of alerts. By automating the triage process, the pipeline can filter out false positives and prioritize high-risk incidents for further investigation.

This phase involves setting up predefined rules and thresholds that help determine the significance of each alert. For example, an alert about a suspicious login attempt might be assigned a higher priority if it originates from an unfamiliar IP address or if it follows a series of failed login attempts.

- **Automated Triage**: Automation allows for real-time analysis of alerts, categorizing them according to risk level and assigning priority based on factors like user roles, system access, and attack context.
- **Incident Enrichment**: During triage, the pipeline can also automatically enrich alerts with additional context, such as threat intelligence data (e.g., IP reputation), user information, or historical context from past incidents.

This process helps security teams to focus their attention on the most critical incidents and reduce the time spent on investigating low-priority alerts.

c. Incident Analysis and Investigation

Once an alert has been triaged, the pipeline moves to the analysis and investigation phase. In this phase, the automated response pipeline can collect additional information to confirm whether an incident is a legitimate threat. While this stage still involves some human decision-making, automation can greatly speed up the process by gathering data and providing context automatically.

Automation can assist in the following ways:

- **Correlation of Data**: Automating the correlation of different data sources helps to form a clear picture of the incident. For example, an analyst can receive automated alerts about a potential phishing email combined with relevant metadata from email servers, web logs, and endpoint logs, which accelerates the investigation.
- **Threat Intelligence Integration**: By integrating threat intelligence feeds into the pipeline, automated systems can identify whether the observed attack matches known attack patterns, such as specific malware families or IP addresses associated with malicious actors.

- **Automated Forensic Analysis**: Automated tools can also perform forensic analysis, such as reviewing network traffic for anomalies, checking for file integrity changes, and analyzing system configurations. This allows the analyst to rapidly understand the scope and impact of the attack.

d. Automated Response Actions

One of the key benefits of building an automated incident response pipeline is the ability to trigger response actions based on predefined workflows. Automation reduces the response time significantly by executing predefined actions based on the severity of the incident.

Common automated response actions include:

- **Network Isolation**: Automatically isolating affected systems or devices from the network to prevent lateral movement.
- **Account Lockdown**: If an account is suspected to be compromised, the pipeline can automatically trigger the process of disabling the user account or resetting their credentials.
- **Blocking Malicious IPs**: Upon identifying an IP address associated with an attack, the system can automatically block or blacklist the IP on the firewall or intrusion prevention system.
- **Incident Containment**: Automation can also help contain the spread of a threat by applying containment measures such as disabling ports, limiting user privileges, or enforcing access control restrictions.

Automating these steps ensures a swift and consistent response to security incidents, minimizing the impact and reducing the chances of human error.

e. Incident Resolution and Recovery

Once the immediate threat has been mitigated, the pipeline will move to the incident resolution and recovery phase. While this often requires some level of manual intervention, automation can still assist in tasks like restoring compromised systems from backups, applying security patches, or rebuilding affected configurations.

Automated tools can assist in:

- **Patch Management**: Automatically applying security patches and updates to vulnerable systems identified during the investigation phase.

- **System Restoration**: If systems were compromised, automation can help restore systems to a known good state using backup data.
- **Post-Incident Reports**: Automatically generating incident reports that document the timeline of events, actions taken, and lessons learned. These reports can be used for compliance purposes or to improve future incident response.

By automating the resolution and recovery steps, organizations can ensure that their systems return to a secure state as quickly as possible with minimal downtime.

2. Best Practices for Building Automated Incident Response Pipelines

Building an automated incident response pipeline requires careful planning, design, and implementation to ensure it aligns with the organization's security objectives and operations. Here are some best practices for creating an effective pipeline:

a. Define Clear Response Playbooks

A critical part of automation is creating clear and well-documented response playbooks. These playbooks outline the steps to be taken during different types of incidents, such as malware infections, data breaches, or insider threats. The playbooks should include:

- The criteria for when an automated response should be triggered
- The tools and systems involved in the response process
- The actions that need to be taken, such as isolating endpoints, blocking IPs, or notifying stakeholders
- These playbooks should be regularly reviewed and updated to account for new threats and changes in the organization's security posture.

b. Integrate Multiple Security Tools

An effective automated incident response pipeline requires the integration of various security tools and platforms to gather data, analyze incidents, and trigger responses. This integration ensures that automation flows smoothly across systems. Common tools to integrate include:

- SIEM systems for event aggregation and correlation
- Endpoint Detection and Response (EDR) for endpoint monitoring
- Firewalls and intrusion prevention systems for automated network defense
- Threat Intelligence Platforms (TIPs) for real-time threat data
- Incident management platforms for tracking incidents

c. Test and Optimize the Pipeline

Automation is only effective when it has been thoroughly tested. Organizations should regularly simulate real-world incidents to test the pipeline's response. This includes validating automated actions, ensuring that alerts are correctly categorized, and refining workflows to address gaps in response efficiency.

d. Monitor and Improve

Once the pipeline is up and running, continuous monitoring and feedback loops are essential for improvement. Security teams should regularly evaluate the effectiveness of the automated responses, adjust configurations based on new attack vectors, and use the insights gained to enhance the pipeline's efficiency.

Building automated incident response pipelines significantly enhances an organization's ability to detect, respond to, and recover from security incidents. By automating routine tasks and orchestrating workflows across multiple security tools, organizations can reduce response times, minimize human error, and improve overall security efficiency. The integration of data sources, triage processes, analysis, and response actions ensures that security incidents are handled swiftly and effectively, leading to stronger protection against evolving cyber threats.

7.3 Leveraging AI in Threat Containment and Mitigation

In the face of increasingly sophisticated and fast-evolving cyber threats, organizations must adopt more advanced methods of threat containment and mitigation. Traditional approaches, relying on static rules and human intervention, are no longer sufficient to handle the speed, complexity, and scale of modern attacks. Artificial Intelligence (AI) plays a pivotal role in this transformation, enabling organizations to detect, contain, and mitigate threats in real-time with greater precision, efficiency, and scalability.

This section delves into how AI can be effectively leveraged for threat containment and mitigation. By automating and enhancing response processes, AI helps organizations not only respond more rapidly to threats but also anticipate and neutralize them before they cause significant damage. We will explore various AI-driven techniques, tools, and frameworks for threat containment and mitigation, illustrating how they empower security teams to stay ahead of malicious actors.

1. AI-Powered Threat Detection and Containment

Threat containment is the process of isolating or mitigating the impact of a detected attack in real-time to prevent further compromise. Traditional methods often require human intervention to assess the situation, which can delay the response time and allow the attack to spread. AI, on the other hand, can automate detection, correlate data, and trigger appropriate containment measures without human intervention.

a. Real-Time Detection with AI

AI and machine learning (ML) algorithms are capable of analyzing vast amounts of security data in real-time, identifying anomalous patterns that signify potential threats. For example, AI can detect unusual network traffic, unusual user behavior, or the presence of known malware signatures by analyzing network logs, endpoint data, and other sources of telemetry. Once a threat is identified, AI can immediately initiate containment actions, such as isolating infected devices or blocking malicious IP addresses.

Machine learning models trained on large datasets can quickly recognize both known and novel threats. Unlike traditional signature-based systems, AI models do not rely on pre-existing knowledge of specific attacks; they can detect new, previously unseen attack vectors by recognizing anomalies in the data.

b. Automated Containment Actions

Once a threat is identified, AI can automate containment actions to prevent further damage. These actions may include:

Network Isolation: AI can automatically identify compromised systems and isolate them from the network, preventing lateral movement by the attacker. This is crucial for containing threats like ransomware or advanced persistent threats (APTs), which rely on moving laterally across the network to escalate privileges or exfiltrate data.

Endpoint Isolation: If an endpoint such as a server, laptop, or mobile device is found to be compromised, AI systems can isolate the device from the network, cutting off any communication between the compromised endpoint and external servers or other devices.

Blocking Malicious IPs: AI can instantly block IP addresses that are known to be part of a botnet or associated with a malicious attack. By leveraging threat intelligence feeds, AI can continuously update its database of known bad IPs and IP ranges.

Disabling Accounts: If a threat involves compromised user credentials, AI can automatically disable user accounts or force a password reset to stop attackers from exploiting them further.

c. Adaptive Threat Containment

An AI-powered threat containment system can adapt to the evolving nature of cyber threats. For example, as new attack techniques emerge, AI models can be retrained on new data, enabling them to detect and respond to emerging threats more effectively. AI also enables dynamic containment measures, adjusting containment actions based on the severity of the attack, the type of threat, and the specific environment.

For instance, if an AI system detects that a device is part of a botnet, it may take more aggressive actions, such as disconnecting it from the internet, while for a less severe threat, such as an attempted phishing attack, AI might only flag the suspicious activity for further investigation.

2. AI for Mitigation: Reducing the Impact of Cyberattacks

While containment aims to stop the attack from spreading, mitigation focuses on reducing the impact of the attack on the organization. AI plays a key role in both reactive and proactive mitigation strategies by not only stopping the immediate threat but also ensuring that the organization recovers quickly and with minimal damage.

a. Predictive Mitigation with AI

AI can be used to predict potential threats based on historical data, trends, and attack patterns. By analyzing threat intelligence and behavioral data, AI can forecast potential vulnerabilities that attackers may target, allowing organizations to take preemptive actions before an attack happens. For example:

Vulnerability Management: AI can predict which systems or applications are most likely to be targeted based on historical attack trends and threat actor behavior. By prioritizing patching efforts for those vulnerable systems, organizations can reduce their attack surface and mitigate potential damage.

Predicting Attack Paths: AI can simulate potential attack paths to predict how attackers might exploit system weaknesses to escalate privileges or move laterally within the network. By understanding these potential attack chains, AI can automatically implement countermeasures or adjustments to prevent them from being exploited.

b. Automating Remediation Actions

Once an attack has been contained, AI can assist in the mitigation phase by automating remediation tasks. These tasks are designed to neutralize the threat, restore normal operations, and ensure that any lingering issues are addressed quickly. Some AI-driven remediation actions include:

Patching Vulnerabilities: After containment, AI systems can automate the application of patches to vulnerable systems to prevent further exploitation by the same or similar attacks.

Restoring Systems: For attacks that involve system compromise, such as malware infections or ransomware, AI can assist in recovering affected systems by restoring them from backups or repairing corrupted files.

Clearing Malicious Artifacts: AI can help in the automated removal of malicious files, scripts, and registry entries left behind by attackers, reducing the chances of reinfection.

c. AI-Powered Incident Response and Analysis

AI also enhances the post-attack mitigation process by assisting in forensic analysis and incident response. Once the containment and immediate mitigation measures have been applied, AI can help analyze the incident in-depth to identify the root cause, track the attack's progression, and understand the full scope of the damage. This analysis can be used to improve future incident response and refine defense strategies.

Root Cause Analysis: AI-driven analysis tools can sift through large volumes of data to determine how the attack started, how it spread, and what systems were impacted. This helps security teams gain a better understanding of the incident and apply appropriate remediation measures.

Automated Reporting: AI can generate detailed incident reports, which are valuable for compliance, auditing, and continuous improvement. These reports can include a timeline of the attack, the effectiveness of the containment and mitigation measures, and recommendations for improving security posture.

3. Integrating AI in the Incident Response Lifecycle

The integration of AI into the incident response lifecycle enables a more proactive and holistic approach to cybersecurity. AI-driven threat containment and mitigation do not only help during an active attack; they also enhance the preparation and recovery phases:

a. Preparation and Prevention:

AI can help organizations by continuously monitoring network traffic and endpoint behavior to detect early signs of vulnerabilities or emerging threats. This proactive monitoring can lead to better prevention strategies, such as patching vulnerabilities before they are exploited.

b. Detection and Identification:

AI can automate the detection of potential threats, enabling quicker identification of attacks before they escalate. By analyzing a broad range of data from different security layers, AI can identify previously unknown threats and respond faster than traditional detection methods.

c. Response and Containment:

As discussed, AI automates containment actions like network isolation, blocking malicious activity, and isolating compromised devices. It ensures that incidents are handled swiftly and effectively, minimizing the time an attacker has within the system.

d. Recovery and Remediation:

Post-attack, AI continues to assist in restoring affected systems, removing malicious artifacts, and applying necessary patches. The ability to automate remediation tasks speeds up the recovery process and helps the organization resume normal operations quickly.

4. Challenges and Considerations in Leveraging AI for Threat Containment

While AI presents significant advantages in threat containment and mitigation, there are some challenges and considerations to keep in mind:

False Positives and Negative Impact: AI systems are not perfect and can generate false positives or take overly aggressive actions, such as blocking legitimate users or services. Fine-tuning and continuous monitoring are essential to minimize the impact of these false alerts.

Training and Data Quality: AI models rely heavily on high-quality training data. Without access to diverse, accurate datasets, AI may not be able to detect or respond to evolving threats effectively. Organizations must invest in continuously updating and refining their data sources.

Ethical and Legal Issues: Automated containment actions, such as isolating a device or blocking a user account, must be performed within the bounds of legal and ethical frameworks. Organizations must ensure that their AI-driven containment measures comply with privacy regulations and organizational policies.

Leveraging AI in threat containment and mitigation enables organizations to stay one step ahead of cyber attackers, ensuring faster response times, more accurate decision-making, and reduced impact from security incidents. By automating threat detection, containment actions, and mitigation tasks, AI allows security teams to address attacks more efficiently and effectively. As the sophistication of cyber threats continues to grow, AI-powered solutions will become increasingly indispensable in maintaining robust cybersecurity defenses.

7.4 Human vs. Machine Decision-Making in Incident Response

In cybersecurity, the effectiveness of incident response heavily relies on timely and accurate decision-making. Traditionally, human experts have been responsible for detecting, analyzing, and mitigating cyber threats. However, the rapid evolution of cyberattacks, coupled with the complexity and volume of data, has led to the integration of machine-driven technologies, such as Artificial Intelligence (AI) and Machine Learning (ML), to aid in decision-making. This shift presents both opportunities and challenges, as both human and machine decision-making approaches have distinct advantages and limitations.

In this section, we will explore the interplay between human and machine decision-making in the context of incident response, highlighting the strengths and weaknesses of both approaches and discussing how combining them can optimize incident response efforts. We will also discuss the evolving role of security professionals in an increasingly automated and AI-driven security landscape.

1. The Role of Humans in Incident Response

Human decision-making has been the backbone of incident response for decades. While automation and AI are playing an increasingly important role, human expertise remains critical, especially when it comes to contextual understanding, decision-making in uncertain scenarios, and applying ethical judgments.

a. Expert Judgment and Contextual Awareness

One of the key advantages of human decision-making is the ability to understand the broader context in which a security incident occurs. Human analysts can assess the situation by considering factors that machines might overlook, such as organizational priorities, business objectives, and nuances of the attack environment.

For example, during a suspected data breach, a security analyst may need to prioritize containment actions based on the value and sensitivity of the data affected, considering business impact and regulatory compliance requirements. Human judgment allows analysts to make decisions that align with both security needs and organizational goals, such as determining which departments or systems need to be isolated first or which incident response steps should be escalated to higher management.

b. Adaptability and Problem-Solving

Humans excel at adaptability and creative problem-solving in scenarios where new or unknown attack vectors are encountered. In incidents that involve novel or highly sophisticated attacks, humans can analyze incomplete or ambiguous data to develop hypotheses, adjust tactics, and explore unconventional solutions. This flexibility allows human experts to respond to incidents in ways that machines, which rely on historical data and predefined patterns, may not anticipate.

c. Ethical Decision-Making

Incident response decisions often have ethical and legal implications. Human involvement is crucial in ensuring that actions taken during an incident, such as isolating a system or blocking a user account, comply with privacy regulations, internal policies, and ethical standards. For example, AI might recommend locking out an account based on suspicious login patterns, but a human analyst may need to assess whether the user has legitimate access or whether blocking the account could affect critical business operations or disrupt workflows.

d. Communication and Collaboration

Effective incident response often requires collaboration across teams, such as IT, legal, compliance, and public relations. Humans are skilled in communicating complex technical issues to non-technical stakeholders, making decisions based on input from various departments, and managing the social and organizational aspects of incident response. They are also responsible for documenting the incident for future learning, compliance, and reporting purposes.

2. The Role of Machines in Incident Response

Machines, specifically AI and ML algorithms, have revolutionized the incident response process by automating many of the tasks traditionally handled by human analysts. These technologies excel in handling large volumes of data, detecting patterns, and responding to threats in real time, all of which are essential in today's fast-paced cybersecurity landscape.

a. Speed and Scalability

One of the most significant advantages of machine-driven decision-making is its speed and ability to scale. Cyberattacks can unfold quickly, and threats can evolve rapidly. AI and ML systems are capable of processing vast amounts of data from multiple sources—such as network traffic, endpoint logs, and threat intelligence feeds—at speeds that no human could match. This allows for real-time detection of threats, with AI systems able to trigger automated containment and mitigation actions without delay.

For example, machine learning models can identify malicious traffic patterns and automatically block IP addresses associated with an attack, significantly reducing response time compared to manual intervention.

b. Data Analysis and Pattern Recognition

AI and ML systems excel in identifying hidden patterns and anomalies in large datasets, especially when these patterns deviate from historical norms. By analyzing historical attack data, AI systems can detect new, previously unknown attack techniques, such as zero-day exploits or sophisticated APT tactics. This capability allows machines to provide early warnings of emerging threats that may not yet be recognized by traditional signature-based detection systems.

Furthermore, AI and ML systems can detect subtle anomalies in user behavior, network traffic, or system performance, enabling them to identify threats that would otherwise go unnoticed by human analysts. This proactive detection can greatly reduce the time between initial compromise and containment.

c. Consistency and Accuracy

Unlike humans, machines do not suffer from fatigue or bias. AI systems are capable of performing the same tasks with the same level of accuracy and consistency at all times. In the context of incident response, this means that AI can reliably process and analyze data, identify potential threats, and take action in a consistent manner.

For instance, once a machine learning model has been trained to recognize a specific type of malware, it can reliably identify that malware in future incidents, without being influenced by distractions, human error, or judgment calls. This makes AI-driven systems especially useful for handling repetitive tasks, such as scanning for malware or filtering out false positives, that would be time-consuming and prone to errors if done manually.

d. Automation of Repetitive Tasks

Machines excel in automating repetitive tasks that are essential to incident response but do not require complex decision-making. For example, AI can automatically collect logs, perform initial analysis, and identify potential indicators of compromise (IOCs). These routine tasks are essential for identifying threats but can be time-consuming for human analysts, particularly when dealing with large volumes of alerts or data.

By automating these tasks, AI allows human responders to focus their efforts on higher-priority decisions, such as analyzing complex threats, determining the impact of an attack, and developing mitigation strategies.

3. The Synergy of Human and Machine Decision-Making

While both human and machine decision-making have distinct advantages, they are most effective when used together in a complementary manner. Rather than replacing human decision-making, AI and ML should be viewed as tools that enhance the capabilities of human analysts, allowing them to respond more effectively to cyber threats.

a. Augmented Decision-Making

AI can augment human decision-making by providing additional context, insights, and recommendations. For example, during an incident, an AI system might detect unusual network behavior and recommend isolating a particular endpoint. A human analyst can then evaluate the recommendation in the broader context, considering business priorities, the scope of the attack, and any potential collateral damage before making the final decision. This augmented decision-making process enables the human expert to respond more quickly and accurately, leveraging the strengths of both human intuition and machine intelligence.

b. Continuous Learning and Improvement

AI systems learn and evolve based on the data they process. Similarly, human analysts bring experiential knowledge and intuition into the response process. By combining both approaches, organizations can create a feedback loop where machines continuously improve their ability to detect and mitigate threats, while humans provide valuable insights that help refine the models.

For instance, after an attack, human analysts can review the AI-generated decisions and provide feedback, which can then be used to retrain the machine learning models to improve their accuracy and reduce false positives in future incidents. This collaboration helps ensure that the AI systems evolve in tandem with the emerging threat landscape.

c. Decision-Making in Complex Scenarios

While AI excels at handling well-defined, repetitive tasks, human decision-making is essential in complex or novel scenarios. When facing sophisticated, multi-stage attacks or when contextual information is critical, human analysts can leverage their experience and critical thinking skills to make informed decisions.

For example, an attack involving advanced social engineering techniques or a zero-day exploit may require a deeper understanding of the organization's infrastructure, user behavior, and potential business impact. In such cases, AI can assist by providing data analysis and identifying potential risks, but the final decision will likely rest with a human expert who can factor in the nuances of the situation.

Human and machine decision-making each have their strengths, and their combination is the key to effective incident response. AI and machine learning enable faster, more consistent, and scalable responses to threats, while human decision-making brings contextual understanding, ethical considerations, and adaptability. By leveraging the strengths of both, organizations can create a more efficient, accurate, and dynamic incident response process. As the cybersecurity landscape continues to evolve, the integration of human expertise with AI-driven technologies will become increasingly essential for staying ahead of advanced cyber threats.

8. Reinforcement Learning for Adaptive Security

Chapter 8, Reinforcement Learning for Adaptive Security, introduces readers to the concept of reinforcement learning (RL) and its application in developing adaptive security systems that evolve in response to changing threat landscapes. This chapter explains how RL algorithms can train systems to make decisions based on feedback from the environment, enabling security measures that continuously adjust to new attack methods. Readers will explore how RL can be used to optimize defense strategies, dynamically allocate resources, and strengthen response protocols. By focusing on real-world examples, this chapter demonstrates how RL enables proactive, self-learning systems that can outpace traditional, static security measures.

8.1 Introduction to Reinforcement Learning in Security

Reinforcement Learning (RL) is a type of machine learning where an agent learns how to make decisions by interacting with an environment and receiving feedback in the form of rewards or penalties. Unlike traditional machine learning, which relies on supervised learning from labeled datasets, RL allows agents to explore and learn from their actions in an environment, optimizing their behavior over time through trial and error. This paradigm is particularly well-suited to environments where decision-making is sequential and outcomes are influenced by a series of interdependent actions, which is precisely the nature of cybersecurity challenges.

In the context of cybersecurity, RL can be a powerful tool for building adaptive security systems that can continuously learn from and react to evolving threats. It empowers systems to dynamically adjust defense strategies, detect new vulnerabilities, and respond to incidents with minimal human intervention. The ability of RL to model complex decision-making processes makes it a promising approach for areas such as intrusion detection, network security, attack mitigation, and even the automatic tuning of security controls.

This chapter introduces the concept of Reinforcement Learning (RL) and its potential applications in the field of cybersecurity. We will explore how RL works, its key components, and the ways in which it can be used to create more autonomous, adaptive, and effective security solutions. Additionally, we will address some of the challenges and considerations when applying RL to security tasks and provide insights into how organizations can begin to implement RL-based security systems.

1. What is Reinforcement Learning?

Reinforcement Learning is a branch of machine learning that is based on the concept of agents interacting with an environment. The agent's goal is to learn a policy (a strategy for decision-making) that maximizes cumulative rewards over time. The RL process can be described as follows:

Agent: The decision-maker that performs actions within an environment. In the case of cybersecurity, this could be a system or a model tasked with detecting attacks, mitigating risks, or adjusting security configurations.

Environment: The external system or world that the agent interacts with. In cybersecurity, the environment could be the network, endpoints, or cloud infrastructure being protected.

Actions: The decisions or operations performed by the agent that influence the environment. For example, in an intrusion detection system, actions might include flagging traffic as suspicious or blocking certain IP addresses.

State: The current condition or configuration of the environment. In a cybersecurity context, this could refer to the state of the network, ongoing security alerts, or the current status of an attack.

Reward: The feedback received by the agent after performing an action. Rewards are used to evaluate how well the agent is performing. In a security system, a reward could be positive for successful threat detection or mitigation and negative for a failure to respond appropriately.

Policy: The strategy or mapping from states to actions that the agent follows to maximize long-term rewards. The policy is refined over time as the agent learns from its interactions with the environment.

Over time, through continuous interaction with the environment, the agent learns to make better decisions by refining its policy. The key benefit of RL is its ability to operate in dynamic and complex environments where the agent can continually learn from the results of its actions, adjusting and improving its strategy without requiring predefined labels or exhaustive datasets.

2. Applications of Reinforcement Learning in Cybersecurity

Reinforcement Learning has significant potential in the field of cybersecurity, particularly in areas that involve decision-making in complex, ever-changing environments. Below are several ways in which RL can be applied to improve security measures:

a. Intrusion Detection Systems (IDS)

An IDS is designed to identify malicious activities or policy violations within a network. Traditional IDS often rely on predefined patterns or rules to detect known threats. However, new attack techniques or zero-day exploits may evade these systems. Reinforcement Learning can be employed to build an adaptive IDS that learns to identify abnormal behavior based on real-time data. The system would continuously update its detection strategy based on rewards for correct identification and penalties for false positives, ultimately becoming more effective at spotting novel attack patterns.

b. Network Traffic Classification

RL can be applied to network traffic analysis to differentiate between benign and malicious activities. In this application, an RL agent would monitor network traffic and learn over time which actions (such as blocking IP addresses or flagging traffic) reduce the likelihood of a cyberattack. The agent would receive positive rewards for reducing suspicious traffic and negative rewards for allowing malicious activities to bypass security measures.

c. Automated Vulnerability Management

Vulnerability management involves the identification, assessment, and mitigation of security vulnerabilities within a system. Reinforcement Learning can be used to optimize vulnerability patching by determining the best course of action to prioritize vulnerabilities based on factors like exploitability, criticality, and the system's current security posture. The RL model would evaluate different patching strategies and continuously improve its decisions over time based on the outcomes of previous actions.

d. Attack Mitigation and Response

In an ongoing cyberattack, traditional automated response systems often follow pre-configured rules that can be inflexible and inadequate in novel situations. Reinforcement Learning can help security systems adapt in real-time by dynamically adjusting defense strategies. For instance, if a security breach is detected, an RL agent could autonomously deploy a series of countermeasures, such as isolating affected systems, blocking malicious IP addresses, or executing security scripts, based on the evolving nature of the attack. The RL model would continuously refine its decision-making process based on the success or failure of its actions.

e. Adaptive Security Configuration

Organizations often have complex security configurations that need to be fine-tuned to prevent unauthorized access while ensuring minimal impact on legitimate users and operations. RL can be used to automatically adjust security policies, such as firewall settings, user access controls, or encryption protocols, based on current network conditions, user behavior, and potential threats. By learning from feedback, the RL system can dynamically optimize these configurations to balance security with performance, effectively adapting to changing environments.

3. Challenges of Implementing Reinforcement Learning in Security

Despite its promise, applying Reinforcement Learning to cybersecurity presents several challenges:

a. Data Complexity and Quality

Security environments are inherently complex, and gathering high-quality, labeled data for RL systems can be difficult. For example, it is challenging to simulate all possible attack scenarios in a controlled environment, making it hard to train an RL agent effectively. The data available may also be noisy or incomplete, affecting the RL model's performance.

b. High Computational Costs

Reinforcement Learning requires significant computational resources to simulate and evaluate the results of various actions, especially when dealing with large-scale networks or complex attack scenarios. The training process can be computationally expensive and time-consuming, requiring powerful hardware infrastructure, which can be a barrier to entry for smaller organizations or those with limited resources.

c. Exploration vs. Exploitation Dilemma

RL agents need to balance between exploration (trying new actions to learn more about the environment) and exploitation (taking the action that maximizes known rewards). In cybersecurity, this balance is crucial because exploration may expose the system to risks or attacks while exploiting known strategies might miss novel threats. Striking the right balance is key to ensuring that RL models are both effective and safe when applied to security tasks.

d. Ethical and Legal Implications

As with other AI-driven technologies, the use of RL in security raises concerns about privacy, data security, and ethical decision-making. Automated security systems must be carefully designed to ensure that they do not violate legal or regulatory requirements, such as those related to data protection (e.g., GDPR). Additionally, RL models that automatically respond to threats might make decisions that could negatively affect users or the organization if not properly managed.

Reinforcement Learning has the potential to revolutionize the way organizations approach cybersecurity by enabling adaptive, real-time decision-making and response. By allowing security systems to continuously learn from their environment and improve over time, RL can enhance threat detection, vulnerability management, and attack mitigation strategies. However, deploying RL in security requires careful consideration of challenges like data quality, computational costs, and ethical concerns. As the field of cybersecurity evolves, reinforcement learning will play an increasingly critical role in enabling more autonomous, intelligent, and effective security systems.

8.2 Building Agents for Dynamic Threat Mitigation

In the realm of cybersecurity, one of the most critical tasks is the ability to identify, assess, and mitigate threats in real time. Cyberattacks evolve quickly, often using sophisticated techniques that can bypass traditional defense mechanisms. To combat these dynamic threats, Reinforcement Learning (RL)-based agents can play a crucial role by providing autonomous, adaptive decision-making in the face of unknown and emerging threats. These agents learn and improve their ability to mitigate security risks over time through interaction with their environment, responding to changes in network traffic, attack patterns, and system vulnerabilities.

In this section, we explore how to build RL agents specifically designed for dynamic threat mitigation, focusing on their architecture, training process, and deployment in real-world security scenarios. These agents are designed to automatically adjust security measures, make real-time decisions, and evolve their strategies as new threats emerge, significantly enhancing an organization's cybersecurity posture.

1. Key Components of RL Agents for Threat Mitigation

Building effective RL agents for dynamic threat mitigation involves several key components. These include defining the agent's environment, designing its learning mechanism, and setting up appropriate feedback systems to enable continuous learning. Let's break down each of these elements:

a. Environment Design

The environment is a critical element in the development of RL agents, as it defines the context in which the agent operates. In the case of cybersecurity, the environment can be the entire IT infrastructure, which includes networks, endpoints, servers, and applications.

A key challenge in designing the environment is ensuring it accurately reflects the complexity and dynamism of real-world cyber environments. The environment should model different types of attacks, system vulnerabilities, user behaviors, and network traffic. Additionally, it should represent the system's normal state, along with potential deviations due to cyber threats.

For example, the environment might consist of:

- **Normal Network Traffic**: Representing regular operations and communication within the network.
- **Attack Scenarios**: Simulated or real-time attack patterns such as DDoS attacks, phishing attempts, or ransomware infections.
- **System Health**: Representing various conditions of system health, including vulnerabilities, patches, and configuration statuses.

The RL agent must interact with this environment and observe changes in real-time, using this information to make decisions about how to respond to potential threats.

b. State Representation

A critical aspect of an RL agent's ability to function effectively is how it represents and interprets the state of the environment. The state provides the agent with the necessary context to make decisions. In the context of dynamic threat mitigation, the state could include a variety of factors such as:

- **Network Activity**: Real-time data on network traffic, including IP addresses, ports, and protocols being used.

- **System Health Indicators**: Information regarding vulnerabilities, software patches, configurations, and resource usage.
- **Threat Intelligence**: Indicators of compromise (IOCs), attack vectors, and ongoing attack activities.
- **User Behavior**: Any deviations from typical user actions, such as access patterns or login locations that could indicate a compromised account.

An effective state representation should encapsulate all the relevant variables necessary for the agent to make informed decisions about threat mitigation. The state is updated continuously as the environment changes, providing the agent with fresh data to inform its next actions.

c. Actions and Mitigation Strategies

The RL agent's core task is to determine which actions to take in response to perceived threats. These actions are typically designed to mitigate or neutralize cyber risks, and they can vary widely depending on the context of the threat. Actions might include:

- **Blocking Malicious IPs**: Identifying and blocking suspicious or known malicious IP addresses associated with an ongoing attack.
- **Quarantining Infected Systems**: Isolating affected devices or network segments to prevent lateral movement during a breach.
- **Disabling Vulnerable Services**: Temporarily shutting down specific services or applications that are being exploited by attackers.
- **Deploying Patches or Updates**: Automatically applying critical security patches or updating software to address newly discovered vulnerabilities.
- **Alerting Security Teams**: Generating real-time alerts to notify security personnel about ongoing incidents or when automated responses may not be sufficient.

The actions taken by the agent are designed to either prevent the attack from succeeding or mitigate its impact. These actions can be pre-defined or dynamically learned by the agent over time, as it continually interacts with its environment and assesses the effectiveness of previous actions.

d. Rewards and Feedback Mechanisms

The RL agent learns by receiving feedback in the form of rewards or penalties based on its actions. In a dynamic threat mitigation system, the reward structure is critical because it guides the agent toward making effective decisions that contribute to the overall security of the system.

For example:

- **Positive Rewards**: These could be assigned when the agent successfully blocks an attack, prevents a data breach, or isolates a compromised system without impacting legitimate users or services.
- **Negative Rewards (Penalties)**: These could be assigned when the agent takes a wrong action, such as blocking legitimate traffic, causing system downtime, or failing to mitigate a threat in time.

The goal of the agent is to maximize its cumulative reward by continuously refining its decision-making process. Over time, the agent learns to prioritize actions that lead to higher rewards (effective threat mitigation) while avoiding those that result in penalties (false positives or ineffective responses).

2. Training RL Agents for Threat Mitigation

Training an RL agent for dynamic threat mitigation involves several steps, which may include the creation of a simulation environment, setting up training scenarios, and monitoring the agent's learning progress.

a. Simulated Training Environments

Due to the unpredictable nature of cyber threats, it is essential to train the RL agent in a simulated environment before deploying it in production. The simulated environment should closely resemble the real-world network, systems, and applications that the agent will eventually protect. Training can take place in virtual environments that replicate different types of cyberattacks, from simple exploits to complex, multi-phase attacks.

The advantage of simulated environments is that they provide a safe space where agents can experiment and learn from mistakes without risking actual data or systems. Additionally, simulated environments allow for the creation of diverse attack scenarios, including those that may be rare or hard to reproduce in real-world settings.

b. Exploration and Exploitation

The training process for RL agents involves balancing exploration (trying new actions to see what works) with exploitation (relying on what the agent has already learned). During training, the agent will experiment with various strategies for mitigating threats, such as blocking certain IPs, isolating systems, or deploying patches.

Exploration is important because it allows the agent to discover novel and unexpected strategies that might not have been anticipated during the initial design. However, excessive exploration can lead to suboptimal actions, such as disrupting normal operations or causing unnecessary system downtime. On the other hand, exploitation ensures the agent relies on the most successful actions it has learned so far, but it may miss out on new strategies.

c. Real-Time Adaptation and Continuous Learning

Once deployed, the RL agent must continue to learn and adapt in real-time. Cyber threats are constantly evolving, and the agent's ability to update its strategy in response to new attack vectors is essential for long-term effectiveness. One of the key benefits of RL is that it enables continuous learning: as the agent interacts with the environment, it refines its policy based on its experiences.

This continuous learning approach allows the agent to stay up-to-date with new attack techniques, vulnerabilities, and system configurations, ensuring that the security system remains effective even in the face of emerging threats.

3. Challenges in Building RL Agents for Threat Mitigation

While RL agents hold great promise in cybersecurity, several challenges need to be addressed for their effective implementation:

a. Real-World Complexity

Cybersecurity environments are highly complex and dynamic, making it difficult to model them accurately in a training environment. The diversity of systems, threat types, and attacker behaviors adds complexity, and any inaccuracies in the simulation can lead to ineffective agent behavior.

b. Action Space Explosion

As the number of possible actions increases, the training process for RL agents becomes more computationally intensive. For large-scale environments, where many systems and services must be protected, the agent's decision-making space can become very large, making it harder to find optimal solutions efficiently.

c. Balancing Security and Usability

RL agents must balance effective threat mitigation with minimizing the impact on legitimate users and system performance. Overzealous actions, such as blocking too many IP addresses or isolating critical systems, can lead to operational disruptions. Ensuring that the agent adapts without causing unintended side effects is an important challenge in threat mitigation.

Building RL agents for dynamic threat mitigation offers significant potential for enhancing cybersecurity defenses. By continuously learning from their environment, these agents can automatically adapt their strategies to detect and neutralize new threats. While the development of RL-based threat mitigation systems comes with challenges, such as dealing with real-world complexity and the vastness of potential actions, the ability to create autonomous, adaptive security solutions represents a major step forward in the evolution of cybersecurity. As these systems mature, they hold the promise of providing more resilient and responsive security mechanisms, capable of defending against even the most sophisticated and rapidly evolving cyber threats.

8.3 Training and Optimizing Adaptive Defense Policies

In cybersecurity, adaptive defense refers to the ability of security systems to dynamically adjust their protection strategies in response to evolving threats. As cyber threats become increasingly sophisticated, static defense mechanisms—such as signature-based detection systems—are often inadequate, because they are not designed to recognize or adapt to novel or zero-day attacks. To address this challenge, organizations are turning to Reinforcement Learning (RL) to train and optimize adaptive defense policies that can learn from real-time data, continuously improve, and autonomously adjust defense strategies based on the nature of incoming threats.

This section delves into how to train and optimize adaptive defense policies using RL, focusing on the processes involved in designing these policies, the training methods required for effective defense, and the challenges that organizations must overcome to deploy robust and resilient adaptive security systems.

1. What Are Adaptive Defense Policies?

Adaptive defense policies are security strategies that adjust automatically based on ongoing analysis of an organization's network, user behavior, attack patterns, and other security-related events. These policies aim to protect systems from both known and unknown threats by continuously evolving in response to changes in the threat landscape.

For example, an adaptive defense policy might involve:

- **Dynamic Risk Assessment**: Continuously evaluating the risk of different systems based on real-time data and attack patterns.
- **Response Adaptation**: Automatically shifting between various defense mechanisms (e.g., blocking malicious IPs, altering firewall rules, isolating affected systems) based on the current threat level.
- **Self-Optimization**: Periodically refining defense settings (e.g., intrusion detection thresholds or automated blocking mechanisms) to improve their efficiency in detecting or mitigating new types of attacks.

Reinforcement Learning plays a key role in training and optimizing these policies by enabling security systems to learn optimal actions through interaction with the environment. Over time, RL systems can adapt their policies based on the effectiveness of prior actions, optimizing their defense strategies autonomously.

2. Training Adaptive Defense Policies with Reinforcement Learning

Training an RL model to generate adaptive defense policies involves several important steps, from creating a realistic training environment to refining the model's decision-making process. The key stages in training adaptive defense policies are outlined below.

a. Defining the Environment

The first step in training an RL agent to optimize defense policies is to define its environment. This environment needs to represent the organization's network, systems, and the various types of threats it may face. The complexity of this environment is critical, as the RL agent needs to interact with a realistic representation of how cyberattacks unfold in real time.

A typical cybersecurity environment for RL training might include:

- **Network Topology**: Details about the layout of the network, including communication patterns, endpoints, and connections.
- **Attack Vectors**: A range of potential attacks (e.g., Distributed Denial of Service (DDoS), SQL injection, malware, or phishing).
- **System Vulnerabilities**: The current state of software patches, vulnerabilities, and exposure to specific types of attacks.

- **User Behavior**: Patterns of legitimate user actions that might be deviated from during an attack (e.g., logging in from unusual locations or accessing sensitive files).

The environment should be dynamic and evolve over time to simulate different attack scenarios. It should also provide realistic feedback to the RL agent regarding the effectiveness of its defensive actions, based on real-world cybersecurity dynamics.

b. Designing State, Actions, and Rewards

Once the environment is defined, the RL agent must understand the state, actions, and reward structure that will guide its learning.

State: The state defines the current condition of the system based on observable variables such as network traffic, system health, ongoing attacks, and other threat indicators. For example, a state might capture the number of incoming suspicious IP addresses, the level of CPU usage, or the presence of unauthorized login attempts.

Actions: The actions available to the RL agent represent the possible defense strategies it can implement in response to a given state. These might include:

- Blocking suspicious IPs or users
- Isolating compromised systems
- Deploying patches or updates
- Changing firewall rules
- Raising alerts for security teams
- Adjusting intrusion detection system (IDS) sensitivity thresholds

The RL agent must be able to select the best action based on the current state and its policy.

Rewards: The reward function is critical to guiding the agent's learning. Positive rewards should be given when the agent successfully mitigates a threat or prevents a security breach. For instance, if the agent blocks a DDoS attack in time, it could receive a positive reward. Negative rewards or penalties should be given for ineffective actions, such as false positives (blocking legitimate traffic) or failing to respond to an attack.

The reward structure should align with the goals of the defense system: minimizing security breaches, reducing false positives, and maintaining system availability while blocking malicious activity.

c. Training the Agent

Training an RL agent to optimize adaptive defense policies involves simulating a variety of cyberattack scenarios and allowing the agent to learn from the outcomes of its actions. During the training process, the agent must explore the environment, experiment with different actions, and update its policy based on feedback from the reward function.

Key elements of the training process include:

Exploration: In the early stages of training, the agent needs to explore different defensive strategies (e.g., trying different IP blocking strategies, or applying security patches at different intervals). Exploration is important because it allows the agent to discover novel, potentially more effective defense strategies.

Exploitation: Over time, the agent exploits the knowledge it has gained from previous exploration to choose actions that are likely to result in the highest cumulative rewards. In this phase, the agent relies more on its learned policy, gradually improving its ability to mitigate threats.

Learning Algorithm: The learning process typically involves an algorithm such as Q-learning, Deep Q-Networks (DQN), or Proximal Policy Optimization (PPO), which helps the agent adjust its decision-making process based on experience. These algorithms evaluate the outcomes of actions and adjust the agent's behavior to optimize for long-term success.

d. Continuous Learning and Model Updates

Once trained, the RL agent is deployed in a real-world environment where it can begin to implement its learned defense strategies. However, the cybersecurity landscape is constantly evolving, and new types of threats emerge regularly. To maintain optimal defense, the agent must be capable of continuous learning.

Model Updating: Continuous learning allows the agent to update its policy in real time based on feedback from new attack scenarios or changes in the network environment. For example, as new malware variants or attack vectors are discovered, the agent may adjust its actions accordingly to improve future defense responses.

Adaptive Feedback Loop: The agent should be constantly monitored and fine-tuned to ensure it adapts to the latest threats. If the agent detects a change in attack patterns or experiences a large number of false positives, the feedback loop can adjust its policy, reinforcing better decision-making and eliminating suboptimal defense strategies.

3. Optimizing Adaptive Defense Policies

The optimization of adaptive defense policies requires fine-tuning the RL model and ensuring that the agent can operate efficiently in a production environment. This involves several key strategies:

a. Reducing False Positives

One of the major challenges in dynamic threat mitigation is minimizing false positives—legitimate activities that are flagged as threats. These can lead to disruptions and user frustration. By continuously refining its reward function and policy, the RL agent can learn to better distinguish between benign and malicious activities, ensuring that legitimate traffic is not unnecessarily blocked.

b. Balancing Security and Performance

There is often a trade-off between aggressive security measures and the impact on system performance. For example, while isolating compromised systems may prevent further damage, it may also cause a temporary loss of service. The RL agent must learn to strike the right balance between maintaining security and minimizing disruptions to business operations.

c. Scalability

As organizations grow and add more systems, networks, and users, the RL agent must be capable of scaling its defense strategies to accommodate increased complexity. Optimizing policies for larger environments requires efficient training methods and an adaptable model that can handle more data, interactions, and possible actions.

d. Generalization to New Threats

A key challenge is ensuring that the RL agent can generalize its knowledge to new, previously unseen threats. The agent must be trained with a wide variety of attack scenarios and designed to adapt to new threat intelligence quickly. This is especially important in the case of zero-day attacks or novel attack vectors that the system may not have encountered during training.

Training and optimizing adaptive defense policies using Reinforcement Learning can significantly improve an organization's cybersecurity posture. By allowing security systems to automatically adjust their defense strategies in response to evolving threats, RL agents provide a dynamic, proactive approach to cybersecurity. Through continuous learning and optimization, these agents can reduce the risk of successful attacks, minimize false positives, and ensure that defense strategies remain effective as the threat landscape changes. While challenges remain—such as balancing security with performance, reducing false positives, and ensuring scalability—adaptive defense powered by RL holds tremendous potential for the future of autonomous cybersecurity.

8.4 Use Cases for Reinforcement Learning in Cyber Defense

Reinforcement Learning (RL) has emerged as a powerful tool in cybersecurity, offering organizations the ability to create systems that dynamically adapt to new and evolving threats. By using trial and error to optimize decision-making in a given environment, RL enables autonomous systems to continually improve their defense strategies. In the context of cyber defense, RL offers a variety of practical use cases, helping organizations bolster their security posture while reducing human intervention. This section explores some of the most compelling use cases for applying Reinforcement Learning in cybersecurity.

1. Automated Intrusion Detection and Response

One of the most significant use cases for RL in cyber defense is in intrusion detection and response. Traditional systems rely heavily on predefined rules, which can be ineffective against novel or sophisticated threats, such as zero-day attacks. RL can enhance intrusion detection by enabling systems to continuously learn from the environment and optimize responses to unusual activity.

How it Works:

- The RL agent monitors network traffic, logs, and system activity for any signs of intrusions or deviations from normal behavior.
- When suspicious activity is detected (e.g., a rapid increase in outbound traffic, unusual access to sensitive files, or anomalous login attempts), the RL agent assesses the severity of the threat and determines the most effective countermeasure.
- Over time, the agent learns to distinguish between legitimate activity and potential threats, continuously improving its detection and response strategies.

- The system can autonomously trigger actions such as isolating compromised systems, blocking malicious IPs, or alerting security teams, minimizing response time and preventing widespread damage.

Benefits:

- Real-time detection and mitigation of threats.
- Reduced human intervention and faster response times.
- Adaptability to new and emerging attack techniques.

2. Dynamic Firewall Management

Firewalls are one of the most fundamental security mechanisms in any organization's infrastructure. However, managing and fine-tuning firewall rules can be complex and time-consuming, especially as new threats emerge. RL can be used to optimize firewall rules dynamically, ensuring they are tailored to the current threat landscape.

How it Works:

- The RL agent is trained to assess the traffic passing through the firewall and determine whether the existing rules are sufficient to block potential threats.
- Based on the nature of incoming traffic and evolving attack patterns, the agent can recommend or automatically apply adjustments to the firewall rules.
- The agent continuously monitors the performance of the firewall, adjusting its strategies to reduce the likelihood of false positives and false negatives.
- For example, it could tighten restrictions during a DDoS attack or temporarily relax rules for trusted users while keeping suspicious traffic blocked.

Benefits:

- Continuous optimization of firewall configurations based on real-time data.
- Reduction in false positives and improved security posture.
- Automated adjustments to firewall settings, reducing the need for manual intervention.

3. Adaptive Phishing Detection

Phishing remains one of the most prevalent and damaging cyber threats. Attackers are continuously evolving their phishing tactics to deceive users, making it difficult for traditional detection systems to keep up. Reinforcement Learning can be employed to create adaptive systems capable of detecting phishing attempts, even those using new or previously unknown techniques.

How it Works:

- The RL agent monitors email communications, website links, and other communication channels for potential phishing attempts.
- It assesses the characteristics of messages or URLs, such as the use of suspicious language, unusual sender addresses, or deceptive formatting.
- As the system interacts with new phishing campaigns, the agent learns to recognize patterns of deception, improving its ability to flag phishing attempts with greater accuracy.
- Over time, the RL agent adjusts its behavior based on real-world attack patterns, enhancing its ability to detect even the most sophisticated phishing schemes.

Benefits:

- Real-time detection of phishing attacks, including new and evolving threats.
- Reduced reliance on static rule-based systems that may miss novel phishing tactics.
- Continuous learning and adaptation to new phishing techniques.

4. Autonomous Malware Analysis and Mitigation

Malware remains a significant threat to businesses, with new variants constantly emerging. Reinforcement Learning can be used to improve malware detection, analysis, and mitigation, allowing security systems to adapt to new types of malware dynamically.

How it Works:

- The RL agent interacts with malware samples in a controlled environment (sandbox) to understand their behavior.
- As the agent encounters new malware samples, it learns the most effective techniques for detecting, analyzing, and neutralizing these threats.
- The agent may determine the most effective way to isolate the infected system, block the malware's communication with external servers, or remove malicious code without disrupting system functionality.
- Over time, the RL agent refines its strategies, improving its ability to detect malware based on behavior rather than relying solely on signatures.

Benefits:

- Real-time, behavior-based malware detection and mitigation.
- Continuous learning from new malware samples.
- Automated, dynamic response to malware threats without human intervention.

5. Adaptive Vulnerability Management

Vulnerability management is a critical component of a proactive cybersecurity strategy. However, manually assessing vulnerabilities and applying patches can be an overwhelming task for large organizations with complex networks. RL can automate the vulnerability management process, allowing systems to prioritize vulnerabilities and apply patches based on the real-time risk they pose.

How it Works:

- The RL agent continuously scans the organization's infrastructure for known vulnerabilities, assesses their severity, and considers the current threat landscape.
- It evaluates which vulnerabilities pose the highest risk and determines the optimal time to apply patches or mitigation strategies.
- In the event of an attack, the RL agent can adjust the vulnerability management strategy, ensuring that the most critical vulnerabilities are prioritized and mitigated in real time.
- The agent can also learn from historical data, identifying which vulnerabilities have been most frequently exploited, thereby improving its ability to prioritize future patches.

Benefits:

- Automated, dynamic vulnerability management with reduced manual effort.
- Improved prioritization of vulnerabilities based on real-time risk assessments.
- Reduced exposure to critical vulnerabilities through timely patching.

6. Traffic Anomaly Detection in Network Security

Detecting anomalous network traffic is essential for identifying early signs of cyberattacks, such as Distributed Denial of Service (DDoS) attacks, insider threats, or unauthorized data exfiltration. RL can be used to continuously monitor network traffic, automatically adjusting detection strategies based on new attack patterns.

How it Works:

- The RL agent learns the baseline behavior of the network, including normal traffic patterns, communication frequencies, and bandwidth usage.
- When abnormal traffic is detected, the agent evaluates the situation to determine whether the anomaly is indicative of a potential threat, such as a DDoS attack or data breach.
- The RL agent can then take predefined actions, such as blocking malicious traffic, alerting administrators, or even rerouting traffic to minimize the impact of the attack.
- Over time, the agent adapts to new forms of traffic anomalies, improving its accuracy in identifying legitimate threats.

Benefits:

- Real-time detection and mitigation of anomalous network activity.
- Continuous learning and adaptation to new attack vectors.
- Reduced false positives and improved network performance.

7. Dynamic Access Control and Authentication

Access control is a fundamental security measure to ensure that only authorized users can access sensitive systems and data. Traditional access control systems rely on static rules, such as role-based access control (RBAC) or least privilege models. RL can be used to create adaptive access control systems that adjust access levels based on real-time risk factors, such as user behavior, environmental conditions, and ongoing security events.

How it Works:

- The RL agent assesses a user's behavior in real-time, analyzing factors such as login patterns, device usage, location, and access requests.
- Based on the risk assessment, the agent dynamically adjusts access privileges. For example, it may grant higher privileges to a user logging in from a trusted location but impose stricter controls when the same user logs in from an unfamiliar device or location.
- In case of suspicious behavior or a detected threat, the agent can instantly reduce access levels, require multi-factor authentication (MFA), or temporarily revoke access.

Benefits:

- Dynamic, real-time adjustments to access control based on real-time data.
- Enhanced security by minimizing the impact of compromised credentials.
- Reduction in the risk of insider threats and unauthorized access.

Reinforcement Learning offers numerous transformative applications in the field of cybersecurity, providing organizations with the ability to proactively adapt to new and evolving threats. By leveraging RL in use cases such as intrusion detection, dynamic firewall management, phishing detection, malware analysis, and vulnerability management, organizations can improve their defense systems' responsiveness, accuracy, and effectiveness. As the cybersecurity landscape continues to evolve, RL's ability to learn from real-world data and optimize decision-making processes will play an increasingly critical role in safeguarding digital environments.

9. Deep Learning and Advanced Neural Networks in Cyber Defense

Chapter 9, Deep Learning and Advanced Neural Networks in Cyber Defense, explores the use of deep learning techniques, including Convolutional Neural Networks (CNNs) and Recurrent Neural Networks (RNNs), to enhance cybersecurity defenses. This chapter explains how deep learning models are capable of processing vast amounts of data, identifying intricate patterns, and detecting complex cyber threats such as advanced persistent threats (APTs), malware, and phishing attacks. Readers will learn how these advanced neural networks can improve threat detection accuracy, reduce false positives, and automate the analysis of large-scale security data, such as network traffic and logs. By examining real-world use cases, this chapter highlights the potential of deep learning to revolutionize cyber defense, despite the challenges associated with deploying and scaling these models in dynamic environments.

9.1 Deep Learning Architectures in Cybersecurity

Deep learning, a subset of machine learning, has revolutionized many fields, including cybersecurity. Deep learning architectures, which are designed to mimic the human brain's processing patterns, are well-suited for identifying complex patterns in large datasets, making them an ideal tool for addressing the increasingly sophisticated and diverse range of cyber threats. In cybersecurity, these architectures enable systems to automatically detect malicious activities, identify vulnerabilities, and even predict attacks before they occur, all with minimal human intervention.

This section provides an overview of key deep learning architectures that have found application in cybersecurity, exploring how these models work, their advantages, and specific use cases within the domain of cyber defense.

1. Convolutional Neural Networks (CNNs) for Security

Convolutional Neural Networks (CNNs) are a class of deep learning models most commonly associated with image recognition. However, CNNs are highly effective in cybersecurity applications that involve pattern recognition, anomaly detection, and feature extraction from complex, high-dimensional data. They excel at processing grid-like data structures, such as network traffic logs or time-series data, where spatial and temporal dependencies exist.

How It Works:

CNNs are designed to automatically learn hierarchical features from raw data by applying a series of convolutions. These convolutions allow the network to learn localized patterns at various levels of abstraction, enabling it to recognize both simple and complex structures. The architecture typically consists of multiple convolutional layers, pooling layers, and fully connected layers that work together to extract increasingly complex features as data passes through the network.

Use Cases in Cybersecurity:

- **Network Traffic Analysis**: CNNs can analyze the structure of network packets or the flow of traffic through a system, detecting unusual patterns that may indicate an attack, such as Distributed Denial of Service (DDoS) attacks, botnet activities, or other anomalies in data flow.
- **Malware Detection**: CNNs can learn patterns in the binary structure of malware files, enabling them to identify malicious software by recognizing unique sequences or signatures within the file structure.
- **Intrusion Detection Systems (IDS):** CNNs can be applied to intrusion detection systems that process network logs and system event data to spot potential intrusions, focusing on irregularities and deviations from known normal patterns.

Benefits:

- Automated feature extraction, reducing the need for manual data preparation.
- High accuracy in recognizing complex, subtle patterns.
- Scalability to handle large datasets typical in cybersecurity environments.

2. Recurrent Neural Networks (RNNs) for Temporal Threat Detection

Recurrent Neural Networks (RNNs) are deep learning models designed to handle sequential data and temporal dependencies. Unlike traditional feed-forward networks, RNNs have loops that allow information to persist, making them particularly useful for applications in cybersecurity where time-series data, such as network traffic logs or user behavior patterns, is critical.

How It Works:

RNNs process input data one step at a time, maintaining an internal state (or memory) that helps the model understand dependencies between previous inputs and current outputs. This makes RNNs well-suited for tasks where the context of previous actions influences future outcomes, such as tracking user behavior over time or monitoring continuous data streams for suspicious activity.

However, vanilla RNNs have limitations in handling long-term dependencies due to issues like vanishing or exploding gradients. More advanced versions, such as Long Short-Term Memory (LSTM) networks or Gated Recurrent Units (GRUs), are often used to mitigate these challenges by retaining information over longer periods.

Use Cases in Cybersecurity:

- **Anomaly Detection in User Behavior**: RNNs, especially LSTMs, can be used to monitor user behavior, such as login times, access patterns, and resource usage. Deviations from normal behavior can be indicative of an account takeover or insider threat.
- **Predicting Network Attacks**: By analyzing historical network traffic patterns, RNNs can be trained to predict future attacks or identify emerging threats before they cause significant damage, such as in DDoS attacks or attempted intrusions.
- **Phishing Detection:** RNNs can be used to detect phishing emails by analyzing the sequential structure of email content or the context of links and attachments, helping to recognize deceptive patterns.

Benefits:

- Ability to handle sequential and time-dependent data, which is crucial in cybersecurity tasks.
- Effective for predicting and detecting events that evolve over time.
- Ability to detect subtle anomalies in complex datasets.

3. Autoencoders for Anomaly Detection

Autoencoders are a type of unsupervised deep learning model used primarily for anomaly detection. They work by compressing input data into a lower-dimensional latent space (encoding) and then reconstructing it back to its original form (decoding). The idea is that the network learns to represent normal data more efficiently and struggles to reconstruct data that deviates from the norm, which can then be flagged as anomalous.

How It Works:

An autoencoder consists of two main parts:

- **Encoder**: Compresses the input data into a compact, lower-dimensional representation.
- **Decoder**: Attempts to reconstruct the input data from this compressed representation.

The key to anomaly detection is that the autoencoder is trained primarily on normal data. When it encounters outlier or anomalous data, the reconstruction error (i.e., the difference between the input and reconstructed data) is significantly higher, indicating a potential security threat.

Use Cases in Cybersecurity:

- **Intrusion Detection**: Autoencoders are widely used for detecting intrusions in network systems. By learning the "normal" network behavior, they can identify unusual patterns of traffic or system events that might indicate unauthorized access or data exfiltration.
- **Malware Detection**: Autoencoders can be applied to analyze the features of malware and identify behaviors that differ from normal system operations. For instance, they can identify unusual system calls or file system changes that are indicative of a malware infection.
- **Insider Threat Detection**: Autoencoders can monitor employee activity and identify behavior that deviates from established norms, potentially flagging activities related to fraud, data theft, or sabotage.

Benefits:

- Effective at detecting novel or previously unseen anomalies without requiring labeled training data.
- Scalable for large datasets and capable of detecting subtle deviations from normal behavior.
- Useful for early detection of threats and reducing false positives.

4. Generative Adversarial Networks (GANs) for Cyber Threat Simulation and Defense

Generative Adversarial Networks (GANs) are a class of deep learning models that consist of two neural networks: a generator and a discriminator. The generator creates synthetic data, while the discriminator attempts to distinguish between real and fake data. These two networks compete with each other, leading to the generation of realistic synthetic data as the process evolves. GANs have been applied in various cybersecurity contexts, particularly in threat simulation and improving detection systems.

How It Works:

- The generator creates adversarial examples or synthetic cyberattack data, such as malware or phishing emails, by learning the underlying distribution of real-world threat data.
- The discriminator evaluates whether the generated data is real or fake, improving the generator's ability to produce realistic adversarial data over time.
- Through this adversarial training, GANs can generate diverse, realistic attack samples that can be used to test and improve cybersecurity defenses.

Use Cases in Cybersecurity:

- **Adversarial Training**: GANs can be used to generate adversarial examples to test the robustness of machine learning-based cybersecurity models. By exposing detection systems to simulated threats, GANs help improve their ability to recognize novel or sophisticated attacks.
- **Malware Synthesis**: GANs can be employed to generate synthetic malware variants, which can be used to train malware detection systems on a broader range of attack patterns.
- **Phishing and Fraud Detection**: GANs can generate realistic phishing attempts, helping to train anti-phishing systems and enhance detection capabilities by simulating real-world threat scenarios.

Benefits:

- Enhances training datasets with realistic, diverse adversarial examples, improving the robustness of cybersecurity systems.
- Helps in adversarial testing of machine learning models to identify vulnerabilities and improve detection accuracy.
- Facilitates the development of more resilient and adaptive cybersecurity defenses.

5. Deep Reinforcement Learning (DRL) for Autonomous Cyber Defense

Deep Reinforcement Learning (DRL) combines deep learning with reinforcement learning, enabling systems to learn optimal strategies for sequential decision-making tasks. In cybersecurity, DRL can be used to automate threat mitigation and defense strategies, allowing systems to adapt to new threats dynamically and autonomously.

How It Works:

In DRL, an agent interacts with an environment (e.g., a network, system, or endpoint), making decisions based on the state of the environment. It receives rewards or penalties based on the actions it takes and learns to maximize cumulative rewards over time. DRL models can handle continuous, high-dimensional action spaces, making them ideal for complex cyber defense tasks.

Use Cases in Cybersecurity:

- **Autonomous Incident Response**: DRL can be used to develop systems that automatically respond to threats, such as isolating compromised devices, blocking malicious traffic, or applying patches to vulnerabilities. The system learns from previous incidents to improve future responses.
- **Adaptive Defense Policies**: DRL agents can optimize security policies in real-time, adjusting firewall rules, intrusion detection thresholds, or access control settings based on evolving threats.
- **Adaptive Attack Mitigation**: DRL can dynamically adjust attack mitigation strategies during an active attack, such as adapting DDoS defenses or rerouting malicious traffic in real-time.

Benefits:

- Enables autonomous decision-making for complex security tasks.
- Real-time adaptability to new and evolving threats.
- Improves efficiency and reduces the need for human intervention in critical security operations.

Deep learning architectures, including CNNs, RNNs, Autoencoders, GANs, and DRL, offer substantial advantages in tackling the complex and evolving challenges of cybersecurity. By leveraging these models, cybersecurity systems can improve threat detection, response times, and overall resilience to attacks. As the cybersecurity landscape becomes increasingly sophisticated, the integration of deep learning will continue to play a vital role in creating adaptive, intelligent defense systems capable of addressing both known and unknown threats.

9.2 Convolutional Neural Networks (CNNs) for Phishing Detection

Phishing is one of the most prevalent and dangerous cybersecurity threats, with attackers using deceptive techniques to trick individuals into divulging sensitive information, such as login credentials, financial details, or personal data. Traditional phishing detection methods often rely on signature-based techniques or rule-based filters, which can be ineffective in detecting new, more sophisticated phishing attempts. However, Convolutional Neural Networks (CNNs), a type of deep learning architecture, have proven highly effective in identifying and mitigating phishing attacks by analyzing patterns within data, such as emails, URLs, or website content. This section explores how CNNs can be applied to phishing detection, their benefits, and real-world use cases.

1. How CNNs Work for Phishing Detection

Convolutional Neural Networks (CNNs) are designed to process data with grid-like structures, such as images or text sequences. CNNs are particularly effective at feature extraction, where they automatically learn to detect patterns from raw input data, such as the structure of an email or the visual layout of a webpage. CNNs do not require manual feature extraction, which makes them highly adaptive and capable of learning from complex and diverse phishing patterns.

A CNN typically consists of several layers, including convolutional layers, pooling layers, and fully connected layers. The convolutional layers apply filters to the input data to detect patterns, such as specific keywords in an email or certain visual elements in a website. Pooling layers help to reduce dimensionality and highlight the most important features, while fully connected layers allow the network to make predictions based on the features extracted.

For phishing detection, the model is trained on large datasets containing both legitimate and phishing samples, allowing it to learn distinguishing features such as suspicious URL patterns, email formatting, or the presence of deceptive language.

2. Phishing Detection Using CNNs for Email Classification

One of the most common ways phishing attacks are carried out is via deceptive emails that appear legitimate. These emails often imitate trusted sources, such as banks, e-commerce websites, or government agencies, to trick users into clicking malicious links or opening harmful attachments.

CNNs can be employed to analyze the content and structure of emails, detecting various types of phishing tactics such as:

- **Suspicious sender addresses**: Phishers often use addresses that appear similar to legitimate ones with small variations, such as changing one character.
- **Suspicious language and tone**: Phishing emails often use urgent language, such as "Your account is at risk" or "Immediate action required," which may be unusual for legitimate communication.
- **Malicious links or attachments**: Links in phishing emails often lead to fake websites or download malicious software. CNNs can be trained to recognize these hidden dangers by analyzing the link structure and the context in which they appear.

Using a CNN for email classification involves training the model with labeled data containing phishing and legitimate emails. The network learns to identify relevant features, such as suspicious phrases, abnormal email structures, or unusual metadata, which are then used to classify incoming emails as either phishing or benign.

3. Phishing Detection Using CNNs for URL Analysis

Another common attack vector for phishing is through deceptive URLs that lead users to counterfeit websites designed to steal personal information. Phishers may use obfuscated or misleading URLs that appear similar to trusted websites but contain subtle differences, such as swapped characters or additional subdomains.

CNNs can analyze URLs and detect patterns that are indicative of phishing. For example, a CNN might look for:

- **Suspicious subdomains**: Phishing URLs may include additional words or characters in the subdomain to appear legitimate.
- **Suspicious characters or sequences**: Some phishing URLs contain non-standard characters or use domains that look like popular websites but contain extra symbols or misspellings.
- **Domain age and reputation**: A CNN can also incorporate information about the age or reputation of a domain, flagging newly registered or suspicious-looking domains often associated with phishing attempts.

Training a CNN to analyze URLs typically involves using datasets of known phishing and legitimate URLs, with features such as domain names, path structures, and query strings being fed into the network. The CNN then learns to recognize patterns that distinguish phishing URLs from legitimate ones and can automatically flag potentially dangerous links.

4. Phishing Detection Using CNNs for Website Analysis

Phishing websites are designed to mimic the look and feel of legitimate websites, making it difficult for users to distinguish between the two. CNNs can be applied to analyze the visual features of websites, identifying suspicious elements that may indicate a fraudulent page, such as:

- **Similarities in design**: Phishing websites often copy the layout, color scheme, and logos of legitimate sites, but subtle differences may reveal their true nature.
- **Suspicious UI elements**: Certain UI components, such as fake login forms or deceptive buttons, are common in phishing attempts. CNNs can be trained to detect these patterns in the website's visual content.
- **HTML and CSS anomalies**: Phishing sites may have poorly constructed HTML or CSS, leading to inconsistencies in page rendering that can be detected by a CNN.

To train a CNN for phishing website detection, a dataset of legitimate and phishing websites (often in the form of screenshots or HTML) is used. The CNN learns the differences between authentic and fraudulent websites, enabling it to classify new web pages as phishing or legitimate based on visual cues.

5. Benefits of Using CNNs for Phishing Detection

Using Convolutional Neural Networks for phishing detection offers several advantages over traditional methods, such as rule-based filtering or keyword matching:

- **Automated Feature Extraction**: CNNs automatically learn the most relevant features for detecting phishing attacks, eliminating the need for manual feature engineering. This makes the model highly adaptive to new phishing techniques.
- **High Accuracy**: CNNs are particularly effective at detecting complex patterns, enabling them to identify even subtle differences between legitimate and phishing emails, URLs, or websites.
- **Scalability**: CNNs can handle large amounts of data efficiently, making them suitable for analyzing thousands or even millions of emails, URLs, and websites in real-time.

- **Generalization to New Phishing Techniques**: Unlike signature-based systems that rely on predefined patterns, CNNs can generalize from training data and detect new, unseen phishing tactics, improving defense against evolving attacks.
- **Reduction of False Positives**: By learning from large and diverse datasets, CNNs can minimize false positives, ensuring that legitimate communications are not incorrectly flagged as phishing attempts.

6. Challenges and Limitations of CNNs for Phishing Detection

While CNNs offer numerous benefits for phishing detection, there are some challenges and limitations to consider:

- **Data Quality and Diversity**: CNNs require large, high-quality labeled datasets for training. If the dataset does not adequately represent all types of phishing attacks or is biased, the model may struggle to detect certain phishing techniques or may generate false positives.
- **Computational Resources**: Training CNNs can be computationally expensive, requiring significant processing power, especially when handling large volumes of data. Organizations may need access to powerful hardware or cloud resources to implement CNN-based phishing detection at scale.
- **Adversarial Attacks**: Just as CNNs can be used to detect phishing, attackers can attempt to evade detection by crafting adversarial examples specifically designed to fool deep learning models. Continuous retraining and model updates are necessary to mitigate this risk.

7. Real-World Use Cases and Implementations

Several cybersecurity companies and organizations have begun integrating CNNs into their phishing detection systems with promising results:

- **Email Phishing Detection**: Companies like Google and Microsoft use deep learning techniques, including CNNs, to filter out phishing emails from user inboxes, providing an additional layer of protection to their users.
- **Web Browser Plugins**: Some web browsers, such as Chrome and Firefox, use CNN-based models to analyze URLs in real-time, warning users when they attempt to visit a phishing site.
- **Anti-Phishing Solutions**: Dedicated cybersecurity platforms, such as PhishLabs and Proofpoint, have integrated CNNs into their phishing detection and prevention systems, offering real-time threat intelligence and protection.

Convolutional Neural Networks have proven to be a powerful tool in detecting phishing attacks, leveraging their ability to learn complex patterns and features from raw data without manual intervention. Whether applied to email analysis, URL inspection, or website evaluation, CNNs significantly enhance the ability to detect and block phishing attempts before they can harm users or organizations. As phishing tactics continue to evolve, CNNs represent a dynamic and adaptive solution that can scale and improve over time, offering robust protection against one of the most prevalent cybersecurity threats.

9.3 Recurrent Neural Networks (RNNs) for Log Analysis

Log files are essential sources of data for cybersecurity professionals, containing valuable information about system activities, network traffic, application behavior, and potential security incidents. However, the large volume and complexity of logs make it difficult to manually analyze and detect threats in real time. Traditional log analysis methods rely on predefined patterns and rule-based systems, which can be ineffective at identifying new, sophisticated attack vectors or anomalous behaviors. To address these challenges, Recurrent Neural Networks (RNNs), a class of deep learning models designed to handle sequential data, have emerged as a powerful tool for analyzing logs and detecting security threats. This section delves into how RNNs can be leveraged for log analysis, their advantages, and real-world use cases.

1. Understanding RNNs and Their Application to Log Data

Recurrent Neural Networks (RNNs) are a type of artificial neural network designed specifically for processing sequential data. Unlike traditional feedforward neural networks, which assume that all inputs are independent of each other, RNNs maintain internal states that can capture dependencies and patterns across time or sequence. This characteristic makes RNNs particularly well-suited for tasks where the order of events or data points is important, such as speech recognition, language modeling, and, in the case of cybersecurity, log analysis.

Logs are inherently sequential; the events recorded in log files are generated in a specific order over time. To effectively detect threats or anomalies, it's crucial to understand the temporal relationships between these log entries. RNNs can learn these temporal patterns and make predictions based on the sequence of events, enabling them to identify unusual activities, detect intrusions, and diagnose system errors.

RNNs achieve this by processing each log entry one at a time while maintaining an internal state, or memory, that is updated with each new input. This allows RNNs to capture long-range dependencies in the data, making them especially effective at identifying complex patterns and anomalies that might go unnoticed using traditional techniques.

2. Log Data and the Need for Sequential Analysis

Log data, especially from servers, network devices, and security appliances, typically consists of timestamped entries that record system actions, user activities, access logs, and error messages. For example, logs might capture information such as:

- User login attempts and session durations
- Network traffic patterns
- Error messages and system warnings
- Security alerts and audit trails

These logs often contain valuable indicators of compromise (IoCs) or other signs of a security breach. Analyzing these logs manually or using traditional methods can be time-consuming and error-prone, especially when dealing with large volumes of data. Moreover, the potential threats may not be immediately obvious and often unfold over time, making it necessary to analyze the sequence of events and detect abnormalities in the pattern of activities.

RNNs can address this challenge by learning the temporal dependencies in log entries, making them capable of identifying not only the presence of suspicious events but also their context within a broader sequence. For instance, an RNN could detect an unusual sequence of failed login attempts followed by a successful login, which may indicate a brute-force attack or credential stuffing attempt.

3. How RNNs Work for Log Analysis

To use RNNs for log analysis, the log data is typically preprocessed and converted into a format that can be fed into the model. This often involves tokenizing the log entries into relevant features, such as:

- **Timestamps**: The time when an event occurred, allowing the model to understand the sequence of actions.
- **Log messages**: Descriptive text or codes indicating system events, errors, or security alerts.
- **Event types**: Categories or tags for each log entry (e.g., "login," "error," "suspicious activity").

- **Severity levels**: The level of importance or urgency associated with a given log entry (e.g., low, medium, high).

Once the data is structured, the RNN processes each log entry in sequence, updating its internal state as it progresses through the log file. The RNN learns to recognize patterns, such as the typical sequence of normal system activities, and can flag deviations from the norm as potential threats or anomalies.

There are several types of RNNs that can be used for log analysis, including:

- **Vanilla RNNs**: The basic form of RNNs, which can capture short-term dependencies in sequential data. While effective for simple log analysis tasks, vanilla RNNs can struggle with long-range dependencies due to issues like vanishing gradients.
- **Long Short-Term Memory (LSTM):** A specialized type of RNN designed to mitigate the vanishing gradient problem and capture long-range dependencies in data. LSTMs are well-suited for log analysis, where patterns may unfold over extended periods.
- **Gated Recurrent Units (GRUs):** A variant of LSTMs that offers a simplified architecture while still capturing long-term dependencies. GRUs are sometimes preferred for their efficiency and computational simplicity.

4. Benefits of Using RNNs for Log Analysis

There are several advantages to using RNNs for log analysis, including:

- **Contextual Understanding**: Unlike traditional methods that may treat each log entry independently, RNNs can take into account the full sequence of events, providing a more comprehensive understanding of system behavior and making it easier to detect attacks that involve multiple stages or actions.
- **Anomaly Detection**: RNNs excel at identifying outliers or deviations from established patterns. They can be trained to recognize normal behavior in log data and flag any significant variations as potential security threats.
- **Dynamic Learning**: As new log entries are processed, RNNs continuously learn and adapt to changes in system behavior, making them well-suited for environments where threat patterns evolve over time.
- **Scalability**: RNNs are capable of analyzing large volumes of log data in real-time, enabling automated threat detection across vast networks and systems.
- **Automated Threat Classification**: By learning from labeled training data, RNNs can automatically classify log entries into different categories, such as "normal,"

"suspicious," or "malicious," helping security analysts prioritize their response efforts.

5. Real-World Use Cases for RNNs in Log Analysis

Several cybersecurity applications benefit from the use of RNNs for log analysis, including:

- **Intrusion Detection Systems (IDS):** RNNs can be used to analyze log data from network devices, firewalls, and servers to identify potential intrusion attempts. For example, a sequence of unusual events, such as multiple failed login attempts followed by an elevated privilege access, could indicate a possible attack.
- **Fraud Detection**: In financial systems, RNNs can analyze transaction logs to detect fraudulent behavior. Anomalous sequences, such as large numbers of rapid transactions from the same account, could be flagged for further investigation.
- **Malware Detection**: RNNs can detect patterns associated with malware activity in system logs. For instance, unusual patterns of file access or modification could indicate the presence of malicious software.
- **System Anomaly Detection**: RNNs can help detect operational anomalies, such as server crashes, performance degradation, or misconfigurations, by analyzing system logs over time.

6. Challenges and Limitations of RNNs for Log Analysis

Despite their many benefits, RNNs do present some challenges when applied to log analysis:

- **Data Quality and Labeling**: RNNs require large, high-quality datasets for training. Logs can be noisy, incomplete, or inconsistent, which may affect the performance of the model. Additionally, labeled datasets (i.e., logs marked as "normal" or "malicious") are often required for supervised learning, and obtaining such labeled data can be difficult and time-consuming.
- **Computational Cost**: Training RNNs, especially LSTMs or GRUs, can be computationally intensive, requiring significant processing power and memory, particularly when analyzing large volumes of log data in real-time.
- **Interpretability**: Deep learning models, including RNNs, are often considered "black boxes," meaning that understanding how they arrive at a particular decision or prediction can be challenging. This lack of transparency can hinder the ability of security analysts to trust and verify the results.

Recurrent Neural Networks (RNNs) are a powerful tool for log analysis in cybersecurity, offering the ability to capture temporal patterns and detect anomalous behaviors across large and complex datasets. By leveraging the sequential nature of log data, RNNs can provide valuable insights into potential security threats, enabling automated and real-time detection of attacks. While RNNs present challenges related to data quality, computational cost, and interpretability, their ability to handle dynamic and evolving log data makes them an essential technology for modern cybersecurity defenses. As the volume and complexity of log data continue to increase, RNNs will play an increasingly vital role in securing systems and networks.

9.4 Challenges of Deploying Deep Learning Models in Cybersecurity

The application of deep learning (DL) in cybersecurity offers significant advancements in the ability to detect and mitigate cyber threats. Models such as Convolutional Neural Networks (CNNs), Recurrent Neural Networks (RNNs), and Deep Reinforcement Learning (DRL) have proven to be powerful tools for anomaly detection, threat intelligence, malware classification, and more. Despite the promising results that deep learning has shown in cybersecurity, deploying these models in real-world environments comes with a set of challenges. These challenges must be addressed to ensure that deep learning systems are reliable, effective, and scalable in real-world cybersecurity settings. This section explores the primary hurdles of deploying deep learning models in cybersecurity and discusses potential solutions.

1. Data Quality and Availability

One of the most significant challenges in deploying deep learning models for cybersecurity is ensuring access to high-quality, diverse, and labeled datasets. Deep learning models require vast amounts of data for training to detect patterns and learn relationships within the data. In cybersecurity, data can come from a variety of sources, such as network logs, security events, system behavior, and threat intelligence feeds. However, there are several issues related to data quality and availability that can hinder the effectiveness of these models:

- **Imbalanced Datasets**: Cybersecurity datasets are often imbalanced, with a significantly higher number of normal or benign events compared to malicious ones. This imbalance can lead to biased model predictions, where the model becomes overly conservative and fails to detect rare or new types of attacks.

Addressing this imbalance requires techniques such as oversampling the minority class (malicious data) or generating synthetic data using methods like Generative Adversarial Networks (GANs).
- **Noisy Data**: Log files, network traffic, and security event data often contain noise, errors, or inconsistencies, which can affect the model's ability to learn meaningful patterns. Data preprocessing and cleaning become crucial steps to improve the accuracy of deep learning models.
- **Data Labeling**: For supervised learning models to be effective, labeled data is required. However, labeling cybersecurity data manually can be time-consuming, expensive, and error-prone. Additionally, new and evolving attack types may not have enough labeled examples, making it harder to train deep learning models on emerging threats.

2. Computational Costs and Resource Requirements

Deep learning models are computationally intensive, requiring significant computational power to process large datasets and train models. Cybersecurity environments, particularly in large enterprises or organizations with massive amounts of real-time data, need deep learning models that can handle high-volume, high-velocity data without lag or errors.

- **Training Time**: Training deep learning models, especially those with millions of parameters (e.g., CNNs or RNNs), can take days, weeks, or even months, depending on the complexity of the model and the size of the dataset. The long training times, combined with the need for powerful hardware (e.g., GPUs or TPUs), can be a barrier to implementing deep learning in environments where real-time or near-real-time processing is critical.
- **Inference Costs**: Once the model is trained, the inference process (predicting outcomes based on new data) can still be resource-intensive. Real-time detection systems, such as Intrusion Detection Systems (IDS) or anomaly detection systems, require low-latency predictions, and delays in decision-making could lead to missed attacks or vulnerabilities.
- **Scalability**: As the size and complexity of the network or security infrastructure grow, scaling deep learning models becomes a challenge. Cloud-based solutions may be required for training large-scale models, but the cost and resource management of these systems can add another layer of complexity.

3. Model Interpretability and Transparency

Deep learning models are often referred to as "black-box" models because it can be difficult to understand how they arrive at specific decisions or predictions. This lack of transparency poses several issues in cybersecurity:

- **Trust and Accountability**: Security professionals need to trust the outputs of deep learning models before acting on them. If a model flags an anomaly or a potential attack, the ability to understand the reasoning behind that decision is essential for validating the results. In cybersecurity, incorrect predictions (e.g., false positives or false negatives) could have serious consequences, such as denying access to legitimate users or missing a real attack.
- **Regulatory Compliance**: In some industries, there are strict regulations regarding decision-making processes, especially in sensitive areas like finance, healthcare, or government security. These regulations often require that decisions made by automated systems be explainable and justifiable. The opacity of deep learning models can complicate compliance with such standards.
- **Debugging and Model Improvement**: The lack of interpretability also makes it challenging to debug the models when they fail or underperform. If an AI system misclassifies a threat or generates a false positive, it is difficult for analysts to pinpoint exactly where and why the model went wrong.

To address these challenges, researchers have been developing methods for model interpretability, such as saliency maps, which show which parts of the input data are influencing the model's decision, and explainable AI (XAI) frameworks, which aim to make AI systems more transparent.

4. Adversarial Attacks and Model Robustness

In cybersecurity, one of the major concerns when deploying deep learning models is their vulnerability to adversarial attacks. These attacks involve manipulating input data in subtle ways to deceive machine learning models into making incorrect predictions. This poses a critical risk for deep learning models in security applications.

- **Adversarial Examples**: An adversarial example is a slight perturbation of input data designed to fool the model into misclassifying it. For instance, a malicious actor might modify a file or packet in a way that causes a deep learning model to misinterpret it as benign when it is actually malicious. This can render deep learning-based detection systems ineffective and potentially lead to security breaches.
- **Transferability of Adversarial Attacks**: Adversarial attacks are often transferable, meaning that an attack that fools one model may also deceive others.

This means that attackers can design universal adversarial examples capable of evading multiple models, making it harder for security systems to defend against them.
- **Defensive Strategies**: Several strategies can be used to increase model robustness, such as adversarial training (incorporating adversarial examples into the training process), model ensembling (using multiple models together to make predictions), or defensive distillation (reducing the model's sensitivity to small perturbations). However, these strategies are not foolproof and must be continuously updated to keep pace with new adversarial techniques.

5. Real-Time Detection and Latency

Another key challenge when deploying deep learning models for cybersecurity is ensuring that the model can perform real-time detection with minimal latency. In dynamic environments like networks, system monitoring, or security operations, threats evolve rapidly, and models need to make quick decisions to prevent or mitigate damage.

- **Latency in Deep Learning Models**: Deep learning models, especially those with large architectures or complex computations, may not provide real-time responses needed for immediate threat detection or defense. In environments where speed is critical—such as intrusion detection systems or endpoint protection—delays in prediction could result in missed attacks or extended damage windows.
- **Real-Time Threat Mitigation**: Once an anomaly is detected, cybersecurity systems must respond quickly to mitigate potential threats. Deep learning models must not only identify the problem but also trigger automated responses, such as alerting administrators, isolating compromised systems, or blocking malicious IP addresses. This requires the integration of deep learning systems with automated security orchestration and response platforms (SOAR), which can present additional deployment and integration complexities.

6. Generalization to New Threats and Evolving Attacks

Cyber threats are constantly evolving, and attackers are always developing new techniques to bypass security defenses. This poses a challenge for deep learning models, which must continually adapt to detect novel and previously unseen attacks.

- **Model Adaptation**: Deep learning models can struggle to generalize to new threats that differ from the patterns seen in the training data. Attackers often use variations of known tactics, techniques, and procedures (TTPs) or completely new

methods, meaning that models need to be regularly retrained on updated data to stay effective.
- **Continuous Learning**: In dynamic environments, it is critical for models to be capable of continuous or incremental learning, where the model is regularly updated with new data without retraining from scratch. However, this requires sophisticated infrastructure to manage ongoing training, data updates, and model deployment.

Deploying deep learning models in cybersecurity offers immense potential for enhancing threat detection, response times, and overall security posture. However, organizations must carefully consider and address the numerous challenges involved, including data quality and availability, computational costs, model interpretability, adversarial attacks, real-time performance, and the ability to generalize to evolving threats. By addressing these challenges, deep learning models can become an invaluable tool in the fight against cybercrime, improving the ability to detect and respond to threats in real time while maintaining the necessary reliability and trust for security professionals.

10. Ethical and Legal Implications of AI in Cybersecurity

Chapter 10, Ethical and Legal Implications of AI in Cybersecurity, delves into the complex ethical and legal considerations surrounding the use of artificial intelligence in cybersecurity. This chapter explores the balance between leveraging AI for enhanced security and safeguarding privacy, ensuring fairness, and avoiding bias in AI models. It discusses the ethical dilemmas of AI-driven surveillance, data collection, and decision-making in security operations. Additionally, readers will gain an understanding of the global legal landscape, including data protection regulations like GDPR and CCPA, and how they intersect with AI applications in security. Through this chapter, readers will grasp the importance of ethical AI design and compliance to ensure that cybersecurity solutions remain responsible, transparent, and aligned with legal standards.

10.1 Privacy Concerns and Data Protection Regulations

As artificial intelligence (AI) and machine learning (ML) increasingly play a central role in cybersecurity, they raise significant privacy concerns and bring about the need to navigate complex data protection regulations. The use of AI in cybersecurity often requires the collection, processing, and analysis of large volumes of sensitive and personal data, including network traffic, user behaviors, system logs, and communications. This widespread data collection is crucial for detecting and mitigating cyber threats, but it also introduces significant challenges related to individual privacy rights, data security, and compliance with legal frameworks designed to protect personal information. This section explores the privacy concerns that arise when deploying AI and ML systems in cybersecurity and the critical role of data protection regulations in managing these concerns.

1. Privacy Concerns in Cybersecurity AI Systems

The use of AI and machine learning in cybersecurity frequently involves handling large amounts of sensitive data, which can be problematic for several reasons:

Data Collection: AI-based security tools often require access to a wide array of data sources to effectively monitor and detect potential cyber threats. These can include network traffic, user login histories, browsing habits, emails, and personal devices, all of which contain private information. The collection of such data raises questions about the scope of data collected, who has access to it, and how it is managed and stored. Unauthorized or excessive data collection could infringe upon the privacy rights of individuals.

Data Retention: Cybersecurity systems often store large amounts of raw data over extended periods for future analysis. Long-term retention of personal or sensitive data can pose significant risks if not managed properly, particularly if the data is misused, breached, or accessed by unauthorized parties. Retaining this data for longer than necessary increases the risk of privacy violations, especially in cases of data breaches or misuse.

Surveillance: The deployment of AI and ML-based systems often leads to more intense surveillance and monitoring of user activities across digital environments. While surveillance can be crucial for detecting malicious activities, it can also lead to overreach if not properly controlled. Employees, customers, or users may feel that their privacy is being violated if they are constantly monitored, leading to a trust deficit and potential legal repercussions.

Anonymity and De-anonymization: AI systems often rely on anonymized data to protect user identities while still extracting valuable insights from the data. However, the increasing sophistication of AI models, especially those utilizing deep learning, can enable the re-identification or de-anonymization of previously anonymized data. This raises concerns about how personal data may be reconnected to individuals and whether that could violate user privacy.

2. Key Data Protection Regulations Impacting AI in Cybersecurity

Data protection regulations are established to mitigate privacy risks and ensure that the collection and use of personal data are lawful, transparent, and secure. Several key data protection laws and frameworks govern how AI and ML systems can operate within cybersecurity while maintaining individual privacy rights. These regulations impose specific requirements on organizations using AI-based cybersecurity solutions, ensuring that user data is handled responsibly.

General Data Protection Regulation (GDPR): The GDPR, enacted in the European Union (EU), is one of the most comprehensive data protection laws in the world. It regulates how personal data is collected, processed, stored, and transferred, and it applies to organizations that handle the data of EU citizens, regardless of where the organization is based. Key provisions relevant to AI and cybersecurity include:

- **Right to Access**: Individuals have the right to access their personal data and to understand how it is being used.
- **Right to Erasure**: Individuals can request the deletion of their personal data, which impacts the use of persistent data in cybersecurity systems.
- **Data Minimization**: AI and cybersecurity systems should only collect the minimum amount of data necessary for their intended purpose.
- **Automated Decision Making**: GDPR requires organizations to disclose the use of automated decision-making processes (such as those used by AI models) and provide individuals with the right to contest decisions made solely by automated processes.

Compliance with GDPR means that organizations must ensure transparency in their data processing activities and give individuals control over their personal data. For AI-based cybersecurity systems, this could mean implementing explainable AI (XAI) to ensure that users understand the decisions being made by these models.

California Consumer Privacy Act (CCPA): Similar to the GDPR, the CCPA provides California residents with rights over their personal data, including the right to know what personal data is being collected, the right to delete that data, and the right to opt out of data selling practices. Under the CCPA, businesses must inform individuals when AI or machine learning models are being used to process their data, especially if those models are used for decision-making purposes that may affect the individual. For organizations that use AI-powered cybersecurity solutions, compliance with CCPA means ensuring transparency and user control over personal data while also safeguarding it from unauthorized use.

Health Insurance Portability and Accountability Act (HIPAA): In the United States, HIPAA regulates the use of health-related data. Healthcare organizations that deploy AI and ML systems for cybersecurity must adhere to HIPAA rules when processing Protected Health Information (PHI). This includes ensuring that AI models do not inadvertently expose or misuse health-related data, requiring proper encryption, access controls, and data minimization strategies to protect patient privacy.

Personal Data Protection Act (PDPA): In regions such as Singapore, the PDPA provides guidelines for the collection, use, and disclosure of personal data. Similar to GDPR and CCPA, the PDPA emphasizes the need for organizations to be transparent about data collection and usage practices, ensuring that AI models used in cybersecurity do not breach user privacy. The PDPA also addresses the need for individuals to consent to the processing of their personal data, which is a crucial aspect when dealing with sensitive security data.

Privacy and Electronic Communications Regulations (PECR): In the UK, the PECR governs privacy in electronic communications, including the use of cookies, monitoring of communications, and data breaches. Organizations deploying AI-powered cybersecurity systems must consider how their activities interact with these regulations, ensuring that their systems do not unlawfully intercept, store, or share electronic communications without appropriate consent.

3. Balancing Privacy with Security Needs

The challenge of deploying AI and machine learning in cybersecurity lies in balancing the need for robust security with the privacy rights of individuals. While cybersecurity systems must access and analyze personal data to detect and mitigate threats effectively, they must do so in a way that minimizes risk and complies with data protection regulations. Several strategies can help achieve this balance:

Data Anonymization and Encryption: Encrypting data at rest and in transit, and using anonymization or pseudonymization techniques, ensures that even if personal data is accessed, it cannot be directly attributed to specific individuals without additional information.

Differential Privacy: This is a technique used to enhance privacy in AI models by adding noise to data in such a way that the individual data points cannot be identified, yet the model can still make accurate predictions or decisions. It helps reduce the risk of re-identification of sensitive data and ensures that privacy is maintained.

Privacy by Design: Organizations should adopt a privacy-by-design approach when developing AI-driven cybersecurity systems. This means incorporating privacy considerations into every stage of system development, from data collection and processing to model training and deployment. This proactive approach helps mitigate privacy risks and ensures compliance with regulatory requirements from the outset.

Regular Audits and Transparency: Conducting regular privacy audits and ensuring transparency in data processing activities are essential for maintaining compliance with data protection laws. Providing users with clear privacy notices and the option to opt-out of non-essential data collection helps organizations maintain trust and adhere to regulatory expectations.

The integration of AI and machine learning in cybersecurity presents both opportunities and challenges when it comes to privacy and data protection. While these technologies enable organizations to enhance security, they also create significant risks to personal privacy. By understanding and addressing the privacy concerns associated with AI and complying with global data protection regulations, organizations can strike a balance between robust security measures and the safeguarding of individual rights. Careful consideration of privacy issues in the design and deployment of AI-based cybersecurity systems is essential for ensuring that technological advancements in security do not come at the expense of user privacy.

10.2 Addressing Bias and Fairness in AI Models

As artificial intelligence (AI) and machine learning (ML) become increasingly integrated into cybersecurity systems, ensuring that these models operate fairly and without bias has become a critical concern. AI-driven systems, which are designed to make autonomous decisions based on data, are susceptible to inheriting biases present in the data used to train them. When applied to cybersecurity, such biases can lead to unfair or discriminatory outcomes, potentially undermining the effectiveness and trustworthiness of the systems. This section explores the causes of bias in AI models, the implications of biased cybersecurity systems, and strategies to address these biases while ensuring fairness in the decision-making processes of AI models.

1. Understanding Bias in AI Models

Bias in AI models refers to systematic errors or prejudices in the model's predictions or decisions, which can result from various sources, including the data used to train the model, the design of the model itself, and the underlying assumptions embedded in the algorithms. Bias can manifest in several forms, including:

Data Bias: One of the most common sources of bias is the data used to train AI models. If the data is unrepresentative or reflects historical inequalities, the AI system can perpetuate and even amplify these biases. For example, if a cybersecurity model is trained on data that overrepresents a certain type of cyber threat or attacker behavior while underrepresenting others, the model may perform poorly when confronted with new, unseen threats that deviate from the training data's patterns.

Labeling Bias: In supervised learning, data labels are critical for guiding the AI system to recognize and classify patterns correctly. If the labels are biased or inaccurate, the AI model's predictions will reflect these errors. For instance, if human annotators label cybersecurity threats based on subjective or incomplete criteria, the model might develop skewed or incomplete classifications of what constitutes an attack or normal behavior.

Sampling Bias: Sampling bias occurs when the data used to train the model does not adequately represent the full range of scenarios or environments in which the model will be applied. In the context of cybersecurity, if a model is trained only on data from large enterprises but is then deployed in small businesses or different geographic regions, it may fail to recognize threats specific to those environments, leading to biased or inadequate threat detection.

Algorithmic Bias: Even if the training data is well-balanced and accurate, the algorithmic design itself can introduce bias. Some AI models or machine learning algorithms may favor certain types of patterns over others based on their structure, leading to unintentional discrimination against certain user groups or attack types.

2. Implications of Bias in Cybersecurity AI Models

Bias in AI models can have significant and far-reaching consequences, particularly when deployed in cybersecurity systems. These systems are often responsible for detecting and preventing malicious activities, protecting sensitive data, and ensuring the integrity of organizational infrastructure. When bias is introduced into these systems, it can lead to:

False Positives and False Negatives: A biased model might misidentify legitimate activities as threats (false positives) or fail to detect actual threats (false negatives). For instance, if the model has been trained predominantly on data from one demographic or region, it might inaccurately flag benign activities from other users or underreport attacks from unfamiliar attack vectors, ultimately compromising system security.

Unfair Security Measures: Bias in cybersecurity systems can lead to discriminatory outcomes where certain groups of users are unfairly targeted or treated differently. For example, if an AI model is biased against a specific type of user (e.g., users from a particular region or with certain behavior patterns), they may face more stringent security checks or more frequent false alarms. This can lead to frustration, reduced trust in the system, and, in some cases, legal or reputational consequences for the organizations deploying these systems.

Widening Security Gaps: Cybersecurity systems that are biased may fail to recognize emerging threats or adapt to new attack patterns, particularly if those patterns are not well-represented in the training data. This can create blind spots in the security infrastructure, leaving systems vulnerable to novel or sophisticated attacks that the biased model fails to detect.

Erosion of Trust: For cybersecurity models to be effective, they must be trusted by the organizations and individuals using them. Bias undermines that trust by making decisions appear arbitrary or unfair. When users feel that AI-driven systems are not treating them equitably, they may lose confidence in the system and look for ways to bypass or circumvent it.

3. Strategies for Addressing Bias in AI Models

Addressing bias and ensuring fairness in AI models used for cybersecurity requires a multifaceted approach. The following strategies can help mitigate bias and promote fairness in AI systems:

Diverse and Representative Data: The foundation for minimizing bias in AI models begins with ensuring that the data used to train these models is diverse and representative of the various environments, users, and threats the system will encounter. This includes:

- **Ensuring Data Balance**: Training data should reflect a wide variety of attack types, users, and threat vectors to ensure that the model can detect a broad range of threats and apply appropriate security measures across different scenarios.
- **Incorporating Data from Diverse Sources**: Organizations should aim to incorporate data from different regions, industries, and demographic groups to avoid skewed results. For example, training datasets that account for international cybersecurity threats can help create a more globally aware AI system.

Bias Auditing and Monitoring: Regular audits and assessments of the AI model's performance can help identify any biases that may have developed during training or after deployment. By monitoring the model's outcomes and comparing them across different user groups and scenarios, organizations can ensure that the model is not unfairly targeting or neglecting specific groups or attack patterns. Bias audits should be conducted at multiple stages, from the data collection phase to the evaluation of real-world performance, to detect and correct any unintended biases.

Explainable AI (XAI): One of the key strategies for improving fairness and reducing bias in AI systems is to make the decision-making process more transparent and interpretable. Explainable AI techniques allow security professionals to understand how and why a model made a particular decision, which can help identify and correct sources of bias. When models can explain their reasoning in human-understandable terms, it is easier to spot errors or unfair patterns in the way decisions are made.

Fairness-Conscious Algorithms: Some algorithms are specifically designed to be fair by considering how different groups or characteristics are represented in the model's decisions. Techniques such as fairness constraints or adversarial debiasing aim to minimize bias by ensuring that the model's predictions are not influenced by irrelevant or discriminatory factors. This may involve adjusting the weights assigned to different features in the data or designing loss functions that penalize biased outcomes.

Continuous Model Retraining: AI models should be regularly retrained with updated data to reflect changing user behaviors, new types of attacks, and evolving threat landscapes. By continuously incorporating fresh data, organizations can ensure that their cybersecurity models remain accurate and adaptable, reducing the risk of bias arising from outdated or incomplete datasets.

User-Centric Design: Engaging stakeholders—such as end-users, security professionals, and legal experts—in the design and evaluation of AI systems can help ensure that diverse perspectives are considered. This user-centric approach ensures that the system is built with fairness in mind from the outset and that any issues related to bias or unfairness are addressed early in the design process.

Bias and fairness in AI models are critical considerations, particularly in the context of cybersecurity, where decisions made by AI systems can have significant consequences for both security and privacy. Addressing bias in AI models requires a proactive, comprehensive approach that encompasses diverse data collection, transparent algorithms, ongoing audits, and continuous monitoring. By implementing these strategies, organizations can reduce the risk of biased outcomes, ensure that their cybersecurity systems operate fairly for all users, and maintain the trust of those who rely on these technologies. As AI becomes more integral to cybersecurity, fostering fairness and mitigating bias will be essential for creating more robust, equitable, and effective security solutions.

10.3 Ethical Boundaries in Surveillance and AI for Security

The integration of artificial intelligence (AI) into cybersecurity systems has provided unprecedented capabilities in terms of threat detection, incident response, and overall protection of digital infrastructures. AI's ability to process vast amounts of data, recognize patterns, and make autonomous decisions has led to significant advancements in both security and surveillance. However, these advancements raise a series of ethical concerns, particularly with regard to privacy, individual rights, and the potential for abuse.

In the context of surveillance, AI can significantly enhance security measures, but its use must be carefully controlled to avoid infringing on ethical boundaries. This section delves into the ethical dilemmas associated with AI-powered surveillance in cybersecurity, examining the balance between security needs and individual freedoms, and providing a framework for navigating these challenges.

1. The Role of AI in Surveillance

AI plays a critical role in modern surveillance systems, both in physical and digital environments. From facial recognition technologies to monitoring network traffic and behavior analysis, AI can help identify threats more efficiently and respond to cyber incidents in real time. Some common applications of AI in surveillance for cybersecurity include:

Behavioral Monitoring: AI systems can analyze user behavior patterns across networks to detect suspicious activities, such as abnormal login times, unauthorized access attempts, or data exfiltration. This form of surveillance allows organizations to detect potential insider threats or external attackers early.

Facial Recognition: AI-driven facial recognition systems are increasingly used in physical security, enabling organizations to monitor individuals entering restricted areas. In some high-security environments, facial recognition is also used to track individuals for security purposes.

Predictive Analytics: AI algorithms can predict potential threats by identifying vulnerabilities in a network or a system's architecture. These predictive capabilities allow security professionals to proactively strengthen defenses against possible attacks.

While these capabilities contribute to stronger security, the ethical concerns arise when AI surveillance systems are used excessively, beyond the intended scope, or without proper oversight.

2. Ethical Issues in AI-Powered Surveillance for Security

The use of AI in surveillance for security purposes brings about a variety of ethical challenges that must be carefully considered. These concerns are tied to the potential consequences for individual freedoms, privacy, and human rights.

Invasion of Privacy: AI-driven surveillance often involves the collection, analysis, and retention of large amounts of personal data, such as browsing habits, communication logs, or biometric data (e.g., facial scans). The invasion of privacy can occur when individuals are monitored without their knowledge or consent, or when data is collected in ways that extend beyond what is necessary for the security objectives. The scope of surveillance can quickly grow beyond reasonable security measures and infringe on individuals' rights to privacy and autonomy.

Lack of Consent: Ethical AI surveillance systems require the informed consent of those being monitored. In many cases, individuals may not be fully aware of the extent to which they are being surveilled, especially in environments where AI surveillance operates behind the scenes. For example, network activity is often monitored by AI tools without users being aware that their every action is being analyzed. This lack of transparency raises significant ethical concerns, as individuals may unknowingly become subjects of surveillance without their explicit agreement.

Discrimination and Profiling: AI surveillance systems are only as unbiased as the data used to train them. If AI models are trained on data sets that reflect societal biases or discriminatory practices, the AI can inadvertently perpetuate these biases. For instance, facial recognition technology has been shown to have higher error rates for people of color and women compared to white males, potentially leading to misidentification and discrimination. Additionally, predictive analytics used in AI surveillance can reinforce existing biases, leading to unfair profiling of specific groups, such as ethnic minorities or individuals from particular geographic regions.

Mass Surveillance and Overreach: AI's ability to scale and automate surveillance poses a serious risk of overreach. Governments and organizations may be tempted to deploy AI surveillance systems on a large scale, monitoring vast populations or even entire societies. This type of mass surveillance can undermine the principles of freedom and democracy by creating a culture of constant monitoring. While AI surveillance can be effective in mitigating threats, unchecked or unwarranted surveillance can lead to the erosion of individual rights and create a chilling effect on free speech, dissent, and personal autonomy.

Erosion of Trust: When individuals or groups believe they are being unfairly surveilled or monitored, it can erode trust in both the technology and the organizations deploying it. In the context of cybersecurity, employees, users, or customers may be wary of AI systems that are used for surveillance without clear, transparent policies or without adequate protection of personal data. This distrust can reduce the effectiveness of security measures, as people may actively attempt to circumvent surveillance systems or become less cooperative with security protocols.

3. Establishing Ethical Boundaries in AI Surveillance for Security

To ensure that AI-driven surveillance systems respect ethical boundaries, organizations and governments must implement safeguards and regulations that prioritize privacy and fairness. Several frameworks and practices can help address the ethical challenges posed by AI surveillance in cybersecurity:

Privacy by Design: Ethical AI surveillance systems should be designed with privacy as a foundational principle. This approach, known as "privacy by design," ensures that privacy is incorporated into the system from the outset, rather than being an afterthought. Organizations should limit the amount of personal data collected, ensure that data is anonymized whenever possible, and ensure that any data retained is kept secure and for the minimum necessary duration.

Transparency and Accountability: AI surveillance systems must operate transparently, with clear documentation of how data is collected, processed, and used. Individuals being surveilled should be informed about the scope of surveillance and the purposes for which their data will be used. Additionally, there must be accountability mechanisms in place to ensure that surveillance systems are not being misused or applied in ways that overstep ethical boundaries. Regular audits and oversight can help ensure compliance with ethical standards.

Bias Mitigation and Fairness: As discussed earlier, AI systems are prone to bias, particularly if the training data is not representative or if the model itself is poorly designed. Organizations deploying AI surveillance systems must take proactive steps to mitigate bias by ensuring diverse and representative data collection and using fairness algorithms that help detect and correct any discriminatory practices. Independent audits of AI models for fairness should be conducted periodically to detect and address any emerging biases.

Limited Data Collection and Retention: Surveillance systems should collect only the minimum amount of data required to achieve the intended security goals. Data should be stored for the shortest time possible, with regular purging of unnecessary or outdated information. Any retention of data should be justified with clear security objectives and subject to oversight.

Informed Consent and Opt-Out Options: Where possible, individuals should be given the opportunity to provide informed consent for surveillance and be made aware of the scope of monitoring. In certain cases, such as network security monitoring, where consent may not be feasible, organizations should provide clear privacy policies and allow users to opt out of non-essential data collection where possible. By doing so, organizations demonstrate respect for personal autonomy and privacy.

Ethical Guidelines and Governance: Governments and international bodies should develop ethical guidelines and governance frameworks for the use of AI in cybersecurity surveillance. These frameworks should outline the principles of transparency, fairness, privacy, and accountability that must govern the deployment and use of AI systems in surveillance. Regulatory oversight and legal frameworks should be established to prevent abuse and ensure that AI-driven surveillance remains focused on legitimate security concerns.

AI-powered surveillance systems offer tremendous potential for improving cybersecurity by detecting and mitigating threats in real time. However, these technologies raise serious ethical concerns that must be addressed to ensure that security is balanced with the protection of individual rights. By adopting ethical frameworks such as privacy by design, transparency, accountability, and fairness, organizations can ensure that AI-driven surveillance systems are deployed responsibly. The key to navigating the ethical boundaries of AI surveillance is ensuring that it serves legitimate security purposes without infringing upon personal freedoms or creating undue harm. Only by addressing these ethical concerns can AI and cybersecurity systems be trusted to protect users while respecting their privacy and autonomy.

10.4 Compliance with Global Standards (GDPR, CCPA, etc.)

As AI technologies become more deeply embedded in cybersecurity systems, the need for organizations to ensure compliance with global privacy regulations has never been more critical. The intersection of AI-powered security solutions with personal data raises significant legal and ethical considerations, particularly around data collection, processing, and storage. These regulations, such as the General Data Protection Regulation (GDPR) in Europe, the California Consumer Privacy Act (CCPA) in the United States, and various others worldwide, aim to protect individuals' privacy rights and regulate how personal data is handled. Compliance with these standards is not only necessary for avoiding hefty fines but also for building trust and ensuring that AI surveillance and cybersecurity systems are used ethically and responsibly. This section explores the key global standards, their implications for AI-powered cybersecurity, and best practices for ensuring compliance.

1. Overview of Key Global Privacy Regulations

Several global privacy laws govern the collection, processing, and use of personal data, particularly with regards to AI and cybersecurity technologies. The most influential of these regulations include:

General Data Protection Regulation (GDPR): Enforced by the European Union (EU), the GDPR is one of the most comprehensive and stringent privacy laws globally. It mandates strict controls on how personal data is collected, stored, processed, and shared. GDPR emphasizes principles such as:

- **Data Minimization**: Collect only the data that is necessary for the specific purpose.
- **Transparency and Accountability**: Organizations must inform individuals about how their data will be used and ensure accountability for data protection practices.
- **Right to Access and Erasure**: Individuals have the right to access their personal data and request its deletion when it is no longer necessary for processing.
- **Data Portability and Consent**: Users should be able to move their data between service providers, and organizations must obtain explicit consent for data collection and processing.

GDPR applies to all organizations that process personal data of individuals residing in the EU, regardless of where the organization is located.

California Consumer Privacy Act (CCPA): The CCPA, enforced in California, is one of the most significant privacy laws in the United States. It grants California residents specific rights regarding their personal data, including:

- **Right to Know**: Consumers can request to know what personal information is being collected about them.
- **Right to Delete**: Consumers have the right to request the deletion of their personal data.
- **Right to Opt-Out**: Individuals can opt out of the sale of their personal information.
- **Non-Discrimination**: Businesses cannot discriminate against consumers who exercise their privacy rights, such as denying services or charging higher prices.

While the CCPA applies primarily to businesses operating in California, it can have global implications for companies that collect data from California residents.

Other International Regulations: In addition to GDPR and CCPA, several other countries have enacted data protection laws:

- Personal Data Protection Act (PDPA) in Singapore and Data Protection Act in the United Kingdom regulate personal data handling.
- Brazil's General Data Protection Law (LGPD) mirrors GDPR and applies to any business processing personal data in Brazil or about Brazilian residents.
- Australia's Privacy Act provides protection against unauthorized use of personal information.

These regulations are designed to give individuals more control over their data and ensure that organizations handle personal information responsibly and securely.

2. Challenges for AI and Machine Learning in Compliance

AI-driven cybersecurity systems often rely on vast amounts of data for training, analysis, and threat detection. However, adhering to privacy regulations presents significant challenges:

Data Collection and Consent: AI models typically require large datasets to train effectively. However, under regulations like GDPR, collecting personal data without explicit consent is prohibited. For example, collecting user data from a network without informing the user or obtaining their consent can violate privacy laws. Similarly, many AI systems rely on sensitive information (such as network traffic data, user behaviors, or device information) that may fall under stringent data protection regulations.

Data Minimization: AI systems are often designed to collect as much data as possible to improve model accuracy and enhance threat detection. However, privacy regulations, particularly GDPR, enforce the principle of data minimization, which restricts data collection to only what is necessary for the intended purpose. This requirement forces organizations to reconsider how they collect, store, and use personal data, limiting the volume and types of data that AI models can access.

Data Storage and Retention: Both GDPR and CCPA require organizations to limit the duration for which personal data is retained. AI-driven systems that rely on historical data to recognize patterns or detect threats must be careful to comply with these retention periods. Data that is retained for too long or stored without justification could result in regulatory violations.

Right to be Forgotten: GDPR grants individuals the "right to be forgotten," meaning they can request that their data be deleted under certain conditions. For AI systems, this presents a challenge as deleting data might render previous model training incomplete or inaccurate. Additionally, tracking and removing specific data from complex, trained AI models can be technically difficult, leading to potential violations of individuals' rights.

Cross-Border Data Transfers: Regulations like GDPR impose strict conditions on transferring personal data outside of the EU to countries that do not meet the required privacy standards. This becomes an issue for global organizations using AI for cybersecurity, particularly if their AI models are hosted or processed in locations outside the EU. Compliance with cross-border data transfer rules requires careful data handling and may involve implementing safeguards such as Standard Contractual Clauses (SCCs).

3. Best Practices for Ensuring Compliance with AI in Cybersecurity

Organizations must adopt a proactive approach to ensure that their AI systems comply with global privacy regulations. Below are best practices to ensure compliance while still maintaining effective AI-powered cybersecurity:

Data Anonymization and Pseudonymization: One of the most effective ways to address privacy concerns is by anonymizing or pseudonymizing personal data. Anonymization removes identifiable information, making it impossible to link data back to a specific individual, while pseudonymization replaces identifiable information with pseudonyms. This reduces privacy risks while allowing AI systems to process data for cybersecurity purposes without violating privacy regulations.

Consent Management: Organizations should implement robust consent management systems to ensure that users are fully informed about the data being collected, how it will be used, and how long it will be stored. This includes obtaining clear, explicit consent before data is processed by AI models. Moreover, users should have the ability to withdraw consent at any time, as required by laws such as GDPR.

Data Retention Policies: Establish clear data retention policies that comply with global standards. Data should only be retained for as long as necessary to achieve the intended purpose (such as detecting cybersecurity threats). Once the data is no longer needed, it should be securely deleted to comply with the "right to be forgotten" under GDPR.

Privacy Impact Assessments (PIAs): Conduct regular privacy impact assessments to evaluate the potential privacy risks associated with AI-driven cybersecurity systems. PIAs help identify and mitigate risks related to data collection, storage, and use, ensuring that systems comply with privacy laws and respect individual rights.

Data Encryption and Security: Ensuring that data is securely stored and transmitted is essential for compliance with regulations like GDPR. Organizations should implement strong encryption techniques to protect personal data from unauthorized access, especially when transferred across borders or stored in the cloud.

Training and Awareness: Employees involved in data processing and AI model development should receive regular training on privacy laws and regulations, as well as the ethical implications of AI in cybersecurity. This helps create a culture of compliance within the organization and ensures that all relevant stakeholders understand the importance of privacy and data protection.

Third-Party Vendor Compliance: If third-party vendors or cloud providers are involved in data storage or AI model training, organizations must ensure that these partners also comply with relevant privacy regulations. Contracts should outline data protection obligations and include provisions for auditing and oversight.

Compliance with global privacy regulations such as GDPR, CCPA, and others is a critical consideration for organizations deploying AI-powered cybersecurity solutions. As AI continues to evolve and play a larger role in protecting digital infrastructures, balancing effective security measures with the protection of personal data will remain a top priority. By adhering to data protection principles such as consent, data minimization, and transparency, organizations can leverage AI technologies in a way that respects individual privacy while ensuring robust cybersecurity defenses. This not only helps avoid legal consequences but also builds trust with users and stakeholders, ensuring that privacy and security go hand in hand in the digital age.

11. Building Robust Cyber Intelligence Systems

Chapter 11, Building Robust Cyber Intelligence Systems, focuses on the critical aspects of designing and deploying resilient AI-driven cybersecurity solutions. This chapter covers best practices for developing robust machine learning models and AI systems that can withstand adversarial attacks, handle evolving threats, and scale with increasing data complexity. It delves into techniques for ensuring model robustness, such as adversarial training, and discusses the importance of system resilience, continuous monitoring, and regular updates to keep defenses strong. Readers will also learn how to balance security and efficiency when building cyber intelligence systems, ensuring that they are both effective in detecting threats and efficient in processing data. Through practical insights, this chapter emphasizes the need for ongoing adaptation and maintenance to keep systems secure in the face of ever-changing cyber risks.

11.1 Best Practices for Model Robustness and Scalability

In the realm of AI-powered cybersecurity, building robust and scalable models is essential for effectively detecting, preventing, and mitigating cyber threats. Robustness ensures that models remain effective even when exposed to unexpected or adversarial conditions, while scalability guarantees that these models can handle large datasets, operate across diverse environments, and accommodate the growing complexity of cybersecurity challenges. The following section discusses best practices for ensuring both model robustness and scalability in AI-powered cybersecurity applications.

1. Building Robust Models

A robust AI model in cybersecurity is one that can handle various challenges, such as noisy data, adversarial attacks, or changing threat landscapes, without losing performance. Below are key practices for improving the robustness of AI models in cybersecurity:

Data Quality and Preprocessing: The first step in building a robust model is ensuring that the input data is of high quality. In cybersecurity, data comes from various sources, including logs, network traffic, and endpoint behavior. Ensuring that data is cleaned, normalized, and preprocessed helps the model better understand the underlying patterns, making it less vulnerable to errors caused by noisy or incomplete data. Techniques like data augmentation, outlier detection, and imputation of missing values can significantly improve the quality of data before training.

Adversarial Robustness: Cybersecurity models must be resilient to adversarial attacks, where attackers intentionally introduce malicious input to deceive the model. Techniques like adversarial training, where models are specifically trained on adversarial examples, can improve their resistance to such attacks. Additionally, methods such as gradient masking or input sanitization can be used to block or reduce the impact of adversarial inputs, preventing attackers from manipulating the AI model's behavior.

Cross-Validation and Regularization: To ensure that a model generalizes well to unseen data, it is important to use techniques like cross-validation, which splits the training dataset into multiple subsets to evaluate the model's performance under different conditions. Regularization methods, such as L1/L2 regularization and dropout, help reduce the risk of overfitting to specific data characteristics, thereby increasing the model's robustness to small variations in data and improving its generalization ability.

Model Explainability and Transparency: Robustness also means understanding how models make their decisions. Using explainability techniques like LIME (Local Interpretable Model-Agnostic Explanations) or SHAP (SHapley Additive exPlanations) allows security professionals to interpret the outputs of AI models. This transparency helps identify potential weaknesses and areas where the model may be vulnerable to adversarial manipulation or biased predictions, enabling the development of countermeasures to strengthen the model's robustness.

Continuous Monitoring and Updates: Threat landscapes are constantly evolving, with new attack vectors and techniques emerging regularly. For a model to remain robust, it must be continuously monitored and updated. This includes retraining the model with new data, addressing changes in attack patterns, and incorporating feedback from real-world incidents to adapt to evolving threats. Regular model updates help ensure that cybersecurity defenses remain strong over time and are capable of detecting the latest threats.

2. Ensuring Scalability

Scalability is the ability of an AI model to handle increasing amounts of data, more complex tasks, and larger infrastructures without significant degradation in performance. For AI-driven cybersecurity systems, scalability is crucial because the volume of data in modern networks and the complexity of cyber threats are rapidly growing. Here are some best practices for ensuring that cybersecurity models can scale effectively:

Data Sampling and Distributed Training: One of the first challenges in scalability is the sheer volume of data in cybersecurity. Large organizations may deal with petabytes of network logs, user activities, and other security-related data. To handle this, models can benefit from data sampling techniques, where only a representative subset of the data is used to train the model. Additionally, distributed training across multiple machines or GPUs can help accelerate training time and scale the model to handle large datasets. Frameworks such as TensorFlow and PyTorch provide distributed learning capabilities, enabling more efficient scaling.

Use of Cloud Infrastructure: Cloud platforms provide virtually unlimited storage and computational resources, making them an ideal environment for scaling AI models. Leveraging cloud computing services allows cybersecurity models to handle large datasets without the need for on-premise infrastructure. Platforms like AWS, Google Cloud, and Microsoft Azure offer machine learning services that support scalable model training and deployment, which is essential for ensuring that cybersecurity defenses can be expanded as needed without compromising performance.

Model Parallelism: As AI models grow in complexity, training them on a single machine can become impractical. Model parallelism, where different parts of the model are processed across multiple processors or machines, helps speed up the training process and enables the use of larger models. This approach is particularly useful for deep learning architectures that have numerous parameters, such as Convolutional Neural Networks (CNNs) or Recurrent Neural Networks (RNNs). By distributing the computational load, scalability is enhanced, allowing the model to handle large volumes of data and more complex problems.

Efficient Feature Engineering: Scalable models are dependent not only on computational power but also on the efficiency of the features used for model training. Feature engineering plays a crucial role in determining which aspects of the data are most relevant for threat detection. Optimizing the set of features ensures that the model can operate efficiently even as the size of the data increases. Techniques like Principal Component Analysis (PCA) for dimensionality reduction, as well as automatic feature selection algorithms, can help identify the most important features while reducing computational overhead, enabling better scalability.

Real-Time Processing and Edge AI: In many cybersecurity applications, such as intrusion detection or real-time threat monitoring, models need to operate with minimal latency. To meet this demand, models must be capable of real-time data processing. For distributed or edge-based systems, Edge AI—where AI models are deployed closer to data sources like sensors, routers, or IoT devices—becomes crucial. Edge AI reduces the burden on central servers, allowing faster responses to security events and more efficient handling of data across distributed environments.

Containerization and Microservices: For scalability and easy deployment, AI models should be built using containerization technologies such as Docker or Kubernetes. These technologies package the model and its dependencies in a container, making it easy to deploy and scale across different environments. Microservices architecture allows components of the AI system (e.g., data preprocessing, model training, threat detection) to be independently scaled and updated. This approach enables the system to handle increasing loads and adapt to new threats or changes in infrastructure.

Batch Processing for Large-Scale Data: In cybersecurity, continuous analysis of streaming data might not always be feasible due to the high volume and the need for computational efficiency. For large-scale datasets, batch processing allows organizations to process and analyze data in chunks, optimizing resource use while ensuring that models can handle extensive data inputs. This method is particularly useful for less time-sensitive tasks like identifying trends, detecting periodic attacks, or analyzing historical logs.

3. Evaluating Robustness and Scalability in Production

Once a model is deployed in production, evaluating its performance in real-world conditions is essential to ensure that it meets both robustness and scalability requirements. Here are several methods for evaluating AI models post-deployment:

Stress Testing: In a real-world environment, AI models must be tested against extreme conditions, such as high traffic volumes, noisy data, or adversarial inputs. Stress testing simulates these conditions to determine how the model responds under pressure and identifies weaknesses that could undermine robustness.

Load Testing: For scalable systems, load testing involves simulating increasing amounts of data to assess how well the system handles growing inputs. This helps identify potential bottlenecks or performance degradation as the system scales.

Performance Metrics: Evaluating the performance of AI models should include not only traditional metrics like accuracy, precision, and recall but also real-time performance metrics such as latency, throughput, and resource consumption. These metrics help ensure that models scale effectively in production and perform their tasks in a timely manner.

Building robust and scalable AI models for cybersecurity is crucial for protecting digital assets against an ever-evolving landscape of threats. By following best practices such as ensuring data quality, leveraging cloud infrastructure, implementing adversarial training, and optimizing feature engineering, organizations can build AI systems that are both resilient and capable of handling large-scale data environments. Ensuring continuous monitoring, stress testing, and scaling strategies will help these systems remain effective in an increasingly complex cybersecurity landscape, allowing them to adapt and grow alongside the threats they are designed to protect against.

11.2 Defending Against Adversarial Attacks on AI Models

Adversarial attacks are one of the most significant challenges facing AI models, particularly in the field of cybersecurity. These attacks involve deliberately designed inputs that manipulate the AI system into making incorrect predictions or classifications. In cybersecurity, such attacks can deceive intrusion detection systems, manipulate threat detection, or bypass security measures, allowing attackers to compromise sensitive data or systems. Defending against adversarial attacks is crucial for ensuring the reliability and effectiveness of AI models in protecting against evolving threats. This section will explore strategies for defending AI models against adversarial attacks in cybersecurity.

1. Understanding Adversarial Attacks

Adversarial attacks typically target machine learning models, exploiting their vulnerabilities by feeding in specially crafted inputs (adversarial examples) that are designed to deceive the model. These inputs often appear innocuous to human observers but cause the AI system to make erroneous decisions. In the context of cybersecurity, adversarial examples might manipulate the behavior of a malware detection system, altering network traffic patterns to evade detection, or modifying the inputs in ways that cause an AI-based system to misclassify benign activities as threats.

There are various types of adversarial attacks, including:

- **Evasion Attacks**: In these attacks, the adversary modifies the input data in a way that allows the malicious activity to bypass detection. For example, a network intrusion might be disguised to avoid triggering an intrusion detection system (IDS).
- **Poisoning Attacks**: These attacks target the training data, inserting misleading or false information that can lead to model corruption or inaccurate predictions.
- **Model Inversion Attacks**: This involves extracting information about the training data or the model itself through queries to the AI system.

- **Transferability Attacks**: In these attacks, adversarial examples generated for one model are used to fool another, potentially creating vulnerabilities in different systems or platforms.

The impact of such attacks can be severe, especially in a cybersecurity context, as they can lead to undetected intrusions, data breaches, and compromise of system integrity. Therefore, developing robust defenses is essential for ensuring the resilience of AI systems against these sophisticated adversarial threats.

2. Defensive Strategies Against Adversarial Attacks

There are several approaches to defending AI models against adversarial attacks, ranging from improving the training process to implementing post-processing techniques. Below are some of the key strategies that can be employed to enhance the robustness of AI models:

2.1 Adversarial Training

One of the most widely used techniques for defending against adversarial attacks is adversarial training. In this approach, the model is specifically trained with adversarial examples as part of the training dataset. By exposing the model to adversarial inputs during training, it learns to recognize and resist such attacks. Adversarial training improves the model's ability to generalize and makes it more resilient to adversarial perturbations.

While adversarial training has proven effective in some contexts, it comes with challenges. It can be computationally expensive, as the process of generating adversarial examples during training can require significant processing power. Additionally, adversarial training may not completely eliminate the model's vulnerability to all types of attacks, especially in complex systems where adversaries are highly skilled at crafting sophisticated attacks.

2.2 Input Preprocessing and Sanitization

Input preprocessing is another defense mechanism against adversarial attacks. This method involves transforming or filtering the input data before it is fed into the AI model, removing potential adversarial perturbations. Common preprocessing techniques include:

- **Defensive Distillation**: This technique reduces the sensitivity of a model to adversarial examples by training a second model (a distilled model) on the outputs

of a first, more complex model. The distilled model learns a smoother decision boundary, making it more difficult for adversarial examples to manipulate its predictions.
- **Feature Squeezing**: This involves reducing the complexity of input features by squeezing the feature space, making it harder for adversarial perturbations to manipulate the input data in a way that leads to misclassification.
- **Gradient Masking**: This method tries to obscure the gradients of the model, making it harder for an adversary to calculate the optimal perturbations needed for an attack. However, gradient masking may not provide a foolproof defense, as attackers can still adapt their strategies to bypass these defenses.

2.3 Robust Optimization Techniques

Robust optimization techniques aim to improve the stability of AI models when exposed to adversarial conditions. These techniques modify the training process to account for the possibility of adversarial perturbations and seek to create models that are less sensitive to small, adversarial changes in the input data. Some common robust optimization strategies include:

- **Min-Max Optimization**: This approach seeks to find the optimal model parameters by minimizing the worst-case performance (maximizing the robustness) over a set of potential adversarial perturbations. It trains the model to perform well under the worst-case scenario, effectively making it more resilient to adversarial inputs.
- **Ensemble Methods**: In ensemble methods, multiple models are trained independently, and their outputs are combined. The idea is that adversarial examples that deceive one model may not deceive others. This strategy increases robustness by leveraging diversity in the decision-making process, reducing the likelihood of a successful attack across all models in the ensemble.

2.4 Detection and Mitigation of Adversarial Examples

Another approach is to use a detection-based defense mechanism, where the model is designed to identify adversarial examples before they are processed by the main model. Adversarial detection methods can analyze the input data for signs of manipulation or irregularities that indicate an attack. If an adversarial example is detected, the system can either reject the input or apply additional safeguards, such as reclassifying the data using more secure methods.

- **Statistical Tests**: Statistical tests, such as outlier detection, can be used to identify inputs that deviate significantly from the expected distribution of data. If an input

falls outside the normal statistical boundaries, it can be flagged as potentially adversarial.
- **Ensemble-Based Detection**: Similar to the use of ensemble methods in training, ensemble-based detection involves running multiple models to check for consistency in the outputs. If a large discrepancy occurs between the outputs of different models, it could be an indication that the input is adversarial.

2.5 Model Transparency and Explainability

Model transparency and explainability play a significant role in defending against adversarial attacks, as they allow security teams to better understand the model's decision-making process. If adversarial examples successfully deceive the model, understanding why the model made a particular decision can help identify vulnerabilities or weaknesses that could be exploited by attackers.

Techniques like LIME (Local Interpretable Model-Agnostic Explanations) and SHAP (SHapley Additive exPlanations) provide insight into how specific inputs contribute to a model's decision, helping to detect inconsistencies or unexpected behavior that could indicate an adversarial attack. Furthermore, increased model explainability can help cybersecurity teams anticipate and respond to potential threats in a more informed manner.

2.6 Regularization and Robust Regularization

Regularization methods such as L2 regularization or dropout can also be employed to make the model more robust to adversarial attacks. By introducing penalties for large weights or forcing the model to learn less complex patterns, regularization techniques can prevent the model from becoming overly sensitive to small changes in input, making it more resistant to adversarial perturbations.

In addition, robust regularization techniques, such as adversarial regularization, specifically aim to make the model resilient to adversarial examples by incorporating adversarial perturbations into the regularization process. This form of regularization forces the model to learn features that are less susceptible to attack while maintaining good generalization performance.

Defending against adversarial attacks is a critical aspect of deploying AI models in cybersecurity. As cyber threats become increasingly sophisticated, adversaries are likely to continue developing more advanced techniques to exploit AI vulnerabilities. To build robust, resilient AI systems, cybersecurity professionals must adopt a multi-layered defense strategy, combining techniques like adversarial training, input preprocessing, robust optimization, ensemble methods, and detection mechanisms. Through continuous research and the development of novel defensive techniques, the AI community can strengthen defenses against adversarial threats and enhance the security of AI-powered cybersecurity systems.

11.3 Ensuring System Resilience to Evolving Threats

As the cybersecurity landscape evolves, so too must the systems designed to defend against cyber threats. One of the fundamental principles in modern cybersecurity is the need for resilience: the ability of a system to continuously operate and protect its assets, even in the face of sophisticated and persistent attacks. With the growing reliance on artificial intelligence (AI) and machine learning (ML) in cybersecurity, ensuring system resilience against ever-evolving threats is more critical than ever.

Resilience involves not only the capacity to detect, respond to, and recover from attacks, but also the ability to anticipate and adapt to new and unknown threats. As cyber adversaries become increasingly skilled at bypassing traditional defenses, cybersecurity systems must evolve to continuously adapt to these new challenges. This section will explore key strategies and best practices for ensuring the resilience of AI-driven cybersecurity systems against emerging and dynamic threats.

1. Continuous Learning and Adaptation

Traditional cybersecurity defenses often rely on predefined rules and signatures to detect threats. However, with the rapid pace of change in cyberattack techniques, these static systems are no longer sufficient to protect against new and unknown attacks. To ensure resilience, cybersecurity systems need to incorporate continuous learning capabilities.

Online Learning: This approach allows a system to update its models in real-time based on new data. Online learning techniques enable AI models to adapt to changing threat patterns as they emerge, ensuring that defenses remain effective even as attackers modify their tactics. For example, if an AI-driven intrusion detection system identifies a new type of malware, it can immediately incorporate this knowledge into its threat models and start detecting future instances of similar malware.

Transfer Learning: This technique allows a model trained on one set of data to be adapted to a different but related problem. For instance, if a machine learning model designed to detect network intrusions is trained on data from one company, it can be adapted to detect attacks in a different organization's network with minimal additional training. Transfer learning enables cybersecurity systems to quickly adjust to new environments and threats with relatively little data.

Federated Learning: In a federated learning framework, multiple devices or organizations train machine learning models locally and only share updates with a central model. This technique not only preserves privacy but also enables continuous learning across a distributed network, making it easier for cybersecurity systems to evolve collectively in response to emerging threats. With federated learning, security systems across industries or geographies can learn from each other and rapidly adapt to new attack vectors.

2. Redundancy and Failover Mechanisms

Even the most robust cybersecurity systems can encounter vulnerabilities over time, especially in the face of sophisticated, persistent attackers. To ensure that security is never compromised, it is essential to build redundancy into the system. This means implementing multiple layers of defense, ensuring that if one security mechanism fails or is bypassed, others can take over.

Layered Defense: This approach involves integrating various security technologies—such as firewalls, intrusion detection systems (IDS), antivirus software, and AI-powered systems—so that they work in tandem. By having multiple layers of protection, attackers are less likely to penetrate the entire system, as they must bypass several different types of defenses.

Failover Systems: In the event that a primary security system fails, a secondary system can take over without disrupting the overall defense strategy. This is particularly important for critical infrastructure, where even a short lapse in protection can result in severe consequences. Automated failover processes allow systems to detect when a defense mechanism is no longer functioning and activate a backup to ensure continuous protection.

Redundant Data Sources and Models: In the context of AI and machine learning, ensuring system resilience means relying on multiple data sources and redundant models. If one model becomes corrupted or inaccurate due to adversarial interference, other models or sources can step in to maintain the system's ability to detect and respond to threats.

3. Threat Intelligence Sharing and Collaboration

Cyber threats are constantly evolving, with attackers often adapting their tactics, techniques, and procedures (TTPs) to stay one step ahead of defenders. To keep pace with this evolution, cybersecurity systems need access to up-to-date, actionable threat intelligence. One key strategy for maintaining resilience is collaboration and information sharing.

Threat Intelligence Feeds: Many organizations rely on external threat intelligence sources, such as commercial threat intelligence providers, to stay informed about new threats. These feeds provide up-to-date information on emerging attack techniques, vulnerabilities, and indicators of compromise (IOCs). By integrating this threat intelligence into AI models, organizations can improve their detection capabilities and quickly adapt to new attack strategies.

Information Sharing Between Organizations: Threat intelligence is often more effective when shared between organizations, industry sectors, and even countries. Information sharing enables defenders to learn from each other's experiences and collaborate on understanding the latest tactics used by cybercriminals. In some cases, formal information-sharing programs and platforms, such as Information Sharing and Analysis Centers (ISACs) or Threat Intelligence Platforms (TIPs), facilitate this collaboration.

Public-Private Partnerships: Governments, law enforcement, and private-sector companies can form partnerships to share insights about cyber threats. These partnerships help bridge knowledge gaps between sectors, allowing for a more comprehensive defense strategy. Additionally, governments can support the development of cybersecurity standards and frameworks that improve system resilience across industries.

4. Dynamic Risk Management and Threat Modeling

Cyber threats are not static, and neither should be the approach to managing them. To stay resilient in the face of evolving threats, organizations must continually assess their risk landscape and update their threat models and risk management strategies.

Dynamic Threat Modeling: Threat modeling is a process used to identify potential vulnerabilities and threats within a system. A dynamic approach to threat modeling involves continuously updating threat models based on new data and emerging threats. AI systems can play a key role in this process, helping to identify potential vulnerabilities and suggest mitigations based on the latest threat intelligence.

Automated Risk Assessment: AI and machine learning can automate the process of risk assessment by continuously evaluating the potential risks posed by new and emerging threats. This allows security teams to prioritize their efforts and resources based on the most critical vulnerabilities, ensuring that the system remains resilient even in the face of an evolving threat landscape.

Red Teaming and Adversarial Simulations: Red teaming involves simulating attacks on a system to identify weaknesses in its defenses. Adversarial simulations allow organizations to test their resilience to different types of attacks, including both traditional and novel threats. These exercises help organizations identify gaps in their defenses and refine their strategies for mitigating risks.

5. Scalability and Resource Management

As cyber threats grow in scale and sophistication, ensuring the resilience of AI-based cybersecurity systems requires that these systems are not only robust but also scalable. Scalability allows systems to handle increased volumes of data, more complex attack patterns, and a greater number of potential threats without sacrificing performance or security.

Cloud-Based Solutions: Cloud platforms can scale rapidly to meet the demands of modern cybersecurity needs, providing organizations with the resources they need to process vast amounts of data and apply advanced AI models. Cloud environments also enable organizations to share computing resources and threat intelligence across multiple stakeholders, helping to scale defenses against large-scale threats.

Edge Computing for Real-Time Threat Mitigation: Edge computing brings computation closer to the data source, allowing for faster processing and real-time threat mitigation. This is particularly important for Internet of Things (IoT) networks, where devices often lack the resources to process large amounts of data locally. By utilizing AI models at the edge, organizations can quickly detect and respond to threats before they escalate.

Load Balancing and Distributed Systems: For AI systems to handle growing workloads, implementing load balancing and distributed computing across multiple servers or systems ensures that no single component is overwhelmed by the volume or complexity of incoming threats. This ensures the system remains operational and resilient, even in the face of large-scale attacks.

Ensuring system resilience to evolving threats requires a multi-faceted approach that combines continuous learning, redundancy, collaboration, dynamic risk management, and scalability. As cyber threats continue to evolve in complexity and sophistication, AI and machine learning systems must be flexible and adaptive to meet the challenge. By leveraging these strategies, organizations can build cybersecurity defenses that are not only robust but also capable of anticipating and responding to the ever-changing landscape of cyber threats. This dynamic, proactive approach to cybersecurity will ensure that systems remain resilient, even in the face of the most advanced and persistent adversaries.

11.4 Techniques for Ongoing Model Maintenance and Adaptation

In the rapidly evolving field of cybersecurity, ensuring the long-term effectiveness of AI and machine learning models is crucial. While initial training and deployment may lead to impressive performance, AI models can degrade over time as cyber threats evolve and new attack vectors emerge. To maintain the effectiveness of AI-powered cybersecurity systems, continuous model maintenance and adaptation are necessary. This section will explore key techniques for ensuring that machine learning models remain accurate, resilient, and responsive to emerging threats, while minimizing the risk of performance degradation over time.

1. Continuous Monitoring and Evaluation

The first step in maintaining AI models is to continuously monitor their performance and evaluate their effectiveness. This allows cybersecurity teams to detect early signs of model degradation and take corrective action before a major failure occurs.

Model Drift Detection: Over time, the distribution of data in real-world environments can change, causing the performance of a machine learning model to degrade. This phenomenon is known as concept drift or model drift. Continuous monitoring helps detect these shifts in data patterns, ensuring the model remains aligned with the evolving threat landscape. Techniques such as tracking prediction accuracy over time, monitoring data distribution shifts, and employing statistical tests can alert practitioners to potential drift.

Performance Metrics Tracking: Key performance metrics such as accuracy, precision, recall, and F1-score should be regularly evaluated to assess the health of the AI model. Monitoring these metrics in real-time helps to identify issues, such as increased false positives or false negatives, that may arise due to changes in attack patterns or adversarial interference.

Anomaly Detection in Model Outputs: In addition to monitoring data inputs, it's essential to detect anomalies in model outputs. Significant changes in output can indicate that the model has started to behave unexpectedly, often due to adversarial manipulation or data distribution changes. Automated anomaly detection systems can flag unusual model outputs, prompting further investigation or model retraining.

2. Incremental Learning and Online Updates

Traditional machine learning models are often trained in a batch process, with the model trained on a fixed dataset and deployed once the training is complete. However, in dynamic environments like cybersecurity, this approach is insufficient for long-term model adaptation. Incremental learning and online updates are two techniques designed to address this challenge by enabling AI models to adapt to new data over time without the need for full retraining.

Incremental Learning: Incremental learning techniques allow models to learn from new data continuously without forgetting previously acquired knowledge (catastrophic forgetting). In cybersecurity, this is particularly valuable because new attack types, vulnerabilities, and threat patterns are constantly emerging. Incremental learning ensures the model remains current without the need to retrain from scratch, which can be resource-intensive and time-consuming.

Online Learning: Online learning is a subset of incremental learning that processes one data point at a time, allowing the model to update its parameters as new data arrives. This approach is particularly useful for cybersecurity systems that require real-time updates based on evolving threat data. Online learning helps to maintain model performance in the face of rapidly changing threat patterns, allowing systems to detect new and previously unseen attacks as they occur.

Streaming Data and Adaptive Models: Cybersecurity environments generate large volumes of data in real-time, and AI models must be able to process and adapt to this incoming stream of information. Techniques such as data stream mining and adaptive models enable continuous learning from streaming data, allowing models to adjust to new attack strategies or changes in user behavior dynamically.

3. Retraining and Fine-Tuning

Even with continuous monitoring and incremental updates, there will be times when models need to be retrained from scratch or fine-tuned on new data. Retraining ensures that the model remains effective at detecting and responding to new types of cyber threats.

Scheduled Retraining: Regular, scheduled retraining is essential for maintaining model accuracy over time. This process involves retraining the model on a fresh dataset that includes the most recent cyber threat data. By doing this, the model remains up-to-date with the latest attack patterns, reducing the likelihood of it becoming obsolete. Scheduled retraining may involve retraining the model every few weeks, months, or after a significant change in threat trends.

Active Learning for Data Collection: When retraining is necessary, active learning can be a powerful technique for efficiently selecting the most informative data for retraining. In active learning, the model identifies which instances in the dataset are most uncertain or ambiguous, allowing the model to prioritize learning from these examples. This approach ensures that the model is exposed to the most relevant data, reducing the need for large-scale retraining with uninformative data.

Transfer Learning: Transfer learning can be particularly useful when retraining a model on new data. This technique allows a model to leverage previously learned features and knowledge, improving the efficiency of the retraining process. For instance, a pre-trained model on general cybersecurity tasks can be fine-tuned to specific new attack patterns, reducing the time and data needed for retraining.

4. Adversarial Training and Robustness Enhancements

As AI systems become more integrated into cybersecurity, they are increasingly susceptible to adversarial attacks—deliberate attempts to mislead or manipulate the model into making incorrect decisions. To maintain the model's resilience against these attacks, it is essential to regularly enhance its robustness through adversarial training and defensive techniques.

Adversarial Retraining: One of the most common methods for defending against adversarial attacks is adversarial retraining, which involves augmenting the training dataset with adversarial examples. By exposing the model to adversarial inputs during the retraining process, the model learns to identify and mitigate such inputs in the future. Regular adversarial retraining helps the model maintain its effectiveness in the face of evolving adversarial attack strategies.

Robust Optimization: To strengthen models against adversarial examples, robust optimization techniques can be employed. These methods modify the training process to ensure the model is less sensitive to small perturbations in input data, making it more resilient to adversarial manipulation. Regular updates to the optimization strategies can help ensure the model maintains robustness over time.

Testing for Adversarial Vulnerabilities: In addition to retraining, cybersecurity teams should periodically test AI models for vulnerabilities to adversarial attacks. By simulating different types of attacks, such as evasion or poisoning attacks, organizations can identify weaknesses in their AI models and take corrective actions before attackers can exploit them.

5. Cross-Validation and Ensemble Learning

Ensuring ongoing model adaptation and performance also involves leveraging cross-validation and ensemble learning techniques. These methods help to maintain model reliability by ensuring that the model's predictions are stable across different subsets of the data.

Cross-Validation: Cross-validation is a technique that involves splitting the data into multiple subsets, training the model on one subset, and testing it on others. This process helps ensure that the model generalizes well across different data and reduces the risk of overfitting. Regular cross-validation during model updates can prevent performance degradation and ensure that the model remains stable over time.

Ensemble Methods: Ensemble learning combines the predictions of multiple models to improve overall performance. By using a diverse set of models, ensemble methods can increase resilience to changes in the threat landscape. If one model's performance drops or becomes ineffective against certain types of threats, other models in the ensemble can compensate, ensuring that the overall system remains robust.

6. Collaborative Learning and Feedback Loops

Collaboration between systems, organizations, and even industries can play a significant role in model maintenance and adaptation. Collaborative learning and feedback loops facilitate ongoing improvement through shared insights and the exchange of threat intelligence.

Federated Learning: In federated learning, multiple organizations or devices train models locally on their data, then share model updates rather than raw data. This decentralized approach helps the model stay up-to-date across a wide range of environments, with each participating entity contributing to the collective learning process.

This collaboration helps mitigate the risk of data leakage while ensuring models remain current with evolving threats.

Feedback Loops: By incorporating real-time feedback from the environment, AI models can continuously adjust to new types of threats and anomalous behaviors. For example, if a model flags a potential security incident, the response to that incident can be used to further refine and improve the model's accuracy.

Ongoing model maintenance and adaptation are essential to ensuring the long-term success of AI-powered cybersecurity systems. By implementing techniques such as continuous monitoring, incremental learning, retraining, adversarial training, and collaborative learning, organizations can ensure that their models remain effective and resilient in the face of evolving threats. The ability to adapt quickly to new attack patterns and maintain system robustness in a changing environment will be critical to staying ahead of cyber adversaries and ensuring the continued security of sensitive systems and data.

12. Case Studies in AI-Powered Cybersecurity Solutions

Chapter 12, Case Studies in AI-Powered Cybersecurity Solutions, provides real-world examples of how AI and machine learning are being successfully implemented across various industries to combat cyber threats. This chapter showcases detailed case studies from sectors like finance, healthcare, and government, highlighting specific AI-driven cybersecurity solutions that have enhanced threat detection, response times, and overall security posture. Each case study illustrates the practical challenges faced by organizations and the strategies they used to integrate AI into their existing security frameworks. Through these examples, readers will gain insights into the practical benefits and limitations of AI in cybersecurity, as well as lessons learned that can inform their own security strategies.

12.1 AI in Financial Sector: Fraud Detection and Prevention

The financial sector has long been a prime target for cybercriminals, given the large volumes of sensitive transactions and personal data that flow through it daily. Fraud, including identity theft, phishing, and credit card fraud, is a persistent and growing issue. In response, financial institutions have increasingly turned to artificial intelligence (AI) and machine learning (ML) to bolster their defenses and enhance fraud detection and prevention systems. AI offers advanced techniques that can analyze vast amounts of transaction data, detect suspicious patterns, and take preemptive measures to minimize financial losses. This section explores how AI is reshaping fraud detection and prevention in the financial sector.

1. Machine Learning for Real-Time Fraud Detection

One of the most powerful applications of AI in the financial sector is its ability to detect fraudulent activity in real-time. Traditional rule-based systems often fall short in identifying new or evolving types of fraud because they rely on predefined patterns. Machine learning, on the other hand, can identify subtle anomalies and emerging patterns by continuously learning from vast amounts of transactional data.

Anomaly Detection: Machine learning models can analyze historical transaction data to learn what constitutes normal behavior for individual users or organizations. Once trained, these models can flag transactions that deviate from this baseline as potential fraud. For instance, if a user makes an unusually large transfer from an account that has a history of low-volume transactions, the system may flag it for further investigation. The ability to detect outliers in real-time allows for quick action, preventing fraudulent transactions from being completed.

Supervised and Unsupervised Learning: Both supervised and unsupervised machine learning techniques are employed in fraud detection. In supervised learning, models are trained on labeled datasets where transactions are marked as either legitimate or fraudulent. This allows the model to learn patterns and classify future transactions accordingly. On the other hand, unsupervised learning techniques do not require labeled data and can discover hidden patterns or clusters in the data, which is particularly useful for identifying novel types of fraud that haven't been seen before.

Real-Time Transaction Scoring: AI can assign a risk score to each transaction based on factors such as the amount, location, time, and behavior history. These risk scores are computed in real-time and help flag high-risk transactions that require immediate attention. Financial institutions can set thresholds for transaction approval, where transactions exceeding a certain risk score are automatically flagged for manual review or even blocked.

2. Behavioral Analytics for Fraud Prevention

Behavioral analytics, a subfield of AI, plays a significant role in preventing fraud by analyzing user behavior patterns over time. By establishing a user's normal behavior profile—such as transaction size, frequency, and geographic location—AI systems can quickly identify deviations that may signal fraudulent activity.

User and Entity Behavior Analytics (UEBA): UEBA solutions use machine learning to detect anomalies in the way users interact with financial systems. These systems learn a user's typical behavior, such as login times, payment patterns, and even device usage. When there are significant deviations—like accessing an account from an unusual location or making a large transfer after a period of inactivity—the system triggers alerts, helping prevent fraud before it happens.

Biometric Authentication: AI-powered biometric systems, such as facial recognition and fingerprint scanning, add an additional layer of security by ensuring that only authorized users can access accounts and perform transactions. These systems analyze unique biometric data from the user to verify identity, adding an extra layer of defense against fraudsters attempting to steal credentials.

Continuous Authentication: Unlike traditional authentication systems that rely on a one-time password or PIN, continuous authentication constantly monitors user behavior throughout the session. This ongoing assessment helps detect suspicious activities in real-time, even if an attacker has gained access to a legitimate account. For instance, AI can track typing speed, mouse movements, and browsing patterns to continuously verify the user's identity, adding an extra layer of fraud prevention.

3. Predictive Analytics for Early Detection of Fraudulent Trends

AI's predictive analytics capabilities allow financial institutions to forecast and prevent fraud before it happens. Predictive models analyze historical data, transaction trends, and external factors to anticipate potential threats and proactively mitigate risks.

Risk Prediction Models: AI models use historical transaction data to build predictive risk models that can forecast future fraud risks. For example, predictive models can assess the likelihood of a particular customer or account being targeted for fraud based on various factors, including transaction frequency, credit scores, and demographic information. By identifying high-risk clients or transactions early, financial institutions can take preventive actions such as restricting access, flagging accounts for review, or alerting customers.

Clustering and Segmentation: AI can also segment customers and transactions based on similarities in their behavior, identifying groups that are more likely to be targeted by fraudsters. By clustering transactions into different risk categories, financial institutions can focus their attention on the most vulnerable segments and allocate resources more efficiently.

Real-Time Threat Forecasting: AI models can analyze external data sources, such as news, social media, or market trends, to identify emerging fraud patterns and predict future threats. This helps financial institutions stay one step ahead of fraudsters by adapting their defense strategies to new fraud tactics, such as phishing campaigns or synthetic identity fraud.

4. Automated Fraud Response and Prevention

Once a fraud alert is triggered, AI systems can automate much of the response process, reducing the time it takes to mitigate the impact of fraud and preventing further losses.

Transaction Blocking and Alerts: AI-powered fraud detection systems can automatically block suspicious transactions and freeze accounts when fraud is detected.

This immediate response helps limit financial losses and prevents further fraudulent activity. Customers can also be notified in real-time via SMS, email, or app notifications, allowing them to verify the transaction and confirm their identity if necessary.

Fraud Risk Mitigation: AI can automatically adjust the fraud prevention measures applied to accounts based on the detected risk level. For example, if a high-risk transaction is detected, the system may automatically require additional authentication steps (e.g., multi-factor authentication) or restrict certain account functionalities until the user's identity is verified.

Customer Verification and Alerts: AI systems can send alerts to customers when suspicious activities are detected in their accounts, prompting them to verify the transaction or change their passwords. This adds an additional layer of protection by allowing customers to act quickly when fraudulent activity is detected.

5. Challenges and Future Directions in AI-Powered Fraud Prevention

While AI offers significant benefits in detecting and preventing fraud in the financial sector, there are challenges to its widespread adoption and effectiveness.

Data Privacy and Security: Financial institutions must ensure that the personal and transactional data used to train AI models is protected and complies with data privacy regulations, such as the General Data Protection Regulation (GDPR). Maintaining data security is essential to prevent data breaches that could expose sensitive customer information.

Evolving Fraud Tactics: Fraudsters are becoming increasingly sophisticated, often using AI and machine learning themselves to bypass traditional fraud detection systems. As a result, financial institutions must continuously update and adapt their AI models to counteract these evolving threats.

Bias and Fairness: AI models must be trained on diverse and representative datasets to avoid bias, ensuring that fraud detection systems are fair and equitable for all users. Ensuring that AI algorithms do not disproportionately target certain groups or individuals is essential for maintaining trust in the system.

Explainability and Trust: One of the key challenges of using AI in fraud detection is ensuring the explainability of the model's decisions. Financial institutions need to ensure that AI models can explain the reasoning behind their fraud detection decisions to regulators and customers. This transparency helps build trust in the system and ensures that AI decisions are fair and accountable.

AI is revolutionizing fraud detection and prevention in the financial sector by enabling real-time analysis, predictive modeling, and automated responses. With the help of machine learning, behavioral analytics, and predictive technologies, financial institutions are better equipped to detect fraudulent activity, mitigate risks, and protect their customers. While challenges such as data privacy, evolving fraud tactics, and algorithmic bias remain, AI continues to be a powerful tool in the ongoing battle against fraud. As AI technology continues to evolve, its capabilities in fraud detection and prevention will only become more advanced, offering even more robust defenses against cybercriminals.

12.2 Healthcare Industry: Protecting Patient Data with AI

The healthcare industry has become one of the most critical sectors in terms of data privacy and cybersecurity. With the rise of electronic health records (EHR), telemedicine, and digital health platforms, vast amounts of sensitive patient data are being collected, stored, and transmitted. This data is a prime target for cybercriminals due to its high value on the dark web, where it can be sold for identity theft, insurance fraud, or other malicious purposes. To combat these risks, the healthcare sector is increasingly turning to Artificial Intelligence (AI) and Machine Learning (ML) to safeguard patient information and strengthen overall security infrastructure.

AI's capabilities in healthcare security are multi-faceted, spanning data protection, threat detection, access control, and anomaly detection. This section explores how AI is revolutionizing the way healthcare organizations protect patient data, focusing on AI's role in preventing data breaches, securing medical devices, and ensuring regulatory compliance.

1. AI-Driven Threat Detection and Prevention in Healthcare

With the vast amount of patient data stored across healthcare systems, it is vital to detect and respond to potential cyber threats quickly and efficiently. AI offers sophisticated capabilities that help healthcare organizations proactively identify and mitigate security threats.

Real-Time Cyberattack Detection: Traditional methods of detecting cyberattacks, such as signature-based detection, rely on known attack patterns. However, cybercriminals are constantly evolving their methods, making it difficult for signature-based approaches to keep up. AI-powered systems can detect zero-day attacks and new types of malware by analyzing real-time traffic and behavior. Machine learning algorithms monitor network traffic, login patterns, and user activity to identify suspicious behavior. For example, if an employee accesses a large number of patient records they don't typically interact with, the system can flag this as unusual and alert administrators for further investigation.

Advanced Threat Intelligence: AI can integrate with external sources of threat intelligence to detect emerging threats that specifically target healthcare systems. By leveraging data from cybersecurity forums, government agencies, and private threat intelligence firms, AI models can stay ahead of new attack techniques used by hackers. This integration allows healthcare organizations to adjust their defense mechanisms accordingly, such as blocking new malware or identifying compromised users more quickly.

Phishing Detection: Healthcare workers often fall victim to phishing attempts, where cybercriminals impersonate trusted entities to steal login credentials and gain unauthorized access to patient data. AI-powered email filtering systems can analyze incoming communications for signs of phishing attacks, such as suspicious links, unusual sender addresses, or mismatched sender names. The system can automatically quarantine such emails and alert the healthcare staff, minimizing the risk of phishing attacks.

2. Protecting Patient Data Through Secure Access Control

Patient data is sensitive, and healthcare organizations must enforce strict access controls to ensure that only authorized individuals can view, modify, or transmit it. AI can help enhance these security measures, ensuring that healthcare organizations can balance user convenience with robust access protection.

AI-Powered Biometric Authentication: One of the most promising applications of AI in healthcare security is biometric authentication. AI-driven facial recognition, voice recognition, and fingerprint scanning are increasingly being used to verify the identity of medical staff and patients. These biometric systems provide a more secure and efficient means of authenticating users than traditional passwords or PINs. AI algorithms can also ensure that authentication systems continuously adapt to changes in the user, such as aging or physical appearance, which can increase the reliability and accuracy of identity verification.

Behavioral Biometrics for Continuous Monitoring: In addition to initial user authentication, AI-based behavioral biometrics can monitor how healthcare professionals interact with the system to ensure that the person accessing the data is who they claim to be. This includes analyzing mouse movements, typing patterns, and device usage. If the system detects irregularities in behavior that could indicate unauthorized access, it can trigger an alert, lock down the account, or initiate a multi-factor authentication request to confirm the user's identity.

Role-Based Access Control (RBAC) Optimization: AI can also optimize role-based access control (RBAC) systems within healthcare organizations. By analyzing user behavior and job functions, AI can ensure that individuals have access to only the information necessary for their role, minimizing the risk of unauthorized data exposure. For instance, AI can analyze a doctor's patterns to determine if their access to patient records is consistent with their responsibilities, and it can automatically adjust permissions based on any anomalies or changes in role.

3. Data Encryption and Privacy Protection Using AI

The confidentiality of patient data is a critical concern in healthcare, and AI can play a crucial role in safeguarding this data through encryption and other privacy-enhancing technologies.

Automated Data Encryption: AI can automate the process of encrypting patient data, ensuring that sensitive information is protected when stored or transmitted across networks. By automatically applying encryption protocols based on the sensitivity of the data and the context in which it is being accessed, AI minimizes the risk of human error and ensures that all patient information is encrypted according to best practices. Furthermore, AI models can ensure that data is encrypted with the latest encryption standards, protecting against new vulnerabilities in older encryption methods.

Privacy-Aware AI Systems: AI systems can be designed with built-in privacy-preserving mechanisms that comply with strict healthcare regulations, such as the Health Insurance Portability and Accountability Act (HIPAA) in the U.S. AI models can operate within constraints that prevent them from accessing or processing personally identifiable information (PII) unless absolutely necessary, ensuring that patient privacy is upheld at all times. Additionally, AI-driven tools can assist in anonymizing or pseudonymizing patient data for research or analysis, ensuring that sensitive information is protected.

4. AI for Securing Medical Devices and IoT Systems

With the rise of connected medical devices (IoT), securing healthcare systems has become even more complex. Devices like pacemakers, infusion pumps, and diagnostic machines often collect and transmit sensitive data. However, these devices are also vulnerable to cyberattacks. AI plays a vital role in securing medical devices and preventing cyberattacks that target healthcare's growing network of connected devices.

AI for Device Behavior Monitoring: AI-powered monitoring systems can track the normal behavior of medical devices, allowing them to detect unusual activity or potential threats. For example, if a device begins transmitting data at an unusual time or to an unauthorized location, AI algorithms can flag this as suspicious and automatically shut down the device or isolate it from the network. This minimizes the risk of cybercriminals exploiting vulnerabilities in medical devices to access patient data.

Vulnerability Detection in IoT Devices: Medical IoT devices often have limited computational resources and may lack the security updates required to keep them safe from cyberattacks. AI-driven tools can help identify vulnerabilities in these devices by analyzing their behavior and cross-referencing known vulnerabilities from threat intelligence sources. By proactively identifying weak points, AI can help healthcare organizations patch vulnerabilities before they can be exploited.

AI-Enabled Device Authentication: To ensure that only legitimate devices connect to healthcare networks, AI-powered authentication systems can be used to verify the identity of medical devices before granting them access. These systems can analyze unique device identifiers and biometric data (such as patterns in device usage) to ensure that unauthorized devices are blocked from accessing sensitive healthcare data.

5. Ensuring Compliance with Healthcare Regulations

In addition to protecting patient data from cyber threats, healthcare organizations must ensure compliance with regulations such as HIPAA (in the U.S.) and the General Data Protection Regulation (GDPR) in Europe. AI can help organizations adhere to these regulations while minimizing the administrative burden.

Automated Compliance Auditing: AI can be used to automate the process of compliance auditing, ensuring that healthcare organizations meet the regulatory requirements for data protection. AI tools can regularly review access logs, patient data handling processes, and audit trails to ensure compliance with privacy laws and data retention requirements.

AI-Powered Reporting: Healthcare organizations must submit reports to regulatory bodies to demonstrate their adherence to security and privacy standards. AI can streamline this process by automatically generating compliance reports based on real-time data and providing insights into areas that may require corrective actions.

Predictive Risk Management: By leveraging AI's predictive capabilities, healthcare organizations can identify potential compliance risks and mitigate them before they result in penalties. AI systems can analyze regulatory changes and assist organizations in adjusting their data protection strategies to remain in compliance with evolving healthcare laws.

AI is rapidly transforming the healthcare sector by providing advanced security solutions to protect patient data, secure medical devices, and ensure regulatory compliance. Through AI-driven threat detection, behavior analytics, encryption, and device security, healthcare organizations are better equipped to mitigate cyber risks and safeguard sensitive information. As healthcare systems continue to digitize and adopt new technologies, AI will play an increasingly important role in securing patient data, building trust with patients, and maintaining the integrity of healthcare services. While challenges remain, particularly in terms of data privacy, regulatory compliance, and AI system transparency, the benefits of AI-driven security in healthcare are undeniable, making it an essential tool in the ongoing effort to protect sensitive medical information from evolving cyber threats.

12.3 Government Sector: AI in National Security and Defense

Artificial Intelligence (AI) has become a cornerstone of modern national security strategies, with its transformative potential in defense, intelligence, and cybersecurity being increasingly recognized by governments worldwide. As geopolitical tensions rise, cyber threats evolve, and the complexity of global security challenges deepens, AI offers powerful tools to enhance national defense capabilities, improve decision-making, and respond to emerging threats more swiftly and effectively.

In this section, we explore the role of AI in the government sector, focusing on its application in national security and defense. From military operations to intelligence gathering, AI is reshaping how governments protect citizens, safeguard critical infrastructure, and maintain geopolitical stability. AI's ability to analyze massive amounts of data, automate complex tasks, and predict potential threats is driving significant advancements in both the defense and intelligence sectors.

1. AI for Threat Detection and Surveillance

National security agencies and defense organizations are increasingly relying on AI-driven systems for real-time threat detection and surveillance across various domains—cyber, physical, and geopolitical.

Intelligent Surveillance Systems: AI-enhanced surveillance tools, such as advanced video analytics and facial recognition systems, allow governments to monitor large public spaces, borders, and critical infrastructure. AI algorithms analyze video feeds, detect unusual behaviors, and alert authorities in real-time. For example, AI can identify suspicious individuals or vehicles by matching their features against known databases, helping law enforcement agencies prevent criminal activity or terrorist attacks.

Autonomous Drones and Satellite Systems: The use of AI in drones and satellite systems is revolutionizing surveillance capabilities. AI algorithms enable drones to patrol borders, monitor military installations, or track movements in conflict zones without human intervention. Similarly, satellites equipped with AI can autonomously analyze vast amounts of data to identify potential threats, such as troop movements or missile launches, offering a significant advantage in strategic defense and military intelligence.

Cyber Threat Detection: Governments are also utilizing AI to protect critical national infrastructure from cyber threats. AI-driven cybersecurity solutions help detect and mitigate attacks on government systems, networks, and military assets. AI systems can recognize abnormal patterns in network traffic, identify sophisticated malware, and detect vulnerabilities in government systems before attackers can exploit them, providing a crucial layer of defense against cyber espionage, hacking, and cyber warfare.

2. AI in Military Decision-Making and Strategy

AI's role in military decision-making is growing, as it assists commanders in analyzing vast datasets, making strategic decisions, and simulating various combat scenarios. These capabilities can improve the speed and accuracy of decisions, which is especially critical in high-pressure environments where every second counts.

Data Fusion for Operational Decision-Making: AI can integrate data from a variety of sources, such as satellites, sensors, drones, and military intelligence reports, to provide real-time situational awareness. By processing large volumes of data, AI helps military commanders understand the battlefield, anticipate enemy actions, and make decisions based on the most up-to-date information. This level of data fusion is especially crucial for modern warfare, where success often depends on rapid decision-making.

Predictive Analytics for Defense Strategy: AI's predictive capabilities enable military planners to anticipate potential threats, predict adversary movements, and simulate different strategic outcomes. AI models can analyze historical conflict data, geopolitical trends, and enemy behavior to forecast future events, providing defense agencies with valuable intelligence for preparing responses to potential security threats.

AI-Enhanced Simulation for War Gaming: Military forces use AI-driven simulations and war gaming platforms to evaluate different combat scenarios and test defense strategies. AI can simulate numerous combat situations, incorporating variables such as terrain, weather, enemy tactics, and equipment. These simulations help military leaders assess the potential effectiveness of various strategies before implementing them in the field, reducing the risks associated with real-world military operations.

3. AI-Powered Autonomous Defense Systems

One of the most exciting developments in AI for defense is the emergence of autonomous weapons and defense systems. These systems, powered by AI and machine learning algorithms, are designed to operate with minimal human intervention, making decisions in real-time to respond to security threats.

Autonomous Combat Vehicles: AI has paved the way for autonomous military vehicles, including drones, tanks, and ground robots. These vehicles can operate in combat zones without human operators, reducing risks to personnel while enhancing operational capabilities. AI allows these machines to navigate challenging environments, identify targets, and engage threats autonomously or under human supervision. For example, autonomous drones can carry out reconnaissance missions, drop supplies, or even carry out precision strikes on enemy targets.

Autonomous Defense Systems for Critical Infrastructure: AI can be integrated into missile defense systems, automated air defense platforms, and anti-drone technologies to protect critical national assets, such as power grids, military bases, and communication networks. These AI-powered systems can autonomously track, intercept, and neutralize incoming threats like ballistic missiles, enemy aircraft, or drones, without requiring direct human intervention. The integration of AI into defense systems enables faster, more effective responses to emerging threats, minimizing the risk of human error.

Swarm Robotics for Tactical Operations: AI is also being used to control swarms of autonomous robots, which can be deployed for a variety of military tasks, including surveillance, reconnaissance, and even combat. These robots operate in coordinated groups, autonomously adjusting their behavior in response to changes in the environment. Swarm robotics, powered by AI, can overwhelm enemy defenses, gather intelligence in hostile territory, or provide logistical support in dangerous areas.

4. AI for Cyber Defense and Counterintelligence

Cyber warfare has become a central focus of national security, and AI is being leveraged to protect government networks from cyberattacks and espionage, while also playing a role in counterintelligence operations.

AI-Driven Cyber Defense Systems: Governments are increasingly using AI to bolster their cybersecurity frameworks, helping to defend sensitive data and critical infrastructure from state-sponsored cyberattacks, hacking groups, and cybercriminals. AI-based intrusion detection systems (IDS) and intrusion prevention systems (IPS) use machine learning to analyze network traffic, identify anomalies, and block potential threats in real time. These systems can adapt and evolve with new cyberattack tactics, enabling governments to respond proactively to emerging threats.

Counterintelligence and Threat Hunting: AI is also instrumental in counterintelligence efforts, where it helps security agencies identify and neutralize foreign espionage operations, cyber espionage, and insider threats. AI-powered tools can analyze communication patterns, monitor social media activity, and track suspicious behavior to uncover covert operations. Additionally, AI can assist in identifying connections between adversaries and their assets, making it easier to dismantle enemy networks.

AI for Cyberattack Attribution: One of the most difficult aspects of cybersecurity is accurately attributing cyberattacks to specific actors. AI models can help government agencies pinpoint the origin of cyberattacks by analyzing digital footprints, attack methodologies, and other forensic data. By linking a cyberattack to a particular group, state actor, or organization, governments can respond with appropriate measures, including diplomatic, economic, or military counteractions.

5. Ethical and Legal Implications of AI in Defense

As AI becomes more integrated into national security and defense operations, questions arise around its ethical use and the potential consequences of deploying autonomous systems in military and intelligence settings. Issues such as accountability, the potential for unintended harm, and the risk of AI-driven arms races are being actively debated.

AI and Autonomous Weapons Systems (AWS): The development of autonomous weapons that can independently select and engage targets has sparked ethical concerns, particularly regarding the use of lethal force by machines. Many experts argue that human oversight is essential to ensure that decisions about the use of force are made responsibly. International discussions are underway to establish guidelines and treaties around the use of AI-powered weapons, with the aim of preventing misuse or escalation of conflicts.

Bias and Accountability in AI Models: As AI systems are used to make critical national security decisions, concerns about algorithmic bias and accountability are paramount. There is a risk that AI models, which are trained on historical data, may perpetuate biases or inaccuracies in decision-making, particularly in areas such as surveillance or military operations. Ensuring transparency in AI models, as well as human oversight in key decisions, is essential for maintaining ethical standards in national defense and security.

International Regulation and AI Governance: The global nature of AI innovation in defense requires international cooperation to set clear regulations for the development and use of AI technologies in national security. Governments must collaborate to create frameworks that promote responsible AI use, prevent abuses, and ensure AI technologies do not destabilize global security.

AI is fundamentally transforming national security and defense, providing governments with unprecedented capabilities to safeguard citizens, protect critical infrastructure, and enhance military operations. From real-time surveillance and predictive intelligence to autonomous defense systems and cybersecurity solutions, AI is enabling faster, more effective responses to evolving security threats. However, the integration of AI into defense and national security also raises ethical, legal, and geopolitical challenges that need to be carefully addressed. As AI continues to advance, governments must balance the immense benefits of AI-powered security with the responsibility to uphold ethical standards and protect civil liberties.

12.4 Lessons Learned from Enterprise Security Deployments

As artificial intelligence (AI) and machine learning (ML) continue to gain traction in the cybersecurity landscape, many organizations across various industries have embarked on the journey of integrating these technologies into their security infrastructure. Governments, while different from the private sector in their operations, can benefit immensely from understanding the challenges and successes experienced by enterprises in their AI-powered security deployments. The lessons learned from these implementations offer invaluable insights that can help improve the efficiency, scalability, and resilience of AI-based cybersecurity initiatives within national security frameworks.

In this section, we explore key lessons learned from enterprise security deployments of AI and ML technologies, and how these insights can be leveraged by government agencies and defense organizations to enhance their own security operations.

1. Data Quality and Availability Are Crucial

One of the most critical lessons from enterprise deployments is the importance of high-quality, relevant, and readily available data. AI models thrive on data, and the quality of the data used for training and analysis can significantly impact the effectiveness of a security system. Enterprises that have successfully integrated AI into their cybersecurity practices often emphasize the need for clean, accurate, and comprehensive data sources.

Data Preparation and Cleansing: In many cases, enterprises have found that raw data must be extensively cleaned and preprocessed before it can be used in AI models. This process includes filtering out noise, handling missing or incomplete data, and ensuring that the data is properly labeled. Without such preparation, AI models can produce inaccurate or unreliable results, leading to inefficiencies and security vulnerabilities.

Data Integration Across Silos: Many enterprises struggle with integrating data from disparate sources, including network logs, endpoint data, cloud services, and third-party security tools. AI systems require data to be well-integrated and accessible in a centralized format to derive meaningful insights. Governments, which often deal with siloed data between departments and agencies, must prioritize data sharing and integration to enable AI models to work effectively across the entire security landscape.

Real-Time Data for Continuous Monitoring: Enterprises with effective AI security systems often focus on real-time data collection and analysis. AI and ML systems need to process data as it is generated to provide timely threat detection and response. For governments and national security agencies, this lesson emphasizes the importance of developing real-time data pipelines to improve situational awareness and enable swift reactions to security incidents.

2. AI Models Require Continuous Training and Adaptation

A key challenge faced by enterprises in deploying AI-powered security solutions is that these models require continuous training and adaptation to stay effective in the face of evolving cyber threats. AI models are only as good as the data they are trained on, and as new attack techniques emerge, models need to be retrained to recognize new patterns of malicious activity.

Evolving Threat Landscape: One of the most common pitfalls in enterprise AI security implementations is assuming that once a model is trained, it is set for the long term. In reality, threat actors constantly evolve their tactics, which means that AI models must evolve alongside these changing tactics. Enterprises have learned that to remain effective, security models must be regularly updated with new data, threats, and attack vectors.

Feedback Loops for Model Refinement: Many organizations have implemented automated feedback loops where AI models learn from false positives, false negatives, and new attack data to improve over time. These feedback loops help enterprises continually refine and adapt their models to ensure they stay relevant in detecting emerging threats. For government and national defense sectors, integrating such feedback mechanisms can ensure long-term reliability and resilience in security operations.

Challenge of Overfitting: Another lesson from enterprises is the challenge of overfitting in AI models. Overfitting occurs when an AI model becomes too specific to the training data and loses its ability to generalize to new, unseen threats. To avoid this, enterprises focus on using diverse training data and regularly testing models against fresh data sets. This is especially important in national security, where the adversaries' tactics are often unpredictable and diverse.

3. Managing AI's Complex Decision-Making in Security

AI-based security systems often operate in environments where the decision-making process is highly complex and involves trade-offs between multiple factors such as threat severity, system impact, and resource availability. Many enterprises have struggled with effectively managing AI's autonomous decision-making capabilities, especially in areas where human judgment is still necessary.

Transparency and Explainability: A critical lesson from enterprises is the need for transparency and explainability in AI decision-making. Enterprises deploying AI in security often face challenges when AI systems generate alerts or responses that are not easily understood by security analysts. This lack of transparency can lead to trust issues and a reluctance to adopt AI solutions. To address this, many enterprises have focused on developing AI models with explainable decision-making processes, which offer clear insights into how and why a particular decision was made.

Human-in-the-Loop (HITL) Approach: In many cases, enterprises have found that fully autonomous AI systems in security can be too risky, especially when they are responsible for critical decisions, such as blocking network traffic or shutting down services. Therefore, many organizations have implemented a human-in-the-loop approach, where AI systems assist analysts by providing recommendations, but human oversight is maintained for critical actions. Governments must consider this approach in sensitive national security contexts, where the consequences of errors can be catastrophic.

Balancing Speed and Accuracy: Another important lesson from enterprises is the delicate balance between the speed of AI responses and the accuracy of those responses. In fast-paced environments like cybersecurity, decisions often need to be made quickly. However, too quick a response from an AI system can lead to false positives or missed threats, while too slow a response might allow threats to escalate. Enterprises have learned that optimizing AI systems to strike the right balance is crucial for effective threat detection and mitigation. This is equally true in government security deployments, where rapid, yet accurate responses are essential in defending national interests.

4. The Importance of Cross-Disciplinary Collaboration

Enterprise deployments of AI in cybersecurity often require collaboration across different organizational departments, such as IT, security operations, data science, and legal teams. Successful integration of AI into security infrastructure necessitates alignment between these departments to address technical, operational, and ethical considerations.

IT, Security, and Data Science Collaboration: AI models in security are only effective when they are closely integrated with existing security tools and workflows. In enterprises, security and IT teams often work closely with data scientists to ensure that AI models align with real-world security requirements. For example, data scientists must understand the constraints of the IT environment, while security teams must communicate their needs for specific threat detections. Governments will need to establish similar interdisciplinary collaboration to maximize the effectiveness of AI in national security and defense.

Legal and Ethical Considerations: Enterprises also highlight the importance of involving legal teams to navigate privacy regulations, data protection, and ethical concerns in AI deployments. Governments must ensure that AI systems used in national security adhere to privacy laws and ethical guidelines, while also safeguarding critical data from malicious actors.

Training and Knowledge Sharing: Finally, enterprises have learned that training employees and stakeholders on the capabilities, limitations, and ethical implications of AI is essential. Security analysts need to understand how AI models work, how to interpret their outputs, and when human judgment should intervene. Governments should prioritize training for national security personnel to ensure they can effectively utilize AI-driven systems.

The lessons learned from AI deployments in enterprise cybersecurity can offer valuable insights for government agencies and defense organizations as they integrate AI into national security systems. High-quality data, continuous training of models, transparency in decision-making, and cross-disciplinary collaboration are all crucial components for success. By understanding and applying these lessons, governments can enhance the resilience of their national security frameworks, ensuring that they are better equipped to defend against increasingly sophisticated and dynamic threats.

13. The Future of Cyber Intelligence: Trends and Emerging Technologies

Chapter 13, The Future of Cyber Intelligence: Trends and Emerging Technologies, looks ahead to the evolving landscape of cybersecurity, focusing on the cutting-edge technologies and trends that will shape the future of cyber defense. This chapter explores the potential impact of emerging technologies like quantum computing, edge AI, and blockchain on cybersecurity, examining how they could revolutionize threat detection and response. It also discusses the growing role of privacy-preserving machine learning techniques, which aim to protect sensitive data while enabling advanced AI analysis. By forecasting the next generation of cyber threats and the corresponding defensive innovations, this chapter prepares readers for the challenges and opportunities that lie ahead in the rapidly advancing field of cyber intelligence.

13.1 Emerging AI Trends: Quantum Computing and Edge AI

The field of artificial intelligence (AI) is rapidly evolving, with new technologies emerging that promise to reshape how AI is integrated into cybersecurity and other domains. Among these transformative technologies are Quantum Computing and Edge AI, both of which are poised to revolutionize the landscape of cyber intelligence and security. As we enter an era of more complex threats and faster technological advancements, these trends offer unique opportunities and challenges that must be addressed for AI in cybersecurity to reach its full potential.

In this section, we will explore the fundamentals of quantum computing and edge AI, highlighting their respective roles in the future of AI-powered security systems. We will also discuss how these technologies are expected to complement existing AI systems, providing unprecedented capabilities in areas like data processing, threat detection, and defense automation.

1. Quantum Computing: A New Paradigm for Processing Power

Quantum computing represents a fundamental shift in computational power, utilizing the principles of quantum mechanics to solve problems that are currently intractable for classical computers. Unlike classical computers, which process data in binary format (0s and 1s), quantum computers operate using qubits, which can exist in multiple states simultaneously (superposition). This ability to handle multiple possibilities at once opens up the potential for exponential increases in computing power.

In the context of AI and cybersecurity, quantum computing could have profound implications, especially in areas that require high computational capacity such as cryptography, machine learning model training, and large-scale data analysis.

Encryption and Cryptography: Quantum computers have the ability to break current encryption methods (such as RSA and ECC) that secure much of the internet today. With quantum algorithms like Shor's Algorithm, quantum computers can factor large numbers exponentially faster than classical computers, undermining the security of traditional encryption protocols. This poses both a threat and an opportunity for the field of cybersecurity. On one hand, quantum computing could render existing encryption obsolete; on the other hand, it also paves the way for quantum-resistant encryption algorithms and new cryptographic methods that leverage quantum properties to create virtually unbreakable security.

Accelerating Machine Learning: Quantum computing's computational power could significantly speed up the training of machine learning models, making it possible to handle much larger datasets and more complex algorithms. This is particularly important in cybersecurity, where real-time detection of threats often depends on analyzing vast amounts of data quickly. By using quantum computing to perform operations in parallel, AI models could process data much faster and more efficiently, allowing for more timely threat detection and response.

Optimization and Simulation: Quantum computing excels in solving complex optimization problems and simulating environments that are otherwise computationally prohibitive. In cybersecurity, this could help in areas such as intrusion detection, anomaly detection, and vulnerability assessment, where solutions require optimizing vast combinations of variables and simulating potential attack scenarios to predict future threats.

While quantum computing remains in its early stages, its implications for AI and cybersecurity are enormous. Governments, financial institutions, and other security-sensitive organizations are already investing heavily in quantum research to prepare for this next wave of computational power. However, significant challenges remain, including overcoming quantum noise, stabilizing qubits, and developing scalable quantum systems.

2. Edge AI: AI at the Edge of the Network

Edge AI refers to the deployment of AI models directly on devices and sensors at the edge of the network, as opposed to relying solely on centralized cloud-based systems. This trend is driven by the increasing need for low-latency processing, data privacy, and bandwidth efficiency in IoT (Internet of Things) devices, mobile devices, and other distributed systems.

By processing data closer to its source, edge AI reduces the time it takes for AI models to analyze and respond to security threats, which is crucial in real-time cybersecurity applications.

Real-Time Threat Detection and Response: One of the most important applications of edge AI in cybersecurity is its ability to enable real-time detection of threats directly at the point of entry. For example, edge AI can be used to monitor network traffic, analyze behavioral anomalies on individual devices, and detect suspicious activity without the need for data to be sent to a centralized server for processing. This reduces the response time to potential threats, making it more difficult for adversaries to succeed in a cyberattack.

Data Privacy and Security: Edge AI offers enhanced privacy benefits by keeping sensitive data on local devices and processing it locally, rather than transmitting it to the cloud. This minimizes the risk of data exposure during transmission, making it more difficult for attackers to intercept valuable information. Moreover, edge AI allows for more stringent control over data, as it enables organizations to implement privacy policies at the device level, protecting against breaches and ensuring compliance with data protection regulations.

Reducing Bandwidth and Latency: By processing data on the edge, organizations can reduce the demand on bandwidth, as only essential data or insights need to be transmitted to centralized servers. This makes edge AI particularly effective in environments with limited connectivity or in situations where rapid responses are required, such as in autonomous vehicles, smart cities, and remote industrial systems. Edge AI also helps to mitigate network congestion and reduces reliance on cloud infrastructure, making systems more resilient in the event of network failures.

Decentralized Security Architecture: The distributed nature of edge AI can provide a more resilient and decentralized approach to cybersecurity. Traditional cybersecurity systems rely on centralized data centers and cloud infrastructure, which can become single points of failure in the event of an attack. By incorporating edge AI, organizations can create more distributed, fault-tolerant security architectures that are harder for attackers to target. Even if one part of the system is compromised, the impact is limited to that specific edge device or node, preventing widespread disruption.

While edge AI holds tremendous potential for cybersecurity, it also comes with its own set of challenges. These include the need for robust security on edge devices (as they are often vulnerable to physical tampering), limitations in computing power on smaller devices, and the complexity of managing and securing vast networks of distributed AI systems. To address these challenges, organizations must invest in secure hardware and software, develop standards for edge AI security, and ensure that edge devices are continuously monitored and updated.

3. The Convergence of Quantum Computing and Edge AI

As both quantum computing and edge AI continue to evolve, an exciting possibility emerges: the convergence of these two technologies. Imagine quantum computing algorithms running on edge devices, where real-time data is processed and analyzed on-site with quantum-enhanced capabilities. Such a combination could revolutionize the security landscape, providing unprecedented computational power and enabling ultra-fast, real-time threat detection and response across distributed systems.

Quantum-Enabled Edge Devices: One possible future application is the integration of quantum computing capabilities into edge devices, which would dramatically increase their ability to process data and run AI models. For example, quantum-assisted AI on edge devices could enable more complex, nuanced decision-making, and provide powerful new methods of encryption and decryption to protect sensitive data in transit. This could be particularly valuable for sectors that require both real-time analysis and robust security, such as autonomous vehicles, industrial control systems, and critical infrastructure.

Decentralized Quantum Security: Quantum-enhanced edge AI could lead to the development of decentralized, quantum-resistant security solutions, particularly in IoT networks. By combining quantum cryptography with edge AI systems, organizations could create more secure, private, and resilient networks, capable of defending against emerging threats like quantum-enabled cyberattacks.

While the integration of quantum computing and edge AI is still in its infancy, its potential for cybersecurity is enormous. Researchers are already exploring the fusion of these technologies, and it is likely that over the next decade, we will begin to see early-stage implementations of quantum-enhanced AI running on edge devices, transforming how cybersecurity operates in the digital world.

Both quantum computing and edge AI are pivotal emerging trends that hold significant promise for the future of AI-powered cybersecurity. Quantum computing offers unprecedented computational power that can enhance machine learning models, improve encryption protocols, and optimize cyber defense strategies. At the same time, edge AI allows for faster, more efficient, and privacy-conscious security operations by processing data locally and enabling real-time threat detection. As these technologies evolve, they will play a crucial role in shaping the future of cyber intelligence, enabling stronger, more resilient defenses against increasingly sophisticated threats.

As we move into the future, organizations and governments must be prepared for the rapid adoption and integration of these technologies, ensuring that they are leveraged responsibly, securely, and effectively to safeguard sensitive data and systems against emerging cyber threats.

13.2 Advances in Privacy-Preserving Machine Learning

As machine learning (ML) and artificial intelligence (AI) technologies become more prevalent in various industries, the importance of privacy and data protection has never been more critical. With the growing reliance on personal and sensitive data to train AI models, there is an increasing need to protect this data while still enabling the capabilities of machine learning. Privacy-preserving machine learning (PPML) has emerged as a key area of research and development, aiming to strike a balance between powerful AI-driven insights and the protection of individuals' privacy.

In this section, we will explore the advancements in privacy-preserving machine learning techniques, focusing on the latest innovations and their potential to address privacy challenges in AI and cybersecurity. These technologies are particularly significant in fields such as healthcare, finance, and law enforcement, where sensitive information must be safeguarded while still enabling powerful data-driven decision-making.

1. Overview of Privacy-Preserving Techniques in ML

Privacy-preserving machine learning refers to the use of techniques that enable machine learning models to be trained on sensitive data without exposing or compromising the privacy of that data. These techniques allow organizations to extract valuable insights from data while adhering to privacy regulations, such as the General Data Protection Regulation (GDPR) in Europe or the California Consumer Privacy Act (CCPA) in the United States.

Several privacy-preserving techniques have gained traction in recent years, including:

Differential Privacy (DP): Differential privacy is a framework that adds statistical noise to data in a way that prevents the identification of individual data points while still enabling meaningful analysis. By incorporating noise during the data analysis process, differential privacy ensures that the output of machine learning models does not reveal private or sensitive information about any individual in the dataset. This technique is particularly useful when working with large datasets containing personal information, as it minimizes the risk of individual data leakage while maintaining the accuracy of the model.

Homomorphic Encryption: Homomorphic encryption allows computation to be performed on encrypted data without first decrypting it. This means that sensitive data can be analyzed and processed without exposing the actual data to the machine learning model. Homomorphic encryption enables secure computations on encrypted datasets, ensuring that data privacy is maintained throughout the analysis process. This method has the potential to revolutionize data sharing, as organizations can collaborate and analyze data without ever exposing sensitive information.

Secure Multi-Party Computation (SMPC): Secure multi-party computation is a cryptographic technique that allows multiple parties to jointly compute a function over their private inputs while keeping those inputs secret from one another. In the context of machine learning, SMPC enables collaborative model training where multiple organizations can pool their data to improve the performance of AI models without sharing sensitive information directly. This allows for privacy-preserving collaborative efforts while preventing the exposure of sensitive data to any single party.

Federated Learning: Federated learning is a decentralized machine learning approach that enables models to be trained across distributed devices or nodes without the need to share the data itself. Each device trains the model locally on its own data, and only the model updates (rather than raw data) are shared with a central server for aggregation. This ensures that the individual data on each device remains private, while the system can still benefit from the collective intelligence of the distributed network. Federated learning is particularly useful in applications such as mobile phones and IoT devices, where local data privacy is a concern.

2. Recent Advances in Privacy-Preserving ML

While the techniques described above have been around for some time, there have been significant advancements in the efficiency, scalability, and practical application of privacy-preserving machine learning in recent years.

Improved Differential Privacy Algorithms: Researchers have made substantial progress in improving the accuracy of differential privacy methods without compromising privacy. Traditional differential privacy algorithms often introduced a trade-off between privacy and accuracy. New techniques, such as adaptive noise addition and privacy budget management, are now able to strike a better balance, reducing the impact on model accuracy while preserving privacy. These improvements make differential privacy more viable for real-world applications, where both privacy and precision are essential.

Scalable Homomorphic Encryption: Homomorphic encryption has traditionally been computationally expensive and slow, making it difficult to apply at scale. However, advancements in Fully Homomorphic Encryption (FHE) and partially homomorphic encryption have made it more practical for machine learning applications. New optimizations, such as bootstrapping and parallel processing, have reduced the computational overhead associated with homomorphic encryption, allowing for more efficient processing of encrypted data in machine learning models. These advances open the door to secure machine learning applications in highly regulated industries like healthcare and finance.

Federated Learning with Privacy Enhancements: Federated learning has become one of the most promising approaches for privacy-preserving machine learning, particularly for applications where data cannot be easily centralized (such as on personal mobile devices). Recently, there have been significant advancements in enhancing federated learning with additional privacy protections. For instance, techniques like secure aggregation, where the individual model updates are encrypted and aggregated in a privacy-preserving manner, have been developed to prevent malicious participants from accessing individual updates. Federated learning has been successfully implemented in sectors like healthcare, where patient data privacy is paramount, and in financial services, where regulatory compliance is essential.

Privacy-Preserving Transfer Learning: Transfer learning, where a pre-trained model is adapted to a new task with minimal data, has also seen advancements in privacy-preserving versions. By utilizing techniques such as differential privacy or federated learning in combination with transfer learning, it is now possible to fine-tune models on sensitive data without compromising the privacy of individuals. This is especially valuable in applications where limited labeled data is available, but privacy must be maintained, such as in medical diagnosis or fraud detection.

Integration with Blockchain for Data Provenance and Auditing: Privacy-preserving techniques are being integrated with blockchain technology to enhance transparency and accountability in machine learning. Blockchain's decentralized nature allows for secure, tamper-proof logging of machine learning processes and data usage, ensuring that privacy-preserving mechanisms are being followed. Blockchain can track the provenance of data used in federated learning or multi-party computations, providing verifiable proof that privacy and compliance requirements are met.

3. Applications in Cybersecurity and Beyond

The application of privacy-preserving machine learning techniques is not limited to data privacy and compliance alone—it also has critical implications for cybersecurity. As the threat landscape continues to evolve, protecting sensitive data while still enabling effective cybersecurity measures is becoming increasingly important. Privacy-preserving ML is playing a crucial role in developing secure AI models that can detect and mitigate cybersecurity threats while ensuring that individuals' privacy is upheld.

Threat Detection: Privacy-preserving machine learning can be used to train models for threat detection, such as identifying malware, phishing attempts, or insider threats, without compromising the privacy of the data being analyzed. With techniques like federated learning, organizations can collaborate to detect emerging threats without exposing sensitive information about their internal operations.

Secure Authentication and Fraud Prevention: In financial services, privacy-preserving ML can be used to detect fraudulent transactions or to develop biometric authentication systems, such as facial recognition or fingerprint scanning, without exposing sensitive personal data. Homomorphic encryption and secure multi-party computation can ensure that these systems are both effective and privacy-conscious.

Healthcare Data Protection: In healthcare, where data privacy regulations like HIPAA and GDPR are particularly stringent, privacy-preserving machine learning allows for the development of AI models that can analyze medical records, predict disease outbreaks, and optimize treatment plans without violating patient privacy. By using federated learning or differential privacy, healthcare organizations can collaborate on AI models without sharing private patient data.

IoT and Smart Cities: With the proliferation of IoT devices and the development of smart cities, privacy-preserving machine learning will play a key role in enabling data-driven services while preserving user privacy. Edge AI and federated learning allow IoT devices to process data locally and collaborate without transmitting sensitive data to centralized servers, ensuring privacy in applications such as smart home security, environmental monitoring, and traffic management.

4. Challenges and the Path Forward

Despite the advancements, there are still several challenges that need to be addressed before privacy-preserving machine learning can be widely adopted. These include:

Scalability: Privacy-preserving techniques like homomorphic encryption can be computationally expensive, which limits their scalability for large datasets and complex models. Further research is needed to improve the efficiency of these techniques, making them practical for real-time applications.

Interoperability: Privacy-preserving machine learning techniques must be compatible with existing AI and machine learning frameworks. Ensuring that these privacy enhancements can be easily integrated into current systems and workflows is essential for widespread adoption.

Regulatory and Ethical Considerations: Privacy-preserving techniques must not only protect individuals' data but also ensure that the use of AI complies with evolving privacy regulations and ethical guidelines. As data privacy laws become more stringent, organizations will need to keep up with compliance requirements, especially as new privacy-preserving technologies emerge.

Privacy-preserving machine learning is a rapidly advancing field that is reshaping how sensitive data is handled in AI applications. The techniques discussed—differential privacy, homomorphic encryption, federated learning, and secure multi-party computation—are essential for enabling secure, privacy-conscious AI systems. As these technologies continue to improve, they will allow for greater collaboration and innovation in fields like cybersecurity, healthcare, finance, and IoT, all while ensuring that individuals' privacy is protected. However, addressing scalability, interoperability, and regulatory challenges will be key to unlocking the full potential of privacy-preserving machine learning in the future.

13.3 Anticipated Cyber Threats and Defensive Technologies

As the digital landscape continues to evolve, so do the threats facing organizations, governments, and individuals. Cybersecurity has become more complex as attackers employ increasingly sophisticated techniques to breach systems, while the tools and strategies to defend against these threats also grow in sophistication. The future of cybersecurity will be marked by a combination of emerging cyber threats and the development of advanced defensive technologies. This section explores the anticipated cyber threats on the horizon and the corresponding defensive technologies designed to counter these evolving challenges.

1. Anticipated Cyber Threats

The cybersecurity landscape is dynamic, with new threats emerging regularly. Several trends point to what we can expect in the near future:

AI-Powered Attacks: Just as artificial intelligence and machine learning have revolutionized cybersecurity defense, cybercriminals are increasingly leveraging these technologies to launch more sophisticated and automated attacks. AI-powered attacks will be capable of performing tasks at speeds and scales that humans cannot, such as generating highly convincing phishing emails, detecting vulnerabilities faster, and deploying malware that can learn to adapt and evade traditional security measures. These threats could target individuals, businesses, or even critical infrastructure.

Ransomware Evolution: Ransomware attacks have been a growing concern for several years, and they are expected to evolve further. Attackers will continue to enhance their strategies, using more advanced techniques such as double extortion, where attackers not only encrypt data but also steal it and threaten to release it publicly unless a ransom is paid. The rise of ransomware-as-a-service (RaaS) also lowers the barrier to entry for cybercriminals, making these attacks more widespread and damaging.

Quantum Computing Threats: Quantum computing promises to revolutionize many industries, but it also presents a significant threat to current encryption standards. As quantum computers become more powerful, they could be used to break traditional cryptographic algorithms like RSA, which underpins many of today's cybersecurity systems. This could have widespread implications for securing communications, transactions, and personal data. While quantum computing is still in its infancy, it is a challenge that the cybersecurity industry must prepare for.

Internet of Things (IoT) Vulnerabilities: With the growing adoption of IoT devices in both consumer and enterprise environments, the potential for large-scale vulnerabilities increases. Many IoT devices are not designed with robust security measures, leaving them open to exploitation. Cybercriminals could exploit these vulnerabilities to launch large botnet attacks (as seen in the Mirai botnet), hack into critical infrastructure, or gain unauthorized access to networks via poorly secured devices. As more connected devices become part of our daily lives, ensuring the security of the IoT ecosystem will be a critical challenge.

Supply Chain Attacks: Supply chain attacks, where attackers target a third-party vendor with access to an organization's systems, have gained prominence in recent years. These attacks can bypass traditional security measures, as trusted vendors are often granted elevated access to sensitive systems. The SolarWinds attack in 2020 was a stark reminder of how devastating these kinds of attacks can be. As organizations increasingly rely on third-party vendors and software providers, the risk of a supply chain compromise will continue to rise.

Deepfakes and Synthetic Media: The rise of deepfakes, where AI algorithms are used to create hyper-realistic but fake videos or audio recordings, is posing new challenges for cybersecurity. Attackers could use deepfake technology to impersonate high-profile individuals, tricking employees into disclosing sensitive information or authorizing financial transactions. The use of synthetic media for social engineering attacks could also increase, making it more difficult for individuals to distinguish between real and fake communications.

Advanced Persistent Threats (APTs): APTs are highly organized, long-term cyberattacks aimed at stealing data or causing disruption, often by state-sponsored actors. These attacks are carefully planned and executed, often with the objective of spying on governments, corporations, or individuals for geopolitical or economic gain. APTs evolve over time, using a variety of tactics and technologies to maintain their presence within targeted organizations for months or even years.

Cloud Security Breaches: As organizations increasingly migrate to cloud environments, the attack surface expands, creating new security challenges. Misconfigurations, insufficient access controls, and vulnerabilities within cloud services could lead to data breaches or exposure of sensitive business information. Cybercriminals will continue to target cloud services and cloud-hosted applications, making effective cloud security management essential for enterprises.

2. Defensive Technologies to Combat Evolving Threats

In response to these anticipated threats, cybersecurity technologies must continue to evolve to ensure that defenses remain robust and resilient. Several key technologies and strategies are being developed and refined to address these emerging threats:

AI and Machine Learning for Threat Detection: AI and machine learning (ML) will play an even more prominent role in the detection and mitigation of cyber threats. With the ability to analyze large volumes of data in real-time, AI-driven systems can identify anomalies, detect malware, and predict potential attacks based on patterns in historical data. These systems can adapt and learn from new data, enabling them to identify previously unknown threats and respond to them before they escalate. For example, machine learning-based anomaly detection systems can spot suspicious behavior across networks or devices, while AI-powered malware detection tools can automatically identify new strains of malware based on their behavior.

Zero Trust Architecture (ZTA): Zero trust security is rapidly gaining traction as a method to combat internal and external threats. The concept of zero trust revolves around the idea that no user or device should be trusted by default, regardless of their location within or outside of the network perimeter. Every access request is thoroughly verified before granting access to any system or data. With zero trust, even if an attacker gains access to a network, they will not be able to move laterally and gain access to critical systems. As organizations shift towards remote work and cloud services, zero trust will become a foundational security model to protect sensitive data.

Quantum-Resistant Cryptography: In anticipation of the future threats posed by quantum computing, researchers are working on developing quantum-resistant cryptographic algorithms that will remain secure in a post-quantum world. These algorithms are designed to resist the decryption power of quantum computers, ensuring that encrypted data remains safe even as quantum computing technology advances. Governments and organizations are already beginning to invest in quantum-resistant cryptography to future-proof their security infrastructure.

Advanced Endpoint Detection and Response (EDR): Traditional antivirus and firewall technologies are no longer sufficient to address the sophisticated nature of modern cyberattacks. Advanced Endpoint Detection and Response (EDR) solutions provide continuous monitoring of endpoint devices and allow for the detection of advanced threats. EDR platforms leverage AI and machine learning to detect suspicious activity, analyze attack patterns, and automatically respond to incidents in real time. These systems are designed to detect not only known malware but also novel threats that have evaded traditional security measures.

Blockchain for Secure Data Integrity: Blockchain technology is being increasingly explored for its potential to ensure the integrity and transparency of data transactions. Blockchain provides a decentralized, tamper-proof ledger, making it an ideal solution for securing transactions and protecting data from malicious alteration. In the context of cybersecurity, blockchain can be used to create secure supply chains, protect critical infrastructure, and verify the authenticity of digital identities.

Extended Detection and Response (XDR): XDR is an integrated security solution that provides a unified approach to threat detection, investigation, and response across multiple layers of an organization's infrastructure, including endpoints, networks, and cloud environments. XDR platforms offer a holistic view of an organization's security posture, enabling security teams to quickly identify and respond to threats across various attack surfaces. By combining data from multiple sources and leveraging AI and automation, XDR solutions can significantly improve an organization's ability to detect and mitigate attacks in real time.

Biometric Security Systems: With the rise of deepfake attacks and increasingly sophisticated phishing techniques, traditional authentication methods like passwords are becoming more vulnerable. Biometric authentication—including facial recognition, fingerprint scanning, and voice recognition—provides an additional layer of security, ensuring that only authorized individuals can access sensitive systems and data. As biometric systems improve and become more widely adopted, they will play an essential role in safeguarding against impersonation-based attacks.

3. Preparing for the Future

The cybersecurity landscape is rapidly evolving, and organizations must proactively prepare for the threats that lie ahead. This means adopting a multi-layered defense strategy that incorporates the latest technologies, promotes a culture of security awareness, and continuously monitors and adapts to emerging threats. The future of cybersecurity will not only involve adopting new tools and technologies but also embracing collaboration between organizations, governments, and the cybersecurity community to stay ahead of attackers.

By staying informed about the latest trends, leveraging cutting-edge defensive technologies, and fostering a proactive approach to security, organizations can mitigate the risks posed by anticipated cyber threats and protect their assets in an increasingly complex and hostile digital world.

13.4 Future Challenges and Ethical Considerations

As the landscape of cyber threats evolves and AI-driven technologies continue to reshape the cybersecurity sector, the future will undoubtedly present both new opportunities and formidable challenges. In the quest to build more intelligent, adaptive, and automated security systems, there are significant ethical considerations and complex challenges that must be addressed. This section explores the primary future challenges in cybersecurity and AI, and the ethical dilemmas that arise as organizations, governments, and individuals strive to safeguard privacy, fairness, and security in an increasingly interconnected world.

1. Ethical Dilemmas in AI-Powered Security

The integration of AI in cybersecurity introduces new ethical questions that need careful consideration. While AI provides powerful tools to detect, respond to, and mitigate threats more effectively than traditional methods, it also carries the potential for misuse or unintended consequences. Some of the major ethical concerns include:

Privacy Concerns: As cybersecurity technologies, particularly AI systems, increasingly rely on vast amounts of data to function effectively, concerns about privacy are growing. AI-driven systems often require access to large datasets, which may contain sensitive personal information, financial data, or communications. In the process of gathering this data, there is the risk of infringing on individual privacy rights. The challenge lies in finding the right balance between ensuring robust cybersecurity protections and respecting individuals' privacy. How much data should be collected, and how should it be stored or processed? Organizations must consider how to safeguard privacy while using AI technologies to enhance security.

Bias and Discrimination: AI systems learn from data, and if the data used to train machine learning models is biased or incomplete, the models can perpetuate and even amplify those biases. In the context of cybersecurity, this could mean that certain groups of people, based on characteristics such as race, gender, or geographic location, might be unfairly targeted or profiled by security systems. For example, facial recognition technologies that are trained on biased datasets could lead to false positives, impacting certain demographics disproportionately. It's essential to ensure that AI models used in cybersecurity are designed to be unbiased, fair, and equitable, particularly when they are deployed in high-stakes areas like surveillance, authentication, and threat detection.

Transparency and Accountability: AI and machine learning algorithms, particularly deep learning models, are often seen as "black boxes" due to their complex and opaque nature. This lack of transparency presents an ethical dilemma when AI systems make decisions that affect individuals or organizations. In cybersecurity, when AI models autonomously detect threats, block access, or flag behaviors as suspicious, there may be a lack of clarity regarding how these decisions are made. For example, if an AI model wrongly classifies an individual as a potential insider threat, it could lead to false accusations, loss of access to resources, or even legal consequences. Ensuring transparency in AI decision-making processes and establishing accountability is vital to maintaining trust and preventing potential misuse.

Autonomy and Control: As AI systems become more autonomous, particularly in incident response and threat mitigation, ethical questions arise around the level of control that should be afforded to AI versus human decision-makers. In situations where an AI system autonomously takes action to mitigate an attack (e.g., blocking a malicious IP address or isolating a compromised system), there is a concern that these actions might be too aggressive or cause unintended collateral damage. The ethical challenge is determining the extent to which AI should be trusted with critical decision-making, and when human oversight is required to ensure that ethical principles are maintained.

2. The Challenge of Securing Emerging Technologies

As new technologies such as quantum computing, 5G, and the Internet of Things (IoT) continue to advance, they introduce new vulnerabilities and cybersecurity risks that need to be addressed. The following are some of the key challenges in securing these emerging technologies:

Quantum Computing and Cryptography: One of the most pressing challenges on the horizon is the potential disruption of current encryption standards by quantum computing. While quantum computing holds great promise for solving complex problems, it also threatens to undermine the security of traditional cryptographic algorithms like RSA and ECC (Elliptic Curve Cryptography), which secure a vast array of digital communications and transactions today. Preparing for the post-quantum world involves developing quantum-resistant encryption algorithms and transitioning to new forms of cryptographic protection. This is a challenge that will require global cooperation and careful planning to ensure that quantum computing advancements do not create an era of widespread vulnerabilities.

5G and IoT Security: The advent of 5G networks and the continued proliferation of IoT devices open up new attack surfaces that malicious actors can exploit. With 5G, the number of connected devices and the speed of communication will increase exponentially, allowing for more sophisticated and large-scale attacks. At the same time, IoT devices, many of which are not designed with strong security measures, provide a wide range of entry points for cybercriminals. Securing 5G and IoT networks is a significant challenge, requiring the development of new security frameworks, the implementation of robust encryption, and the enhancement of device authentication methods. Additionally, addressing the supply chain security of IoT devices and networks is critical, as vulnerabilities in one component can compromise the entire system.

AI in Cyber-Physical Systems: As AI systems are increasingly deployed in cyber-physical environments, such as autonomous vehicles, industrial control systems, and critical infrastructure, they introduce a host of security and safety challenges. These systems are interconnected with the physical world, making them susceptible to novel attack vectors that could have real-world consequences, such as the manipulation of industrial equipment or autonomous vehicle control systems. The security of these systems is of paramount importance, as any compromise could lead to catastrophic failures. Moreover, the ethical implications of AI decision-making in such environments (e.g., decisions that could impact human lives) must be carefully considered to ensure they align with safety standards and human values.

3. Governance, Regulations, and Accountability

The rapid development of AI technologies in cybersecurity calls for a robust framework of governance and regulatory oversight. Governments, international bodies, and private organizations must work together to establish standards, guidelines, and accountability mechanisms that ensure the responsible use of AI in security contexts. Some of the challenges in this area include:

Global Regulation and Standards: As AI and cybersecurity technologies become more global in nature, establishing universal standards and regulations to ensure consistent ethical practices and security measures will be a challenge. Discrepancies between national and regional laws—such as the GDPR in Europe and CCPA in California—could create inconsistencies in how AI systems are deployed and monitored. It will be crucial for international bodies to work towards harmonizing these regulations to avoid conflicts and gaps in security coverage.

Accountability in AI-Driven Security Systems: As more AI-driven security systems are deployed, especially those that involve autonomous decision-making, establishing clear lines of accountability will become increasingly important. If an AI system incorrectly flags a user as a threat or causes harm by taking an automated action, who is responsible? Is it the developer, the organization that deployed the system, or the AI itself? Legal frameworks must evolve to address these questions, ensuring that AI systems are held accountable for their actions and that victims of AI-driven security failures can seek redress.

4. Balancing Innovation and Ethics

The future of AI in cybersecurity is undoubtedly promising, with the potential to create more secure, efficient, and adaptive systems. However, it is equally important to ensure that these technological advancements do not come at the expense of ethical considerations. Striking the right balance between innovation and ethical responsibility is a challenge that will require careful thought, regulation, and oversight. The principles of transparency, fairness, privacy, and accountability should guide the development of AI in cybersecurity to ensure that it serves the greater good without compromising fundamental rights and freedoms.

The future of cybersecurity will be shaped by emerging technologies like AI, machine learning, and quantum computing, which will present both opportunities and challenges. While these advancements will offer powerful new tools to defend against increasingly sophisticated threats, they also raise significant ethical concerns that must be carefully addressed. As AI becomes more embedded in cybersecurity systems, it is essential to strike a balance between harnessing its capabilities and safeguarding individual privacy, fairness, and transparency. Additionally, securing the technologies of tomorrow, such as 5G and quantum computing, will require concerted effort from the global community. Ultimately, the responsible use of AI in cybersecurity will be defined by a commitment to ethical principles and a proactive approach to emerging challenges.

In an era defined by digital transformation, cyber threats are evolving with unprecedented speed and sophistication. **Cyber Intelligence: AI and Machine Learning Approaches to Security** explores how artificial intelligence and machine learning are reshaping the cybersecurity landscape, equipping organizations to proactively defend against complex, ever-changing threats.

Written by cybersecurity expert *Aloïs Lavigne*, this book guides readers through a comprehensive journey from fundamental concepts to advanced applications of AI in cyber intelligence. Readers will discover how AI-driven approaches enhance threat detection, predictive analytics, and incident response, and gain practical insights into implementing these technologies across diverse sectors. Each chapter dives into essential topics, from anomaly detection and natural language processing to ethical considerations and building resilient, adaptive defense systems.

Through real-world case studies and actionable strategies, Cyber Intelligence provides a powerful toolkit for security professionals, data scientists, and technology enthusiasts seeking to understand and leverage AI in cybersecurity. Packed with insights into the latest trends, challenges, and future directions, this book is an indispensable resource for anyone looking to stay ahead in the fast-paced world of digital security.

With Cyber Intelligence, Aloïs Lavigne offers a compelling roadmap for a more intelligent, adaptive, and secure digital future.

www.ingramcontent.com/pod-product-compliance
Lightning Source LLC
Chambersburg PA
CBHW062101220526
45471CB00010B/3557